Creston Junior High School, a Diary of Schoolyard Basketball

D1520091

Creston Junior High School, a Diary of Schoolyard Basketball

Barry M. Cohen

ISBN-13: 9798581019047

Contents

CHAPTER 1

Creston Junior High School

✳ ✳ ✳

THEY ARE SHADOWS OF PHANTOMS now. Images and memories of boys at play in a schoolyard—happy, rambunctious, free, limber, spry. You may be able to find them behind an invisible curtain in the Bronx. Perhaps in another dimension that has no sense of time but together, learning, talking, exploring, and playing. The big-city chaos surrounds them but does not imbue the Creston Schoolyard. They are playing among themselves, checking out the latest new kid that comes into the schoolyard. "Heah, that kid can really dribble. Wow, what a great shot. Look at that move. Wow, that kid's really good! Look at the way he snaps off that pass. That boy can really run. He can really jump. He's 'taking the elevator to the top floor. He's coming down with frost on his elbows!'" Lots of positive energy, all compliments; they express always encouragement.

If you look carefully, you may be able to see the ghosts still playing at Creston Schoolyard. If you ever played with Dick McGuire, you knew the ghosts and you knew schoolyard basketball.[1]

Public School 79, PS.79, Creston Junior High School, Bronx, New York, in the spring of 1933, was a boys' haven in the fourth year of America's Great Depression.

The brisk white winds of the icy spring morning whirl, whisper, and hiss as they join the winged snow powder flying around the school-yard. The most difficult surly wind gusts unpredictably rant at boys shooting basketballs, who find their attempts sailing wildly off their mark. At the edge of the yard small dancing eddies spin dust balls and candy wrappers, which struggle to escape a vortex. The sun's rays reflect brightly, glimmering off snow that has been shoveled to the side of the courts. Morning springs to life for young boys anxious to play outdoors, bursting with energy. In the very corner of the school-yard there is a gray cyclone fence. A spider web is nestled in a small 3-by-3-inch hole, one of many such holes that are part of the fence, all of which are bound by metal fasteners. The web is almost at the base of the fence, and its host has a bounty of insects spun into the web's fabric of thin thread. It glistens as the sun embraces this nest of a spider. No one notices the organic explosion of babies just released—little wolf spiders that scatter about the ground in different directions, not knowing where to go.

An asphalt baseball field and its backstop at the opposite end of the long full basketball court survey the boys at play. They recognize some of them who have played baseball. The other two baskets on each side of the main court are recessed sufficiently to support half-court games on both sides of the main court. None of the six basketball goals have a net.

The half-courts are always busy, and one of these is dedicated to the youngest of the kid groups. They play 3-on-3 ball. The full court is for young teenagers who wait for the best players, usually older high school, college, and occasional pro players. As the morning and early afternoon progresses the better players come to the schoolyard in waves. The best players get picked first and come last without having to wait. Sometimes the youngest have to wait for an hour to play, wanting to improve their game by matching up with the best ballplayers.

There is a 3-on-3 game on one of the side courts. The game is intense, competitive, and the kids are talking and barking, "pass it," "shoot it," "switch," "I got him"; the ball moves, everyone touches. A thin splinter of a young boy moves with lightning quickness. Another heavyset chunky kid grabs a rebound. The kids are excited. They pass, they talk, they set picks, they move some more, they help each other calling out picks on defense. A tall boy positions himself up at the top of the foul line, waiting for someone to cut off his screen. They pass and bolt to the basket, a "give-and-go." The offensive man without the ball sets a screen on the defender guarding the ball. The dribbler rubs his man off the screen; the screener instinctively goes to the basket, a "pick-and-roll." They score, the other team takes possession. The ball is receipted and quickly passed to the left, and the passer sets a screen for his teammate on the right, who follows by cutting to the hoop.

Quick ball movement and snappy passing accent the play. A defender not guarding the ball gets caught watching. His opponent notices that he is "daydreaming" and cuts stealthily to the hoop, with his eye on his teammate who is dribbling the ball and spots him open. Taking advantage of the mistake, he gets the pass "backdoor" from his teammate and lays the ball off the sheet metal aerated backboard and scores. It's schoolyard basketball. The plays are crafty, deceptive, and reactive.

There's a new member of the schoolyard. He is another slender, graceful boy who has found his prize. Very few boys had enough money to own a ball, but there is one lying on the ground; he picks up the extra ball belonging to another playing on the full court. The ball has lost its shine in favor of the influence of the dirt and grit of black asphalt. He is half watching the game taking place as he shoots, hoping he can continue using the ball and that its owner will not take it from him and depart. He shoots and the basketball spins aerodynamically, piercing the gusty, fickle winds. The ball passes through the target, and the netless rim is surprised. It was not expecting the ball to pass so cleanly through its vigilant eye.

He is the proverbial new kid. It's his first time playing in the schoolyard since moving from Prospect avenue to 2010 Grand Avenue, located just 4 blocks away from the schoolyard.

On an adjacent single basket, there is a little man shooting. He is diminutive, only five foot four, an adult in his forties. His hair is gray at the temples, yet he looks in youthfully excellent physical shape. He shoots a two-handed set shot time after time cleanly through the rim. "Who is that?" one kid asks his pal next to him watching.

"That's Barney, Barney Sedran! He coaches the Brooklyn Jewels professional team in the Metropolitan League. Nat Holman of CCNY said in the papers that Barney was the best little man who ever played the game. He was a great pro ballplayer. He can do it all. Shoot, pass, score, dribble, play defense. They used to call him "Mighty Mite." He couldn't make DeWitt Clinton's High School team, can you believe that? But he went on to be one of the greatest pros ever. Now he's coaching. He's a great guy. He helped me once showing me how to protect the ball when I dribbled. He likes to help kids in the schoolyard and teaches them when he's here, which isn't very often. This is a treat. He must be off from coaching the Jewels. Can you imagine, on his day off coming to the schoolyard to shoot and help kids?" The boys were wowed by the shooting of the "Mighty Mite."

The eleven-year-old newcomer is a boy named Solly. He has long, wavy, dark-black hair flying in all directions and penetrating brown eyes; he takes a couple of shots. Finally, he makes one. Barney Sedran walks over and approaches Solly. "You gotta nice release of the ball on the shot, kid. But can I give you a little advice?"

"Sure," said Solly. "When you shoot, son, always lean in and take a little hop toward the basket. I like the way you keep your elbows in when you shoot, but you missed those shots short because you weren't leaning in and getting the most out of your follow-through. Got it?"

"Yes, sir, thank you," says Solly. So the young boy begins to practice shooting like Barney told him to. After watching about ten shots, Barney nods his head in approval. Soon, Barney starts for the gate to leave the schoolyard. "Bye, Mr. Sedran, thank you so much for the pointers," said Solly in a softer voice than he had hoped. Then, like the whirling eddies of snow dust, the "Mighty Mite" leaves the schoolyard. Barney Sedran did not turn back to face the appreciative boy. But Solly had learned from one of the greatest players of the time, and he began to practice the newly learned shooting technique.

A couple of weeks later, Barney returned to the schoolyard. Once again shooting on a side court at Creston, Solly was approached by Barney. "Hey, kid, I like the way you're shootin' it now. You listened! Let me pass you a couple!" So the trim coach began to pass the ball to Solly. "OK, nice shot, but you are taking too long. Let me see how you hold the ball when I pass it to you. OK, I see now. When I pass you the ball you are shifting it and rotating the ball in your fingers to line up the seams. Don't do that, it wastes too much time. Wherever you receive the ball, just shoot it from there. Don't waste time lining up the seams of the ball. You don't have time to do that in high school. Just let it go when and where you catch the ball in your hands. Got it?" Before Solly could respond, Barney continued, "Now, do you know why they call it a free throw? Because it's like free money. When you are awarded a free throw, you gotta take advantage of it. It should always be a free point for you and your team. You should never miss a free throw. So practice, practice, and practice your shots from the foul line and don't miss them!

"OK, Coach," said the eager eleven-year-old boy, happy for the advice and appreciative of the knowledge he had gained from the voice of the great pro player and coach.

"And one more thing, kid," said Barney, "if you keep on practicing your set shot you will see that it will get 'grooved in,' and almost automatic."

5

A wonderful warm feeling came over Solly. No one had ever offered him such kindness and such generosity of spirit. He was deeply touched by this counsel. He felt like he could play with an advantage now. He had found some special additives to his game to help him shoot and play better. The little man had big ideas and to think that he had offered his time to a young stranger when he had to coach a pro game the next evening. "Wow," he thought. "What a good guy!" Solly was impressed by Barney, whom he would meet again, ironically, twelve years later.

The next day, after warming up and practicing his shot once again, the eager boy with the wild black hair got in the first full-court game of the afternoon. He was trying to get into the rhythm of the game, but no one was passing it to him. He decided to sprint up court, open up, and extend his arms to give a good target to the ball handler. This time he got the ball, and instinctively he stepped back to quickly launch his shot. He snapped the shot off with a strong wrist, almost mechanical. He didn't adjust the ball in his hands, shooting it from where he caught it, just like Barney Sedran told him. The ball landed cleanly through the basket. "Winners," a voice called out; he had made the winning game basket. That meant that his team would stay on the court and play another game against the boys who had been waiting to play next. "We got winners," the voice called out again! "You guys staying?" the voice asked Solly. "Yes, we are." After a couple of minutes the new game started with dispatch and the opponent was older, bigger, and stronger. In this game right off the bat the opponents lost the ball, trying to be too fancy. The young Solly then picked up a loose ball, passing and rushing it to the basket. His hustle was rewarded, and he got the ball back on a return pass. He threw up an off-balance short shot about 10 feet from the goal, which appeared to go in the bucket.

"Did that go through the basket or was it short?" asked someone on the other team. "No, it was good," said the brown-haired kid on the shooter's team. "Nice shot!" continued Lester Hirschfield, the smallest boy on the court, but whose importance was not to be underestimated.

He was one of the few whose family could afford to provide him a basketball, Lester's de facto insurance to play in the games. You simply could not play without a ball, and someone that brought a ball was respected for having it. The ball bringer always played!

The next time down the court, Lester dribbled the ball to the top of the key. Lester, remembering Solly's last basket, passed it to him hoping for the new kid to make another basket. Lester was more of a tennis player than basketball player but loved to play the game. He admired those with more talent than him. The shot went up, and the ball, its seams spinning tightly, hit the backboard and ricocheted twice inside the rim almost escaping the cylinder before descending through the hoop. "Nice shot," shouted the smallish Lester with the forearms of Popeye, developed from his tennis. Some kids felt they had to hit their first shot in order to have a good shooting day. The first-shot omen was a superstition to many. The eleven-year-old Solly didn't think that way. He loaded his shooting mechanism each time the same way, focused; and each time he executed the shot in the exact same motion. He could miss his first ten shots, and he would still shoot it the same way. He was not shy about letting it fly.

Lightning quick with his strong hands and feet, Solly hustled up and down the court. He tried to shoot quickly, precisely. The target, a tired metal rim. Each time he scored, he felt the exhilaration of his growing skill. Playing good ball was a confidence booster and allowed him to be more outgoing with the kids in this new schoolyard. He progressed each day, meeting new people playing at the schoolyard. He soon became acquainted with a number of personalities at PS 79, Creston Junior High Schoolyard. A new world opened up to him like petals of the pending spring flowers.

The kids in the schoolyard played ball, but they were also friends, extreme social creatures. They talked constantly about everything that was happening in the schoolyard, and the events going on in "The City," the nation, and the world. Not everyone was interested in playing basketball, some played handball or baseball. Many engaged in all sports shifting from one to the other with the different seasons, like different rotating crops in the fields of a working farm. Solly found his passion in basketball, like many in the schoolyard; he loved the game and could not think of anything else.

The backdrop of the schoolyard was the busy city. More and more people were moving there. Every morning, the Bronx cleared its throat and exhaled the steam of its subways and reverberated with screeches of trolleys, subways, and buses. The sidewalks were replete with the chatter of pedestrians moving and talking—a cacophony, marinading man and machine. It was an eclectic borough. Solly hustled home from school and didn't go to the schoolyard. He was excited. Uncle Jack was coming to take him to a very special dinner. Jack was taking Solly and his brothers to the famous "Ratner's," a classic dairy delicatessen with soul, located on Delancey Street, in the Lower East Side section of Manhattan.

Solly loved the experience of eating out at a restaurant. His uncle had taken him to Ratner's for the very first time several months earlier. It was his first time eating out at a restaurant. His mother's cooking was good, but he found excitement in the variety of spices used in the food at Ratner's. He found the people dining and talking intriguing. Ratner's had been around forever, and the waiters were vocal, and they were all comedians in unique ways. Each of the servers was talented, charming, and knowledgeable, yet they could serve food with aplomb, remember even the smallest order details, and tell jokes at the same time. "What did the hat say to the hat rack? You stay here. I'll go on a-head!" Then, "My wife dresses to kill. She cooks the same way! I've been in love with the same woman for forty-one years, if my wife finds out, she'll kill me!" Or more jokes such as "Why don't Jews drink? It interferes with their suffering!" They were the same jokes from the same waiter Uncle Jack always gravitated to when he came to Ratner's. Each time Uncle Jack would laugh fiercely, taking out his handkerchief to wipe his smooth well-oiled bald head, and brow. The tall, thin bushy-haired waiter would always end with the same joke that made Jack laugh almost uncontrollably. "Which one of you ordered the clean glass?" Solly and his brothers enjoyed having a laugh with their uncle.

The Ratner's waiter warriors were genial, hardworking, dedicated, and a one-of-a-kind breed we shall likely never see again. It was at Ratner's that Solly fell in love with potato blintzes—soft folded dough tightly packed with mashed potatoes and spices; he found them more savory by enhancing them with sour cream. "Out of this world," he exclaimed upon the first taste! His mother had made him blueberry-filled blintzes and potato blintzes on holidays before, but there was something special about going out to eat the delightful blintzes at Ratner's. Jack, their favorite uncle, was a successful real estate man who worked seven days a week and wore a suit and tie every day, seemingly always at the ready for a business encounter. While his sister, Jennie, thought him a rake and cavalier, she enjoyed it when he took her boys out for a nice meal. Uncle Jack had tragically lost his first wife from cancer at an early age. Jack's first wife and only true love had been a star singer at the Metropolitan Opera House. After she passed on, he was overcome with melancholy and sought the company of younger woman to soothe his suffering. His sister did not understand that, but Jack remained who he was for his entire life.

At home, "Uncle" Morris Black was especially kind to Solly. A Russian immigrant, Uncle Morris read stories to Solly in broken English. He liked to read to his nephew. Solly's favorites were "A Tale of Two Cities" by Charles Dickens and the stories by Mark Twain about Tom Sawyer and Huckleberry Finn. While Morris's reading could be slower than what one might have hoped, his young listener loved to hear his uncle's deep husky Russian voice.

Morris was not legally the boy's uncle, but rather, he was one of Abraham Cohen's foremen in the demolition contracting business. Abraham, Solly's dad, took Morris in as a boarder renting the worker a room in their Prospect Avenue apartment. One day when Solly was nine, Uncle Morris didn't come home from a job. There had been a run-in with a recalcitrant worker who had jostled with Morris in a dispute, pushing Morris over a nine-story building roof. Uncle Morris did not survive the fall. The matter was not discussed at home, but Solly would remember his "Uncle Morris." He remembered his storyteller "Uncle" Morris with great fondness his entire life.

While there were opportunities in the City, symptoms of the Depression lingered. Some families in the neighborhood did not have jobs. Every day was a struggle, a trial of survival. The streets were filled with people working legitimate jobs and those who sought to make a quick buck through less-than-legal means. The tough times struck the many and not the few. A decent meal was appreciated with soulful smiles of joy. During the Depression securing food was truly difficult. You were fortunate to be able to eat a nice hot meal. If you were lucky enough to get some chicken on a bone, the meat was eaten and the bone cleaned to the point of being polished, with not an iota of meat wasted or spared.

Solly would never forget the deprivation of the Depression. His drive and hunger to make something of his life was inspired by those difficult times. Many neighborhood boys took to the game of basketball. It was an escape. It seemed like bad news was all around. There were people out of work, and there were bread lines and soup kitchens, which were the only ways to secure food for the many. Jews in Germany were being oppressed, and the formation of the Fascist Nazi party led to the beginning of violent persecution of priests, Jews, and Gypsies in Germany. Harrowing events were being reported from Europe. Basketball became a liberator of boys of the schoolyards. Passion and aspiration were invested in a game that became the fabric of souls in young boys. It didn't matter where the schoolyard was. There were like schoolyards all over New York City—in the Bronx, Brooklyn, Manhattan, and Queens. The love of the city game that started at this time was perpetuated through the years and is described by Pete Axthelm. He quotes Willie Hall, a playground ballplayer from the 135th Street Park in Harlem, New York, "There's a love of the game in this city that is very difficult to put into words. You start off when you are very young and you can't get it out of your system. You might get married to a woman, but basketball is still your first love."[2]

There were well-known rules of engagement in schoolyard basketball. Ball movement, passing, cutting, using the high post, the give-and-go, the pick-and-roll, and good spacing on offense were part of it. The boys had an unselfish attitude both on and off the court. The fears of the world and the apprehension of their future united them. They were a fraternity.

The energy of youth and the ability to play sports end quickly, suddenly, always too soon. The baton gets passed to the next youth as if on divine command. The years steal youth's vigor in favor of the subsequent generation. One says goodbye to the freedom of a young body and wants "a do-over please, just one more game." The body does not cooperate as it is ruined, the magic gone, the vigor never to return. It leaves the forlorn player to long for a return. You cannot blame the athlete who stays too long in the game. Former New York Yankee's player Roy White describes it aptly, "There's nothing that gives you the same excitement as building your skills for years, then going into a pressure situation and hitting a home run, or getting the hit in the pennant race … For the rest of it he White understands why a man would sacrifice some dignity to play to the last game, the last hit, the last hope."[3] The allure of play, the art of melding one's talent within the game to work with others, and to be part of a team are powerful emotions–athletes work in unison and competing together as one organism, moving and gyrating, a synergy of spirit at a unique time and place.

Ask an athlete given all and who can no longer play, "How much would you give to be able to play one more game?" The answer would invariably be, "Everything I have. I'll figure it out from there!"

When you are young and able to run and jump as you like, a hot sunny day is not sweltering and oppressive. It is the smell of grass, moist heat imbued on skin, demanding your arms to throw, catch, or hit a ball. It is the sound of the basketball bouncing on the asphalt, a pounding incantation, like magnetic drumbeats. Youth is a fortune given at birth; its worth further appreciates over time.

Creston Junior High School was one of the dynamic schoolyards where young men played in New York City in the 1930s. Children of immigrant parents from Italy, Russia, Germany, Ireland, and Poland filled the grounds to play. These immigrants were parents that came to America to find opportunity, freedom, and advancement in the bloom of their new country.

New Yorkers had a demeanor, an air of being proud of being from New York City. They felt like they were the best in the world. The City had the best of everything—the most diverse and authentic foods, the smartest people, and many of the successful families of industry, like the Astors and the Rockefellers. New York had a modern city infrastructure, technology, fine dining, and elite entertainment. The daily electric sounds and the rich smells of New York had a rhythm and bouquet all its own, and the City moved at a pace like no other. It was the place to be. It was a Gershwin Rhapsody.

To walk in its streets or in the subway or to ride on its trolley cars was intoxicating for its inhabitants and visitors. Would-be stars and starlets, models, singers, and musicians came from the Midwest and from across

America in search of New York's opportunities. The sound of car horns and trolley wheels and the steamy hiss of underground subway trains were New York City. The subway's metal vents exhaled from their tireless work each day in a city alive and vibrant.

In New York, people worked like nowhere else. Workers in all businesses strived to bring home enough money to provide for their families during the Depression, from 1929 into the early 1930s. During these hard times, each day was more intense than the one before.

The good played by the rules, but the streets were full of the bad. Immigrant families were mindful and respectful, following the rules. Youths without guidance, however, fell prey to the many temptations of the City. Booze, drugs, gambling, and petty thieves were ubiquitous. The good worked harder each day to get ahead and to keep their nose clean.

Parents worked as hard as they could to put food on the table, while their children were devoted to pursuits of music, drama, literature, science, art, friendships, and the sports of the parks and schoolyards. Their children slowly moved away from the traditions of countries from which their parents had emigrated.

New American youth gravitated to the playing of sports and the camaraderie they shared seeking liberation from customs that were tired and irrelevant in the new country. Their quest was for something new, different, and something that liberated them from the shackles of tradition.

Going to church or temple on the weekends was complimented and sometimes supplanted by basketball, stickball, handball, "Johnny-on-a-Pony," and ring-a-levio. There was no cable TV, no video games, nor skateboards, or smart cell phones. There were few opportunities to watch sports. Boxing, baseball, and horse racing were extremely popular, but not accessible to be viewed by many. The newspapers provided the imagination of its readers a virtual experience of sports.

The schoolyard and parks were a primary way to observe sports for most as the boys could not afford to go to pro or college sporting events. The daily basketball games to seven baskets were also the highlight of the day for the kids who played. The ball had to be taken out beyond the foul line on a change of possession in the 2-on-2 or the 3-on-3 half-court basketball games. They would play until dark, and if it snowed they shoveled it off. If it rained, they figured a way to dry the court, sometimes soiling clothing, rags, newspapers, trash, or towels in order to do so. The schoolyard forged powerful bonds, and many who met there remained friends for life.

Surrounded by tenement buildings, the schoolyard courts were a concrete-and-brick canyon, whose mortar roared with the echoes of Bronx schoolyard play. Amid the sound of the trolleys, buses, cars, and occasional subway, the kids played. They could look up, see the black metal fire escapes and apartment windows, and pretend they were playing in front of thousands of fans at Yankee Stadium, Ebbets Field, the Polo Grounds, or Madison Square Garden.

In spite of the loud chatter and banter of outside merchants hawking their wares, and the trucks that supplied them with everything, boys could still be heard in and out of the schoolyard as they played, laughed, needled, taunted, or shouted in the schoolyard.

The schoolyard friendships would survive marriages, divorces, economic hard times, and World War II.

Thousands of kids embraced playground basketball. On those imaginary fields of glory, competitive skills were honed that would lead to high schools like DeWitt Clinton, James Monroe, Columbia Grammar, Metropolitan colleges, and ultimately to the NBA.

As you might expect, Solly went back to Creston. He began to practice his shooting. He loved the schoolyard, and he loved his older brother Benny. It was a pity that Benny couldn't play anymore, he thought. Solly could still play, and he longed to be the best player in the schoolyard. He practiced shooting a basketball each day he could get his hands on a ball. Sometimes they would roll up newspapers and shoot with crumpled-up newspapers rolled into a ball if there were no spare basketballs. This could suffice until someone brought a ball. There were many good schoolyard players and the competition was swift, although not all schoolyard players fulfilled their dreams of success. There were many city players who were great in the schoolyard but who struggled, giving in to temptation and poor choices. As young waves of immigrant parents worked hard in the new country, their sons enjoyed more free time, and some got into mischief.

Just a block outside the schoolyard, there were a kosher delicatessen, an Italian bakery, a card shop near the popular candy store, and a fruit stand. Many of the boys would hang out in front of the stores, talking and watching the pedestrians cruise by. The favorite drink of most of the schoolyarders was an egg cream, that luscious nectar of seltzer water, ice cream, chocolate syrup, and milk. The carbonation in these ingredients created a delicious sweet fizz that was a mixture of soda, chocolate, and ice cream which oozed a sweet creamy foam over the edge of the glass.

The fruit stand had wonderful offerings of oranges, plums, grapes, peaches, apples, and bananas. The fruit was displayed for purchase on large wooden carts directly on the sidewalk. Inside the wooden carts the prices listed each fruit—apples: 5 cents, pears: 7 cents, etc. The items were neatly displayed, and the price signs in the carts were neatly and impeccably handwritten. The prices were set with those big gray signs.

The signs with their letters and numbers were neatly placed into grooves made to hold them inside the carts. New York had the best fruit shipped fresh daily to its Washington produce market from the finest growers of Georgia, Virginia, South Carolina, rural New Jersey, and upstate New York.

In the neighborhood around Creston, a local police officer patrolled the streets. It soon became a game to some of the boys to figure out how to pick off (steal) the fruits when the officer was not looking. Many of the kids would filch fruits and vegetables in this manner. Some of these boys were from the Creston Schoolyard. Solly never engaged in these misdeeds, but he was tempted by the notion of snacking on delicious fruit, delights that were rarely found at home. He stayed away from mischief and had a good sense of right and wrong. Malfeasance of this sort seemed immoral and evil to him. He later read Nietzsche in college and found a saying which fit his moral rubric. Nietzsche said: "For moral values to gain dominion, they must be assisted by lots of immoral forces and affects."[4] Such was the challenge of temptation in the young boy's life. Fresh fruit was not easy to get and it was costly. He wanted the fruits, but understood it was wrong to steal. Years later when the gambling scandals shrouded the game of college basketball in New York, Solly kept away from gamblers, avoiding any wrong decisions. He had the correct moral compass.

When the Communist Party and philosophy was popular in the late '40s and early '50s, Solly stopped himself short of joining the fashionable tenets of Communism. Lucky that he did as McCarthyism would take a foothold in American life shortly thereafter and wreak havoc with many misguided young adults, in some cases ruining their careers and even their lives.

One early spring morning, one of the kids in the schoolyard started to watch Solly play in a three-man game. Solly was so skinny that you could see his ribs through his skin if he took his shirt off. He made a lightning quick move and stole the ball, making the layup. "Look at that little Spider go," said the random kid waiting to play. The name would stick and Solly became known as "Spider," a nickname he didn't like but which he was helpless to shirk.

The next day, Spider found an extra ball, and instead of playing in one of the side games or the full-court game, he picked it up and began to practice his foul shots. After about twenty minutes he eventually made ten free throws in a row. It was the first time he had ever done that.

The boys played freely in the yards. The best were recruited to play first in the local high schools and later at the great basketball universities like City College of New York (CCNY), New York University (NYU), St. Johns, Long Island University (LIU), Seton Hall, and Fordham. In these New York City metropolitan area colleges, the great coaches of the game commanded their squads with military precision. Discipline and hard practice were promoted by the coaches to breed success. The players greatly respected their coaches, who molded them with intricate systems of play on both offense and defense.

Off the court, the coaches did not tolerate poor sportsmanship or tardiness. They held principles of honesty, integrity, discipline, and fair play to be of greatest importance. No one escaped the wrath of a Nat Holman, Clair Bee, or Phog Allen if there was a transgression. Wrongdoers were not tolerated. In this plenary manner of solid moral values, the best coaches would profoundly impact the lives of their players.

The Cohens at 2010 Grand Avenue, The Bronx, 1940

Photo from: Barry Cohen's Family Album

Saul, Israel, Abraham, Mary, Jennie, Rose, Benny, and Murray

Abraham and Jennie Cohen, Bronx, NY

Photo from: Barry Cohen's Family Album

Many parents of the Schoolyard kids had relatives in Poland.

RUN! This is the Szydlow ghetto, and the man at the left wears the white arm band all Jews over 10 years old must display. The women are running like chickens from the photographer.

A HOUSE DIVIDED... This street car in Cracow, Poland, is divided into two sections. The sign indicates one-half is for Jews, the other half for Aryans. The fare, however, is presumably the same for both ends.

These types of reports preoccupied the American Jewry in the Bronx, Article Appeared in NY Times Jan, 1941.

SCHOOLYARD CREW ALL GROWN UP

Photo from: Barry Cohen's Family Album

Left To Right Clockwise: Lester Hirschfield, Beattie Hirshfield
(Wife), Lester Mintz, Artie Reichner, Philly Rick, Shirley Rick,
Wally Sencer, Lennie Lesse, Norma Sencer, Harriet Wallach,
Genie Wallach

CHAPTER 2

The Bronx

THE BRONX WAS A HAVEN for immigrants in the 1930s and 1940s. Families and individuals fled Europe at the end of the nineteenth century and started to come to America, where they sought freedom from persecution. They were rugged, determined workers, appreciative to have escaped Fascist and Communist regimes.

Solly spent the first four years of his life at 144 Tiffany Street, which housed many Jewish, Irish, Italian, and German immigrants—among others—in the early 1920s and 1930s. When he was five, his family moved within the same area in the Bronx to 171 Prospect Avenue. The forty-eight-year-old Abraham Cohen was tough on all his children, but the one who took it the hardest was his shy, awkward son, Solly, who was the second-youngest of six children. His sister Mary was eleven years older than him, and his brother Benny was just two years younger than Mary.

When the older sons and daughters moved out, the Cohen family was able to move up to 2010 Grand Avenue in an area just south of Burnside Avenue but not far from Creston Junior High School, south of Mosholu Parkway and DeWitt Clinton High School. The head of the household, Abraham, spoke Russian and Yiddish and tried to learn English. Abraham didn't communicate much with his children, leaving that to his wife, Jennie, who ran the household and spoke better English, albeit with a Russian accent. Jennie came to America from Lithuania, which at the time was part of Russia.

Solly leaned on his older sisters Mary and Rose for guidance. They taught him how to read, which he learned quickly, devouring books of poetry by Emerson and Poe and the stories of Mark Twain and Charles Dickens.

Solly truly enjoyed poetry. One of his favorites was "The Wreck of the Hesperus" by Henry Wadsworth Longfellow. He, like his brother Benny, could recite poems one after the other and had a great memory of the words, emphasizing the important phrases in front of his sisters, showing off for them in recital.

Solly loved languages but was not as skilled in Latin or French as his brother Benny, who "had the ear" for languages. Solly's two older brothers worked and were often out of the house. Consequently, he was strongly influenced by his mother and sisters. Encouraged by his sisters, he developed a love of reading and took to school learning rapidly advancing ahead of his class in school at an early age.

He didn't like it when his father made fun of him in front of his siblings or outsiders, especially if it was one of his uncles. Abraham was born of the last name Knobel, with his brothers, at staggered times from Russia at different dates from 1890 to 1901. The family name was changed from Knobel at Ellis Island and became Cohen. Having escaped the hardships of the pogroms and acute anti-Jewish sentiment in Russia, Abraham, himself, emigrated from Russia through England to the United States in 1901.[5] He was a skilled construction supervisor and after a time started his own business. He was frustrated by duplicitous building owners who took advantage of his inability to read contracts written in English. His language difficulties and naivety in regard to New York City business practices often left him with less money than he felt equitable.

"I vudn't give you a nickl for this buoy's fuutcha," growled the white-haired balding Russian man, speaking in broken English. He pointed at his son, who was devastated by the barb. The immigrant loved his son but feared for his vulnerability and wanted to help him overcome the difficulties that had frustrated him in the contracting business. He wanted his son to be better and not to suffer the same failures. Most of all, he wanted his son to be strong enough to earn a good living and have a great family.

The Russian father was a small but fierce 5 foot 5, 150-pound sinewy man. He had come to America as a tailor but couldn't find work. He found that he was skilled at contracting work and decided to pursue that as his livelihood. He liked to meet with one of his brothers to drink slivovitz, a plum brandy. Slivovitz was a popular Eastern European alcoholic drink. Abraham found his calling as a demolition contractor, wrecking dilapidated houses that were beyond repair. Soon he enlisted hardworking Russian workers to work with him. He established himself and earned a living, usually getting salvage rights to the buildings. He earned the right to retrieve scrap materials off the job site to sell for additional profits. He often had his sons round up any valuable scrap metal, such as abandoned copper doorknobs. As the boys grew and matured, Abraham allowed his sons to gather the copper or other valuable scrap, negotiate its sale with his usual buyers, and keep a portion of the proceeds for themselves.

A smart procurer of demolition work, Abraham slowly began the process of expansion and took riskier jobs, which often involved buildings that were health hazards and on the verge of collapse. It was dangerous work, and sometimes workers got injured. There was no workers' compensation or health benefits. He worked in the Bronx and in Lower Manhattan. Immigrants poured into the City, and New York's demand grew for apartments and offices. Abraham was able to modestly provide for his wife and six children.

Abraham didn't speak much, and when he addressed his son, in his broken English, it was limited to but a couple of words. Lacking paternal guidance, Solly struggled to find himself, often feeling lost and lonely. He retreated to his room, frequently reading and keeping to himself. Solly was the third-oldest boy in his family. Very serious, he never seemed to smile, at times lost, at times morose. The language barrier with his parents was difficult. He was intimidated by his father, reticent, and self-conscious. He didn't feel very good about himself. As he matured, he felt estranged. Solly grew up with traditional values, respecting greatly the word of his mother and father. Polite and obedient, Solly worked hard at everything he did. As a boy, he had high expectations. His education was very important to him, and he worked at it, truly enjoying schoolwork. As he got older, schoolwork became easier and he found that he didn't have to study much to get good grades. In grammar school he was placed in the "R" program, which stood for "the Rapids," an accelerated program that enabled him to graduate high school at age sixteen.

Just when Solly was feeling really sad about everything in his life, the fifty-two-year-old Abraham decided to spend some time with his son. It was September 12, 1932. He took a day off and spent it all with his eleven-year-old son, Solly. In the West Farms section of the Bronx, there was an auditorium used for boxing and other large events. The locals called it the Bronx Coliseum, but it was also known as the Starlight Arena, or the New York Coliseum. It seated up to 15,000 fans. Originally, the auditorium was built for the 1926 Philadelphia Sesquicentennial, the 150th anniversary of American Independence. The entire auditorium was transported in components in 1928 to Starlight Park, located at E. 177th Street and Devoe Avenue, in the Bronx. Abraham was taking his son to watch a boxing match. Benny Leonard, "the Ghetto Wizard" and one of the greatest lightweight boxers of all time, was fighting. The Starlight hosted 6,000 in attendance that night, and everyone was rooting for Leonard, undefeated up until his 1925 retirement. Now in 1932, he was making his comeback after losing most of his boxing winnings to investments, forfeited as a consequence of the 1929 stock market crash on Wall Street.

The father and son walked to the arena from their Bronx apartment on Grand Avenue. The son felt proud to be walking with his father along the streets passing by the vendors that usually paid him no mind. They all greeted his father along the way. He was respected. After walking about ten minutes, they were joined by the many spectators that were going to the fight, excited about the big happening. Jews were supposed to be studious, nonathletic. They were associated with professions in law, banking, and moneylending. They were smart with numbers, so they said, but they were not considered athletes.

Benny Leonard was the son of Russian immigrants and was not the stereotypical Jewish boy. He was a "tough" Jew, and like the outstanding pre-World War II European Jewish soccer, boxing, and fencing athletes, he was a great competitor. He grew up on the Lower East Side of Manhattan, not far from Ratner's, and he started fighting in his teens. He was fierce, handsome, well spoken, and very popular with the media. He was a crowd favorite, especially among his ubiquitous Jewish fans. As they got close to the Bronx Coliseum, they heard men chanting, "Benn-ee, Benn-ee, Benn-ee," anticipating a great fight from their Jewish hero, the great, if not greatest, lightweight champion of all time. Fight experts called him an "intelligent" fighter, using his legs to fake and set up his weighty punches. Solly had been to the Starlight Amusement Park when he was five, and he noticed that the park had changed. There had been a terrible fire just a month before this fight, and it had destroyed many of the attractions of the park. The fire started under the roller coaster and destroyed what remained of that section of the amusement park. The coliseum was the largest part of the park which survived the fire. Only the week before the arena had hosted the circus, which Solly's sister Rose attended with her friends.

They approached the arena and the chanting of "Benn-ee" continued. "He'll moyrder dis bum," shouted a fan holding a sign that said simply "Benny" on it on his way to the coliseum. Now entering the auditorium where the fight was to take place, Abraham puffed his chest out, proud of his Benny Leonard, his champion. Abraham loved this fighter who at only 5 feet 5 inches, like himself, was wiry, smart, and tough as nails. He defined the term "tough Jew." He was so popular that his championship bouts sold out Yankee Stadium, with 59,000 fans in attendance.

The fight began, and Leonard came on strong from the start of the match against Mike Sarko, in a six-round match. The father and son were crowded deep in the back of the one-level venue. They craned to see every blow. "What a fight, Benny still has it," they thought. At their home on Grand Avenue, even Abraham's wife, Jennie, listened to the fight intently on the radio broadcast of the event.

As Leonard landed a right hook, Solly thought he heard the sigh of Mike Sarko grunting as he recoiled and grimaced from Leonard's punch. It was a vicious blow, and Solly couldn't believe how hard the punches were as they landed on Sarko's face. The roar of the crowd went up with each Benny blow. Solly watched his father leap up and yell out in broken English, "Das a good boy, Benny, Mensch!" He, like many of Leonard's fans, lived vicariously through Leonard's tenacity and integrity. He was an honest fighter, and that made him popular as well. Amid rampant anti-Semitism, Leonard gave Jews everywhere a good feeling and they identified with him. He was so popular that people came from all over the city to watch him fight.

As the fight progressed, each time Benny landed a smart punch, the largely Jewish crowd cheered. Abraham didn't say much else during the fight, but Solly was glad to be with his dad, and he knew his dad was trying to show him something, although at the time he was having a good time and didn't reflect on the lessons to be learned. It was simply excellent to be with his father alone together for the only time he could remember. Abraham was concerned about his son's love of poetry and such things, which he felt did not prepare him for life and how to earn a good living. His son would need to be strong, educated, and tough to protect himself and prosper.

The night was a success. Benny Leonard won the fight on points after the end of the six-round affair was over. After the bout, Solly and his dad walked around, and they saw the burnt grounds of Starlight Amusement Park in the distance. It was sad to see the destruction, but the evening was a joyous one and Solly appreciated Benny Leonard and his father for having shown him what Benny could do. The last time he had been with his dad had been in the temple, and that was with all of his siblings. This time it was just him and his dad, and while not many words were said between father and son, the evening punctuated a change in Solly's outlook on life and gave him a sense of urgency to be capable like Leonard. It was a turning point in Solly's path. Ironically, he would again encounter Benny Leonard later in life. Benny died of a heart attack at age fifty-one refereeing a boxing match at the St. Nicholas Arena in Manhattan in 1947, the same arena that Solly played in for the Gothams in the ABL. Solly would see Benny one last time while leaving the arena after an afternoon practice with the Gothams. Leonard was entering the venue to referee a boxing match, as Solly was exiting the facility. Several weeks later, Leonard collapsed at St. Nicholas and passed away of heart failure.

The school closest to Grand Avenue, grades six to nine, was Creston Junior High School. The Grand Avenue apartment housed Abraham, Jennie, and their sons Murray and Saul. The other children, Mary, Rose, Israel, and Benny had all left by the time the family moved from Prospect Avenue.

Creston Junior High School was the spot. There were always kids ready to play, shooting a basketball, kibitzing, and talking—a lot of talking.

The schoolyard was enclosed by a tall silver metal fence, too high to climb. You could see through the fence as its fabric had small diamond-shaped 3-by-3-inch openings.

The two concrete handball courts had three walls, with the rear of the court open. Behind the open area of the courts was an asphalt baseball field, with no markings for bases, the pitcher's mound, or a batter's box. Small pieces of cardboard were used as bases on the field, and the pitcher's mound was a small white-painted piece of cardboard that was a 2-inch-by-2-foot rectangle 60 feet from the cardboard sliver used as home plate. Left field met the back of the handball courts, and errant handballs harpooned unsuspecting outfielders. Creston Junior High, located at 125 East 181st Street, was a hub of recreation in the neighborhood. Parents worked until dusk, and their children took to the schoolyard, which embraced the boys' desire to play sports and to socialize. Playing basketball in the schoolyard was a great outlet, the most popular sport, and the cool thing to do in the neighborhood.

At first when kids called him "Spider," he rejected it and turned away not wanting to react to the new identifier. No one had to tell him that he was skinny and had thinny thin calves; he already knew that and was especially self-conscious about it. The nickname seemed to fit, however, and the consensus to call him by his new nickname prevailed. Each time he made a quick move someone would say, "There he goes, Spider, Spiiiiider!" The nickname slowly stopped bothering him, and he acquiesced. He was Spider. The newly monikered youngster had jettisoned his middle name, Max, denying its existence, so it was only fitting that he gained another name as recompense, albeit that of an arachnid. Spider let his fingernails grow because he felt he could get a better feel of the basketball. The flick snap of his fingernail on the ball enabled him to get a tight spin on the basketball. When his shot hit the rim, the spin allowed for a "shooter's touch" so that the rotation of the ball kept the ball hovering over the cylinder even after it caromed off the rim and up into the air above it. A "shooter's touch" allowed the ball to hang around the rim and fall into the basket.

He had worked for his father enough, plucking brass doorknobs from rubble at jobsites, and in sifting through the debris, his hands grew strong. Not only were his hands quick but they were very strong and that strength was like a concealed weapon, hidden from most who were fooled by his slender, unimposing physique. He had the strength to shoot the ball accurately from just inside the top of the foul circle, when he was only twelve. His strong hands and great anticipation enabled him to be a good defender who was talented enough to steal the basketball—a skill that not many others shared. He felt quick and bouncy on his feet, and it gave him confidence as a defender. His shyness left him on the basketball court, and he expressed himself through his play. He found that he could be aggressive in schoolyard competition. He was starting to come out of his shell.

Creston had a large asphalt playing area with no grass, but which accommodated the young boys who played there daily. The weekends had festive afternoon games where a larger contingent of local kids would show up to play pickup ball. The competition got better as they day went on and the best high school and college players would join in the games.

When kids came to the schoolyard, their anticipation overwhelmed them. Approaching the tall entry gate, they'd first run then slow up to be cool once they entered. They struggled to conceal their love for their playground. There were kids hanging around the courts at Creston almost all the time except when school was in session. Each day before and after school and all day on the weekends, Spider practiced his shooting, passing, and dribbling, when he was lucky enough to locate a ball. Since having a basketball was a rarity, there was great camaraderie in practicing and shooting around as groups of kids shared both the ball and the passion to work on their game. If someone came to the schoolyard with a ball he quickly became popular, most of the time sharing the ball.

In winter, it was schoolyard tradition to shovel snow off the court. When it rained, the kids cleaned and dried the court with brushes that were kept behind the janitor's office. The janitors of the building liked the boys who played ball in the schoolyard. The preparation of the courts became a pastime in itself, and the youngsters became skilled at drying and cleaning off the courts in all kinds of weather.

Sometimes, when Spider and others shared the court shooting, he would stop and look up at the surroundings—the tall buildings, the baseball field, and the handball courts—and realize that he was very happy, with no afterthought of sadness or inadequacy, thoughts that were seemingly pervasive when he was off the court. On a cold autumn day, or on a windy spring afternoon, the sun's rays would hit his face and radiate throughout his body. It never seemed cold on the courts, in spite of the frequent frosty autumn and spring temperatures.

One late afternoon, the courts were thinning out. It was late spring, a month or so before his twelfth birthday. The country was still in the midst of the Depression. There were bread lines and soup kitchens just several blocks down from the schoolyard, and people were hurting. You were lucky if your family had money for food and if your parents had jobs or some kind of work that earned a fair day's wage. The wind whistled through gaps in buildings while darkness prematurely began to block the light of the schoolyard. Uncle Jack was coming over for dinner. So the olive-skinned, eleven-year-old boy walked around the schoolyard, somewhat reluctant to leave his sanctuary. Finally, he decided to leave the now-deserted grounds, lit only by emergency yellow lights that hung off the school building. The baseball diamond was empty in the back toward the far fence, opposite the schoolyard entry. It was quiet but for the wind and a gentle mist, which began to soak his skin. Just before he turned to go home, a gray-and-white cat cried "meeyow," and the boy turned around to look at the feline. He saw it move through the school-yard and followed its path. Just inside the edge of the fence, the surface sloped, a low spot. There was a small puddle, and in the puddle was a round object that looked like a ball.

His hair started to dampen from the mist. "Someone must have left it," he thought. He didn't want to take something that didn't belong to him. In the fringe groups that frequented the schoolyard there were "lost souls," who gambled, pitched pennies or stole from the adjacent outside fruit and vegetable stands. For a while before the store owners caught on, it was easy to steal produce, but soon the police caught on and some of the juvenile thieves paid for their transgressions. Spider's parents taught him right from wrong and that moral line which could get lost in the temptations of the city. The lessons taught him by his strict parents would become his compass that would lift him up and transcend any odious influence in the schoolyard or neighborhood. For a good ballplayer, resisting temptation and avoiding critical errors were not always easy.

He inspected the ball and grabbed it, thinking that he would bring it back the next day to see if anyone owned it. He started home carrying the ball like he would a new puppy, cradling it in his arms. Then, he started to dribble the ball; he left the yard and continued his dribble onto the concrete Bronx sidewalk by the street just outside the schoolyard. The first dribble was smooth, but the second one got away from him. "Wow," he thought, "I have to practice dribbling, I stink." So he dribbled the ball, and it got away again and rolled down the street. Stabbing at the ball, he retrieved it just before an automobile approached.

He studied the ball under the streetlamp, passing Walton Avenue. The ball had a small bubble in its side, causing it to bounce awry. It must have been left at the schoolyard, abandoned. He brought the ball into the apartment and put it in the hallway closet. No one noticed. It was dinnertime.

His family did not have large dinners, but they always had food for dinner. Abraham, the head of the household, was a smart procurer of jobs.

He was always working and scrapping to get ahead. He was a good provider, and while impacted by the Depression like everyone else, he was beginning to see his way.

The next day, Spider took the ball and asked everyone he knew in the schoolyard about it. No one claimed the ball, and he decided to keep it. He noticed that if he held his hand at an angle while dribbling it, he could compensate for the lump on the side of the ball. He now concentrated more on his dribbling to control the crazy bounces. In his efforts, he practiced dribbling more and more to learn to control the basketball. He practiced without looking down at the ball. It were a thrill to have his own ball, a good omen of things to come.

Throughout the late spring, Spider dribbled and shot for hours at a time. Soon his accuracy became better and better, and free throws became almost automatic. Shot after shot went through the hoop. He moved further away from the basket, expanding his range, slowly. Soon, other kids noticed him shooting.

He really didn't care why they called him "Spider," but somehow the nickname became part of his identity. His family never called him Spider, but when he heard people call him by this new name, it gave him a new strength with other kids in the schoolyard. One day an olive-skinned, slick, dark-haired chatterbox approached him as he was shooting. "Hey, you, not bad, not bad. What's your name?" Spider kept shooting nonplussed, and unresponsive, yet amused by the kind words.

He trained himself to be completely focused when shooting, absorbed, no distraction tolerated. One after another he shot foul shots. The next day once again, the same diminutive twelve-year-old boy with bulging electric blue eyes confronted Spider. "Hey, kid," said the boy with an infectious smile and tightly cropped rich dark-black hair. Again, the boy audaciously moved closer and asked, "How do you make so many in a row?" Spider didn't answer. Then the bubbly energetic youngster gushed, "Hey, let me pass you the ball. I'll feed you?" Spider didn't respond again. Finally, the stranger went off to another basket to mingle with other boys he seemed to know, leaving the shooter to his craft.

The next day, the two boys met again at the schoolyard. After some initial banter, Spider finally replied to the irrepressible stranger, who once again asked him what his name was. "OK, stop calling me 'Hey kid.' I'm Solly."

"Oh, OK, great, my name is Phil, Philly Rick." Philly's cool blue eyes, high-bridged nose, and fantastic smile complemented his words. A magic talker, witty and funny, Phil was a great listener. He made his friends feel like they were being interviewed by a great radio talk show host, with all the right questions that made everyone feel upbeat. He elevated the souls of his friends, asking them questions, really listening to them when they spoke. He cared about what you had to say, and you knew it!

There are two different types of good listeners. There are those who listen and don't speak but don't hear what the other person is saying. They are good at listening, but it is a ruse. They are silent and listen to the speaker only as a springboard to enable them to talk subsequently, most usually about themselves. The entire time they are listening, they are waiting to speak without truly appreciating the other person's thoughts and comments. Often, they tend to filter what is being said to them, and they may be try and judge or change what the person speaking to them is thinking. The speaker may acquiesce at first but ultimately object. The speaker wants to be accepted and respected for who they are and what they have to say.

The second type of listener is one who not only listens but truly hears and cares about what is being said, understanding the content of the spoken words. Phil Rick was this kind of extraordinary listener. He listened, heard, and cared about people, especially in the schoolyard. He did not filter what was being said; he accepted whatever the thought was and did not judge it. It simply was the way he was. People around Phil felt good because Phil accepted them for who they were, viewed them in their most favorable light, and always supported them in the way they wanted to be bolstered.

Anyone who knew Phil Rick left his company a better person, more optimistic. Philly became a schoolyard and gym rat, a "bird dog." From his youth to late in his adult life, Phil studied ballplayers in schoolyards, parks, and gyms all over the City. Soon he would report his observations and evaluations to Howard Garfinkel, who would set the bar for high school player evaluations for colleges and beyond. The "Garf," as Howard was called, rated players on the basis of a five-star system. A five-star ranking was the best, indicating a blue chipper, a "PTPer,"[6] as Dick Vitale says. In the '60s, Garf founded "Five Star Basketball Camp," the gold standard of serious youth basketball camps, with top college coaches participating in the camp each summer. Michael Jordan, Len Bias, and Lebron James, among others, would attend the Five-Star Basketball Camp.

As a kid, Phil developed this wonderful gift of listening and complimenting his friends. Phil always created good karma, good vibrations; this was very important to him. He knew he was not going to be one of the better schoolyard basketball players. He was too small and too slow and lacked great skill on the court. He was, however, an extraordinary observer, evaluator, and fan. Some kids in the schoolyard were fast and shifty, others could rebound, but Phil had a skill that no one else had: HE NEVER TALKED ABOUT HIMSELF! He trained himself to listen, while most were self-absorbed, always preoccupied with hearing themselves talk.

While his friends talked about their own exploits as ballplayers or other egoistic commentary, Philly never used the words "I" or "me" in a sentence. Instead, he saw that he could make people feel really good by listening to them talk about themselves.

In the 1930s a schoolyard ballplayer's "reputation" was developed like layers of paint on a wall, slowly becoming more brilliant, layer after layer, game upon game. The daily games proved a player's worth, and each day the basketballers competed, adjusted, and tried to assert their will against their opponents. Many were friends off the court, but during the games, competition was fierce and reputation had to be earned each game, game after game, until proven, and even then it still had to be asserted in stiff competition to reinforce it.

The most popular schoolyard basketball contests were those 3-on-3 half-court games. There were kids who wanted to play and would shoot around, waiting to take the court. As they waited the boys got to know each other, often meeting new kids who would, in turn, take the court and join in freely. There were never set teams and, like shuffling a deck of cards, different combinations of kids played each day. Dominant players became evident in the games as their teams usually won, regardless of their teammates.

The half-court and the whole court games ended when the first team scored seven baskets. The seventh hoop decided which team stayed on the court to take on the kids waiting to play. In half-court games, schoolyard rules required a "take back" of the ball to the foul line after a change of possession, if the ball hit the backboard or rim. Sometimes they played "make it, take it," which meant that if you made a hoop you got to take the ball out past the foul line and stay on offense until your team didn't score. Sometimes, possession changed hands after a basket depending on the day and the inclination of the players. The possession would still start at the foul line, but the team that got scored on would get the ball out. If there was a change of possession on a steal, turnover, or "air ball," no "take back" was needed, in any event. Fouls were rarely called, and if they were, the defense called them. The games were friendly. The full-court games were more competitive, usually 4-on-4 or 5-on-5 games.

Winning was important, but the thrill of playing with and creating "a game of good ball" with your schoolyard pals was the true objective. When there was a nice play, a pass to someone moving without the ball going to the basket, a "backdoor" cut, "nice play" was the word from fellow participants. Teamwork, passing, movement were the norm. "Hogging the ball" or not passing was rare. Pass and move, pass and cut—every kid was a student of the game. The game was the currency and the vernacular of the schoolyard. The yard was a community with rules of order. The games were fun yet competitive. Boys were mainly from the Bronx at Creston, but on weekends, youngsters would venture over from nearby Manhattan to play. Often excellent African American ballplayers from Harlem would come to show off their skills. Some of these players would go on to play at DeWitt Clinton High School and thereafter to big-time college basketball colleges and the pros.

The schoolyard was a safe haven for sons of persecuted parents that fled Europe, who were delighted to play ball. Some of their fathers wanted them to work full time like they did. This could help take some of the money burden off of the parents. Extra income in the household was expected in many families, forcing some kids to stop playing ball to get a job instead.

The immigrant mothers and fathers wanted more for their children, especially a good education, ascension to a good job, and a healthy and strong family. The older generation worked so hard for a better American opportunity for their kids. The schoolyard became a sanctuary for a great generation of outstanding and productive youth. While the boys were hungry to improve and ascend both professionally and in basketball, they loved to talk to each other, share ideas, and laugh. They had a lot of laughs every day. They shared everything, probing each other and encouraging each other.

Phil Rick was one of the best at making people laugh. He and Spider became great friends for life. They couldn't talk enough basketball. As they grew older, got married, and had families, they continued to ruminate and reminisce about the game seriously, always evaluating the changes in the game and the great athleticism of the then-modern-day players. As they entered their forties and fifties, players like Kareem Abdul-Jabbar, Jerry West, and Oscar Robertson, the "Big O," were their favorites.

Spider and Philly loved to tell stories about the schoolyard and the kids that played there. They told so many stories and seemed to laugh a big belly laugh every time they got together, usually aided by a couple of Scotch drinks. They told the story of the great Max Zaslofsky. Once after a couple of belts of their favorite Scotch, Spider and Philly ran into the great ballplayer Zaslofsky at Toots Shor, a restaurant and lounge located on 51st Street in Manhattan. Spider knew Max, the former Chicago Stags All-NBA player and NBA 1947–48 leading scorer. Spider had played with and against Max in various exhibition games in the basketball circuits of the time. Spider, after several Scotch drinks, was feeling no pain and greeted Zaslofsky with a friendly but intoxicated, "Hello, Maxie, how are ya?" Max smiled and said, "Hello, Solly." Then, with a spontaneous playful gesture, Spider reached out and briskly rubbed Max's hair, jostling Maxie's hairpiece, dislodging the erstwhile elegantly appointed crown. Max's noggin was exposed. Spider didn't mean any harm, but he and Philly had a visceral and rousing laugh, saying "touché" in a play on words with Max's fallen "toupee," chuckling about it when they walked to the subway. The laughs were so intense that they almost began to cry in hysteria.

Solly had a great sense of humor, and he and his friends told jokes, trying them out on each other and sharing the best ones. He truly enjoyed puns and words with double meanings. His knowledge of Latin taught him about the roots and history of most English words. He used his words masterfully. When he came up with a good pun or a play on words, he was pleased and the commentary led to a welcomed laugh or heartfelt smile.

In the '30s and '40s in the Bronx, as elsewhere in New York City, kids broke away from the traditions of the old country. Basketball became a quasi-religion. Kids gravitated to each other to talk basketball, and the boys would leave the schoolyards to go over to the candy store to talk more ball. Soon, the kids from schoolyards would play in gargantuan arenas like Madison Square Garden in front of over 18,000 fans, but they would remain appendages of the schoolyard. The schoolyard was a proving ground, where skills were honed, talents were compared, and both the games of basketball and the events in the world and in one's life were analyzed. It was an eternal light for boys who would never forget it for so many reasons.

CHAPTER 3

"Hooaah" Lucio Rossini

EVERYONE IN THE SCHOOLYARD KNEW Phil Rick. One day he came to the court with another handsome, muscular-looking fellow. The youngster appeared more a football than a basketball player. The black hair brushed back away from his face accented dramatic expressive brown eyes and highlighted his reddish-tan complexion. He looked like Victor Mature of *Samson and Delilah* movie fame. Both Victor Mature and Lucio Rossini were 6 feet, 2 inches tall. The chiseled-chested Lucio was the son of immigrants from a small town in Italy. Mr. Rossini Sr. had little time for his boy Lucio, as the older Rossini busied his day painting and plastering the walls of local buildings in the Bronx.

"Hey, Spider," Philly blurted out to the slim, wild-haired young man shooting a ball, "this is Lucio Rossini. "Looche might be the strongest kid in the city." Phil, while prone to hyperbole, was not to blame for this foible as his intent was merely to bolster and compliment his friends. Phil continued, "Looche can guard anyone in baskets too. When ya play ya wanem on ya team. Look at his neck, he's a bull. Just try and squeeze that baby with both hands as hard as you can; his neck won't budge, and he'll never cry uncle. That's how strong he is. Everyone tries it, and no one can dent him!"

Lucio responded, "Oh, Philly, you are getting a bit carried away. But you are right. No one has ever got me. Wanna try it, kid?"

"What?" said Spider. "Nah, I don't want to do that. I just want to shoot around!"

"What's a matter? You scared, kid?" Not wanting to be called a chicken, Spider acquiesced and after a couple of moments, he approached his new associate.

Moving slowly, Spider put the ball down and moved closer to Lucio. "OK, get ready, here I go," Spider spouted with a burst of reluctant courage. He drew on all the strength he could muster with both hands as he grabbed Lucio's neck. "Uhhh!" grunted Spider as he tried with all his might to penetrate the huge tree trunk of a neck the likes of which he had never seen! "Wow, I can't even budge your neck; it didn't even move, not one inch," said Spider as he released his hands, fingers and both arms spent. His hands began to cramp from the strain of trying so hard. Lucio was smiling and pleased with himself.

Phil was apt to instigate challenges like Lucio's neck challenge, and he was energized by his friends, and especially charged up when there was a competition. Some of his doings might embarrass others, but Philly just promulgated gems like this and everyone seemed to profit. "See, I told you Lucio was strong!" The three boys all had a good laugh, and Lucio invited them all to his momma's house.

"Nice to meet you, Spider! You're a really good shooter. You gotta give me some pointers soon, OK? After we're done playing, come on over. Momma's always cooking, and it's outta this world!" His mother, Momma Rossini, was a fabulous cook, and Lucio on occasion would invite his friends over for wonderful pasta, hot peppers and onions, and Momma's delicious sauce. Kids who were fortunate enough to be invited over marveled at the largesse of Momma Rossini, and her kindness was appreciated by Lucio's friends.

Lucio Rossini had a presence when you met him. He was serious but somehow comical at the same time. His eyes seemed to greet you and smile at the same time. He was intense in a charming sort of way. He had an eternal sort of energy; one seemed invincible. It was as if he derived his enthusiasm from another dimension of life, one that no one else could see. He was so confident in what he believed, mainly about how to win basketball games. As a ballplayer, he hated to lose. Lucio's solid lower body and strong legs enabled him to get good leverage to position and handle opponents on defense. While not a great speedster, he was quick and fearless.

Lucio was intense when he took the court; his hard drives to the basket defined his style of play. On defense, Lucio prided himself on shutting down opponents. He had a way of angling the core of his body so that he could steer the opposing player away from shots near the bucket. His knowledge of how to play good man-to-man defense would form the basis of his success in coaching, teaching tenacious defense. It helped establish him as a renowned college basketball coach. He also never forgot where he came from and taught the concepts of schoolyard ball, one-on-one play, and man-to-man defense. He liked tough physical basketball with quick moves and cuts to the hoop, always finishing hard to the basket. He emphasized the strong defense he played in the schoolyard, and his teams were hard to play against. He was a coaching success first at Columbia University, then at New York University, making the NCAA Tourney three times at NYU, including the Final Four in 1960. He coached players such as Barry Kramer, Satch Sanders, Cal Ramsay, Happy Hairston, Stan McKenzie, and Mal Graham at NYU, and Chet Forte at Columbia University. His NYU players were stars at NYU, and all played professionally. Chet Forte was a phenomenal player at Columbia and went on to a great career at ABC Sports.

The three boys stood in the schoolyard just off the courts as the winds picked up, adding to a chill in the air that they hadn't noticed when they were playing. Lucio extended his hand to Spider, and they shook hands, ratifying their new association. Then spontaneously, Lucio lunged toward Spider, playfully faking a blow with his clenched fist in the direction of Spider's stomach. Just before his fist reached Spider, Lucio pulled his hand back. "Hoouey," said Lucio as Spider recoiled. Then, with a big grin, Lucio's irresistible and loveable smile effected a big laugh from his two friends. Surprised and disarmed at the liberty Lucio had taken at his expense, Spider felt the relief of a good laugh, which was a bridge to an everlasting friendship. The gesture made Spider realize how much he loved to laugh. Philly particularly revered Lucio and enjoyed the way Lucio inspired good cheer with his sense of humor and hint of irreverence. For some inexplicable reason the laughter continued as Lucio's eyes burst with a wild crazed glare that in and of itself was hilarious. Perhaps because Spider didn't really know Lucio or Philly too well for that matter, but they couldn't stop laughing. Spider couldn't catch his breath and began to hyperventilate.

Feeling dizzy and tingly, he gradually let himself slide onto the cold asphalt floor of the grounds. Lucio, laughing uncontrollably, joined Spider on the ground in the hysteria of the moment. Philly seemed to be the only sane one and remained upright, while laughing along with his two buddies.

After a couple more minutes, the wave of laughter which had overwhelmed the boys gave way to relative normalcy, but the boys were still smiling. Their thoughts turned to playing ball, and they looked at each other to get something going as youngsters do.

"Let's shoot around. They'll all start coming in about a half hour," urged Rossini.

"I thought we were going to go over to your house and get something to eat, Rossini?" said Philly.

"Not yet, I was thinking about it, and I remembered that Genie told me Mintz and a couple other guys were coming down today," Lucio said, grabbing the ball.

They continued, and Spider rebounded and passed to Philly. Philly passed Lucio the ball, and they proceeded this way rebounding, passing, and shooting in quiet harmony. They started shooting at the foul line, moved to the top of the foul circle, and then continuing in a 180-degree arc, they shot from spots from baseline to baseline around the perimeter of the basket. They varied their distance from 12 to 15 feet out from the hoop. First Lucio shot for a couple of minutes; then Philly and Spider each did the same.

Lucio liked to talk, if not pontificate, especially about basketball. He and Phil were the perfect pair of friends. Lucio expatiated and Philly listened. Breaking the rhythm of their shooting session, Lucio expressed his passion for one of his favorite subjects, driving hard to the basket. Like opening a shaken can of carbonated soda, the idea gushed out from Lucio. He was transported and zealous when motioning upward with his arms clenched, demonstrating the technique of the hard drive to the hoop.

"You know, when you take a layup you gotta go up and reach out toward the rim, strong to the basket. Boom, like this," said Lucio, and he raised his whole body as if his life depended on it, extending his hands to the goal with a wild look in his eyes.

The three of them continued their practicing, and returned to rebounding, passing, and shooting for another twenty minutes when the courts started to fill with some of the better players. Quickly, pickup games began. Lucio, Philly, and Spider decided to play the three strangers that had just entered their half-court. They didn't know them, but Spider, Lucio, and Philly stayed on the same team to play against the newcomers. They found that they were very comfortable passing to each and looked to move the ball, circulating it fluidly among themselves. They passed and picked away from the direction of the pass. They moved to free up for shots by screening defenders. Sharp cuts to the basket away from the ball were rewarded with crisp passes to the cutter. The result was always a good shot, often a layup. They seemed to instinctively know and anticipate where the other was going. Lucio could pass and set a mean pick, and the boys were unselfish. They won the first game and the second and then lost the third. They left the court. It was getting late, and food was on their minds. By the time the boys left the schoolyard it was already later than expected, and they had to reschedule going to Lucio's for dinner. The next day, when Lester Mintz came down to Creston to play, Lucio and Philly greeted him and introduced him to Spider.

"Nice to meet you, Lester," said Spider, greeting the extra-large man with the big hands and barbarian handshake. He added, "Nice game yesterday. You must've gotten every rebound that came your way!"

"Thank you," replied the upbeat Mintz, and he began to shoot around as he spoke. Lester Mintz was bigger than most, with a large noggin, fair complexion, powder-white skin, and reddish flowing big hair. He just looked bigger than everyone. Lester's high cheekbones distinguished him, and with his big size, he made a powerful form on the court. His large powerful hands gave him the ability to rip 50–50 balls out of his opponent's hands, and this afforded him a profound advantage in rebounding. In basketball games, Lester was a talent playing in the pivot area sporting a good right-handed hook shot.

Lester, or Mintzy, as he was known to some of his friends, was charming. His unique sense of humor captivated his friends.Everyone wanted to hang around with Lester. He was a very popular figure.

Mintzy grew to like Spider, and the two became friends, seeing each other at the schoolyard, playing together often. With Spider's outside shooting and Lester's inside play, they made a strong combination. Lester wasn't fast but his strength and size made him a force in the schoolyard games.

Lester and Lucio had some great schoolyard battles. Lucio was fearless taking the basketball to the hoop, and Lester was a powerful big master defender. Lucio got the better of Lester one day on the court, and the two boys became fiercely competitive. Spider was playing with Lester and Phil Rick with Lucio against them. Lester got the ball on a possession and backed in on Lucio, who stole the ball. Lester didn't appreciate that, as he felt Lucio might have leaned on him a bit much; perhaps it should have been a foul. But Lester, like most, didn't call fouls.

Lester and Lucio were going at it like two young mountain rams locking horns. Neither gave an inch, and neither backed down to the other. Both were trying to dominate, and neither was succeeding. It was a stalemate. Lucio did, however, score the last basket, and he and Philly won the game. When the game ended, Lucio was smiling. He was joking around with Phil. While Lucio never made fun of anyone, Lester thought that Lucio was gloating about his victory. Lester was angry about the loss to begin with, and the laugh was salt on the wound. Mintzy controlled his temper for the moment and joined Lucio, Spider, and Philly in a conversation before leaving the court. Lester noticed a big floppy-eared redheaded boy on one of the half-courts on the other side of the school-yard and laughed. "Hey, look at that fella over there? Doesn't he look like Dagwood, or Blondie?" Lester said sarcastically, referring to the cartoon characters of the same names. The boys chuckled at the unknown boy's big ears. Then Lucio, getting ready to leave, said to his friends, "See you guys tomorrow." Lester interjected. He couldn't let it go after all. He wasn't done with Rossini. He looked at Lucio and pointed to Lucio's neck, "Hey, Rossini, you got lucky last game, but let's see how tough you are?" Lucio nodded his head, and the two moved to the area on the walkway in front of the Creston Junior High School classrooms, away from the playing surfaces. "Let's go, Lucio," said Lester spontaneously. The neck challenge was on! Mintzy flexed his huge hands, looking at the robust dark-skinned Lucio.

Rossini was taken aback. No one ever challenged him like that. He usually had to ask people to try it, not the other way around, and so he asked, "What, now, right here?"

Mintzy nodded his head and said, "Yeah." Lucio hesitated then responded, "OK, let's do it."

They began the battle of the neck. Lucio flexed his neck muscles and upper back with all his might. Lester approached him, facing the Italian bull-necked warrior. Lucio's expressive dark eyes welled with intensity. He prided himself on being the strongman of the schoolyard, and Lester was not going to beat him. Not here, not now, and definitely not in front of his friends at Creston!

"Here we go," said Lucio. "No, stop, stop, we are all friends, guys, cool it," said Philly. "Yeah," said Spider, "let's get something to eat." "No, don't worry, fellas, it's OK," said Lucio.

The giant Lester grabbed Lucio by the neck. Initially, Lucio was calm and appeared to be able to absorb Lester's pressure. Then Lester's massive hands did their work, and Lucio began to suffer. His face began to change color, turning dark red. Slowly, Lester applied more and more pressure using his elbows in tandem with his strong hands. Lester was getting the better of Rossini, and suddenly it looked like Lucio would asphyxiate. Not wanting to blemish his perfect record nor wanting to admit defeat, Lucio continued, steadfast. He would not give in nor cry uncle under any circumstance. Lester went deep into his innermost sanctum of power as he squeezed hard, harder, then hardest. Lucio's emotive eyes fluttered, his neck vulnerable, wearing down. Lucio would never admit defeat; he prepared to go down with the ship.

Johnny-on-the-spot Spider stopped it, getting between the two combatants calling out, "OK, enough, enough, stop, Lester, it's a tie, call it a draw. Both of you did great!"

Lester stopped trying to strangle Lucio and smiled. Philly attended to Lucio, who was a bit shaken up. "I'm fine, guys, I'm OK. Why did you stop it?" the handsome Italian said solemnly. He would never have given up had the competition not been stopped. Phil and Spider would joke about the incident for years and smile. The story became schoolyard legend. Lucio would never admit that he had been glad that it was over or that he was relieved when he was able to catch his breath. His reputation would remain perfect as the schoolyard strongman. Lucio and Lester showed their true grit that day, and they had impressed not only Spider and Philly but others who had watched in the schoolyard and marveled at each boy's tenacity and strength. Lester was plain strong; Lucio would have gone to the hospital before yielding. Good thing his friends broke it up in time. The intervention and the declaration of a draw allowed everyone to go home a winner.

Lucio Rossini would grow up and play for St. Johns University, and Mintzy would play college basketball at New York University, growing to be 6 feet, 5 inches tall, subsequently playing pro ball in the American Basketball League.

The two combatants would remain lifelong friends, and while Philly and Spider would tell the story many times thereafter, Lucio and Mintzy never spoke again of the "Battle of the Neck."

Meanwhile, the game of basketball was experiencing some growing pains of its own. Changes in the rules of the game were being implemented to speed up the game. The game was no longer played in a cage (hence the name "cagers"). There were no more jump balls after every basket. In organized ball there was now a center court line and ten-second rule. The rule changes were resisted by many coaches who didn't fancy changes to what they thought was an already fine game. These changes made the game quicker and provided more freedom and space, rewarding the more athletic players.

The next Saturday, Lucio invited Spider over to his family's apartment. Spider was intrigued by the idea of going over to a new friend's house for dinner. After all, he had heard so much from Phil about Momma Rossini's wonderful cooking. When Spider got there, Lucio required that he take off his sneakers and leave them in the hallway near the front door of the apartment. Lucio's mom immediately fell in love with Spider. She loved his big wild black hair and fussed over it, liking to touch it. It was a funny thing that embarrassed Lucio, but Momma Rossini was the boss and he didn't comment on this. Momma Bella Rossini's real name was Lucy. When she fussed over Spider's hair, she would say, "Solly, put some hot olive oil on your hair to make it nice n thicka. You'll never lose your hair if you soak it in the hot olive oil for twenty minutes every day. Then wash it out!"

Lucio's dad, Archie, didn't like Solly too much because of the way his wife fussed over Spider's hair, but Momma Rossini ruled the roost and Archie left Spider alone.

By today's standards a master chef, Lucy Rossini always had something savory cooking on the stove for the boys, who were always ravenous for her tasty meals, ready to eat, then eat again!

Lucio loved a thick spaghetti with garlicky meatballs basted in tomato sauce, with hot peppers, onions, and some family recipe spices. His mom made the best dishes and sauce in the neighborhood, and all of his friends loved her cooking and appreciated her generosity. Just about all of the Creston crew were visitors to the Rossini home, always enjoying Momma Rossini's fresh homemade dishes.

The schoolyard became haven for most when they were around ten years old, the age at which the boys were skilled enough to play and to walk home on their own. The games and camaraderie brought the boys together to play schoolyard ball even after they moved on to high school and college. As the boys progressed and entered high school, they played against each other, continuing to enjoy their camaraderie.

Chirping or needling to gain an advantage was part of schoolyard ball. Needling your opponent during pickup games became art form. "Hey, hey, miss it, miss it!" Or, "You can't make that. It's waaaay out of your range!" Or, "Watch it, watch it, heads up!" Or, "Watch out!" There were countless variations of ballspeak that activated good-natured competition. It was a weapon to throw opponents off their game. Some kids had rabbit ears and couldn't operate effectively amid chirping; others had sangfroid and collected themselves with grace under pressure.

Talking was a big part of the game in the schoolyard. You encouraged your teammates, helped them, and worked with them. Verbalizing helped on defense, defending against a pick-and-roll, or on offense to generate good passing, picking, and cutting to the basket—integral parts of the schoolyard game. Everyone called picks, and if necessary, they called "switch" to change off of your man to cover your teammate's man in defense of the pick setter and the dribbler using the pick. On offense, you passed and moved, passed and cut, passed and moved, always moving to a good space on the floor. You took good shots and didn't "chuck" or ball-hog. Everyone was engaged. You encouraged your teammates and complimented a good play. Good vibes were put forth by all who played the game in the yard. The positive energy helped better ball play. Verbal communications could be augmented by adding more clandestine forms of communication with teammates. Facial expressions could signal, "Hey, I got you," meaning I was setting a pick on your man and then watch me, I am going to roll to the basket. A raising of the eyebrows to your teammate could signal your teammate to cut "back door." Fouls were not usually called, and if they were, no one abused the rule. Everyone just wanted to play. On the rare occasions that a foul was called, the defense was usually transparent enough to admit the mistake and cede the ball to the opponent to reengage on offense.

Banter and good-natured competitive needling was a nonthreatening and understood part of the game. It was a streetball thing, and the rants would continue after the game as the boys would tease each other in a lighthearted manner. In the schoolyard, no one liked losing. If you lost you took a seat to wait for the next game, or two, or three, or four, until you got back on the court, hoping to win and stay on. Talking a good game became part of your schoolyard bravado, all the while trying to stay on the court, and survive.

There was, however, another aspect of the banter. As the kids got to be more mature, say fourteen or so, some excelled more than others. There were kids who dominated the boards, were faster, or could shoot better. Some had shifty moves, and others could impact a game with expert passes, lifting their teammates and elevating their game as well. Beyond this, there were players who competed harder. Casual schoolyard players were easy prey for their more serious counterparts. Within the ranks of the serious players there was an hierarchy of the very best players. These always wanted to win and assert their will. The fiercest of the competitors dominated games. The dominators were difference makers, and they developed a reputation, usually picked first in making up teams. Trying to beat a difference maker was an exciting challenge. On any given day, a young upstart could "feel it," go up against better players, and prevail. Every game was a quest, and in the best games, the competition was focused and the best of the best were intent on gaining victory.

You became "thick skinned" growing up in the Bronx, playing ball, and hanging out with your friends. You could "needle" endlessly at your pals both on and off the court. On occasion someone could go too far, but there were rarely big disagreements or fights, and all was done in good fun and great spirit.

The Creston Schoolyard crew would go in different directions when they entered high school. Some went to Columbia Grammar, a private school, and others went to DeWitt Clinton, one of the several area public schools just to the north of the schoolyard. Some would move away to Queens, Manhattan, or Brooklyn. No matter which route they took, they all seemed to love to come back to play ball at Creston. After the first year of playing in Creston, Spider continued to practice his shooting religiously. He found a rhythm in his stroke and could reel off basket after basket, practicing his two-handed set shot. He became proficient at foul shots, until he was almost perfect, seemingly never missing as Barney Sedran taught; it was a free point, not just a free throw.

Spider studied shooting and developed his own techniques to gain an edge. The two-handed set shot is an anachronism compared to today's one-handed jump shot, where the shooter can position the ball above his head, jump high, and get off a quick jump shot. Great shooters like Steph Curry can fire off 30- to 35-foot jump shots with lightning quickness. There are many other players today whose skills and quick release are truly extraordinary, as the athletes keep getting better.

Spider worked to get his two-handed shot off quickly. He did this by shooting the ball almost immediately when and where he received the ball without aligning the ball to its seams. Putting into practice the technique taught to him by Barney Sedran his first year in the schoolyard. He had listened to and learned from his mentor. He practiced receiving passes from his friends to get his shot off quickly in this manner. To create space in getting his shot off, he learned to gather himself, turning his body and positioning his feet so he could take a step back, and square his body up to face the bucket while he received the basketball. Sometimes off a screen he would anticipate his shot and take advantage of a split-second opening to get the shot off. He studied shooting and was able to deal with the elements when he practiced or played outdoor games. Wind direction and its speed were taken into account when he shot, like a golfer reading the bend of a green to adjust for slope or the cut of the grass. He began to shoot further and further away from the hoop, increasing his range yearly until he could convert his shots, first 12 feet, then 15 feet, and then 18 feet away from the basket. Each year that followed he sought to increase his range while maintaining his accuracy.

Spider could not get enough ball. He wanted to play more. One night he asked his mom if he could go out to play ball at the night center. He cleaned his place at the dinner table and put away his dishes after the family meal that night. It was almost dark, but he had heard some Creston Junior High Schoolyard kids talking about the night center. He wanted to try to play there. He had heard it was great competition and there were a couple of showstoppers who played there.

His mother, Jennie, with her deep Russian accent replied to him after he asked about the night center, "Have you finished your school voyk? Did you take the garbage down the hall and throw it down ze chute?"

"Yes, Momma, I have done both."

"OK," said the stout, gray-haired matriarch from Kovno, Lithuania. "Just be chome before ten tonight."

Without verbal response, and a quick nod, Spider scurried down the stairs and onto the gray marble foyer lobby of his apartment building. He passed the bronze eagle statue and exited to the street past Creston Junior High School on his way to the basement of a former Bronx Borough office building, which had been converted into a basketball court.

They called it "the night center," and in the darkness of the late-spring evening, the curly haired young boy entered a whole new world. Natural light of day gone, the yellow streetlamps softly issued a fuzzy glow, enough for him to find his way. The day's schoolyard done, play ended, now pro-longed. Spider opened the new door of the new world. The entry door had a steel vertical rectangular lock on each side of the two entry doors.

Spider entered, heart beating rapidly with an anticipation of the unknown; it was a new happening. Adventure was going out into the Bronx night. It thrilled the young boy. He had never gone out at night by himself. The night center was teeming with kids—rivals and friends were competing, altogether ebullient with a wonderful energy. Spider thought of the Fats Waller Song, "The Joint Is Jumping," as he went in.

There was only one court at the night center, and when Spider arrived at the court, there was a game going on. The full court was small, maybe 10 feet shorter than a regulation full court, with 12-foot ceilings and 8-inch black plumbing pipes at the ceiling of this, the bottom floor of a four-story building. It was difficult to shoot a basketball with a normal arc; the night center ceiling taught the boys ingenuity. The only way to make a basket was to adjust the arc of the ball to shoot a flat shot without trajectory. In this "line drive" fashion you could get the ball over the 10-foot rim, through the net, avoiding the ceiling pipes.

Spider didn't know anyone in the gym; he picked up a ball that said "night center" on it and began to shoot on a single practice basket which encroached on the main court. He watched the game as he shot, careful not to interfere with his ball in the game, only shooting when the play went down to the opposite end of the full court. This practice rim was in the small area adjacent to the Jerome Avenue side of the night center. The kids waiting to play sat on the broad window ledge, which was painted pale yellow, covering up a prior coat of white paint which had peeled, but which had been painted over, giving it a dimpled feel to the touch. As they all watched, the players on the sidelines talked about the game and the other players engaged on the court.

The sounds of the game were those of the pure joyful play of the young players—their rubber sneakers squeaking when the players stopped or changed direction, or as their sneakers got traction to leap to the rim.

You could close your eyes and visualize what was going on by the sounds of the sneakers. Players were hustling quick side to side, up and down the brilliantly polished wood floor. Spider was eager to play intense competition; the lure of night ball was a youthful incantation, a siren song, pulling him in. There was a loud cry! The game stopped. A tall Chunkmeister freckled-face boy with the bright ginger hair fell. He held his ankle, unsure of his predicament, unable to get up on his own. He was supported by two others, and he left the game and waited for the night center manager and first aid.

The game paused. There were several other youngsters waiting to play. Then Spider heard a voice. Some blue-eyed young kid was barking at him pointing his finger at him. "You, you, I'm talking to ya, you wanna play?" The skinny brown-haired straight-nosed boy with the blue-green eyes and expressive raised eyebrows launched at Spider like a cat.

"Come on, you wanna play or not?"

"Sure," said Spider in a quiet, almost inaudible whisper. "I'll play."

"OK," said Genie Wallach, about the same height as Spider but even thinner, a wafer in motion playing ball.

Eugene Wallach, the character, the paradox, was affable, complimentary, and friendly. He loved the dramatic, especially in conversation. He looked for the extraordinary in the mundane to enhance interest in what he had to say. "Hey, did you hear so and so said that he was better than you." He loved to stir the pot, making controversial statements about people or events to elicit reaction. "So and so says he's got a better outside set shot than you. Is that true?" He knew full well that so and so hadn't exactly made the assertion. Many of his statements were harmless and meant to get a reaction. Everyone who knew him liked him and found him amusing, but Genie never saw himself that way. He thought he was serious, but he was viewed by his pals as a likeable Danny Kaye-like character, jocular and charming. He was a serious ballplayer at the night center. He was happy in all that he did, never spent a day without smiling, and was a great friend to his schoolyard buddies.

Today, in their first ever meeting, Genie was just a kind soul who by some mystical force had plugged himself into the life of this new boy in the neighborhood, and as Spider didn't know Eugene, he didn't know what to think of him. As the game had not yet started and Spider entered the court, Genie continued his verbal foray and asked the newcomer, "Where are you from? Haven't seen you here before?"

"I live nearby, and I play at PS 79 most of the time. This is my first time here."

Then Genie responded to Spider, "Oh, you play at Creston Junior High School? You must know my pal Lucio Rossini? We are going to Columbia Grammar School next year? It's Lucio's twelfth birthday tomorrow."

"Wow," thought Spider, "my birthday was yesterday, April 22, what a coincidence!"

Spider couldn't utter a word. Eugene didn't give him the chance, but Spider appreciated that Genie got him in the game, and at that moment Genie could do no wrong in Spider's mind. "Let's go. You take that guy over there," instructed Genie, pointing. So Spider entered the court, wiped the street dust off each of his sneakers with his hands, and began to guard the small left-handed ball handler everyone called "Lefty." Genie didn't have time to introduce Spider to the other players on his team, so it took a couple of times up and down the floor to understand who was on his team and who wasn't.

Soon, Spider got the hang of it, learned who his teammates were, and started to blend in well. Genie had randomly picked Spider to play, and their good fortune was that they would develop a friendship and remain friends for the next eighty years. Genie was the same character all his life—friendly and shy but intense when playing ball.

The tough economic times of the early '30s made the schoolyard boys excel in life. They would become doctors, lawyers, insurance agents, ad men, clothing salesmen, coaches, and artists. The boys of Creston Schoolyard and the night center chose different fields of endeavor, yet they remained in contact, always friends. They would share the events of their lives for some seven decades and beyond. Schoolyard basketball was their object of reflection until it wasn't, and they spoke of the game as a science. They exchanged theories and opinions, pensive and analytical.

CHAPTER 4
Shifty Lefty

"OH MY GOODNESS, THIS KID is unbelievable!" thought Spider. "Looks like he's going one way, and then he changes direction on a dime. What springs in his legs, like rubber bands. Holy moley, he's on another level!"

His name was Lefty Levine. His wry smile was etched on his face, lips tilted right, mouth tightly closed like he gritted his teeth when he played. It wasn't a jocular smile, but rather a look of a confident knowledge that no one could beat him. Maybe there was someone somewhere who could beat him, but if there was, Lefty hadn't met him. He did not know failure, and his look was that of the dominant persona on the basketball court. His assertion was always that the court was his and his alone. He could turn on his rocket-quick moves whenever he wanted, and there was no one who could do anything to stop him. Some kids were duly impressed with his game and would attempt to praise him, but Lefty thought talk was cheap, and he looked upon compliments about his play as annoying and unworthy of his acknowledgment. He wore more than a wisp of arrogance about him, a slight young man, of average height, but with a huge, almost incredible game.

With it all, Lefty dominated whatever game he played. He had an air of greatness, a '30s facsimile of Nate "Tiny" Archibald, and like Tiny, Lefty played high school basketball at DeWitt Clinton.

Lefty saw the whole court three seconds before anyone else. As he played, his great peripheral vision helped to anticipate where the ball was going and use that to his advantage. It was almost unfair to play against him, and he was rarely challenged in the local pickup games. He'd compete with anyone and beat them. As Spider tried to guard him, Lefty schooled him. The crafty left-hander could invent passes, moves, or shots that no one had the ingenuity or creativity to execute. Spider dug down in a deep low defensive stance, and with all he had he strained to keep up with Lefty. Suddenly there was a "no look" pass from Lefty to Melvin Fields, who took one step and laid the ball in the hoop. "What a pass!" The pass was as good as anyone had ever seen. Lefty cupped the ball, wrapped the ball around the front of his neck and right shoulder, and in a 360-degree motion passed it over his left shoulder, knowing precisely where his teammate would be. The pass found its mark on the left wing, and Melvin converted it for an easy layup. Lefty passed left but kept his eyes deceptively to his right, not looking at his target.

After the basket, Genie Wallach got the ball and passed it to a speedy, square-shouldered Lenny Lesser, who dribbled it up the court and crossed over on the dribble drive to beat his man. Spider's man came over to help, and Spider cut to the hoop, but the pass went to Artie Reichner on the other wing. Artie fired a running one-handed bank shot and just missed. The ball bounded hard off the backboard, and Lefty gobbled up the rebound. Lefty headed up court the other way and threw a behind-the-back pass that surprised his teammate and went out of bounds. Wallach took the ball out again, this time passing to Spider, who dribbled quickly up court, stopped, faked a shot, and hit Artie Reichner, who fired up a one-handed semi-hook shot from the right side to score.

"Nice pass," said Artie. Spider quickly hustled back down the court to play defense. Lefty got the ball and hit Wally Sencer with a pass that Wally then, in turn, tap-passed like in volleyball to Lefty, who returned it again to Wally with a between-the-legs pass. Wally shot it and missed the driving layup. Lefty darted in and grabbed the offensive board, baseball passing it over to Wally, who shot and missed again. Genie got the rebound and passed to a cutting Lenny Lesser, who passed it back to Genie and then set a pick for Genie. Genie drove to the hoop and scored on a beautiful layup. Losing focus for a moment, Lefty lost the ball off an errant dribble, and Spider grabbed the loose ball after a scramble with Wally Sencer. First fumbling it and then scooping up possession, Spider bolted down the court, passing it back and forth with Lenny and Artie downcourt, with Lenny scoring on an easy layup off of a 3 on 1 fast break. After Lefty missed on a long, long shot, he, looking disinterested on defense, loafed back and tried to steal the basketball from Spider, who darted to the left. Taking two dribbles, Spider set and fired a 14-foot two-handed set shot, which whooshed cleanly through the net.

Genie yelled out, "Nice shot, fella." The play was a short-lived moment of glory. Lefty, agitated, went to work knowing where everyone was positioned at that moment and instinctively knew where they were going. The dimension of time slowed. Lefty saw everything in slow motion. He slowed the game down in his perfect basketball mind, and he could see it all unfold so clearly, like no one else. The flame had been lit. Torched on one end of the court by the slender Spider, Lefty, with a burst of speed dribbled by Spider at mid court; at the foul line an eager Lenny Lesser tried to stop Lefty, and it appeared to work. It looked like the little shifty dribbler was going to get broken up by Lesser, but Lefty had an ace in the hole. He got out of Lenny's snare, and with a quick change-of-direction move, the lightning-quick Lefty put the ball between his legs for fun, looked back to his left and then back to his right and finally passed it back to his left. The fleet-footed Dave Polansky grabbed the gift pass, laying the ball up and in for an easy hoop.

"Whew," cried Lester, "nice move!" Lefty took control of the game after that. He was the best player on the court. The sly Lefty was just a notch above the rest of the players, and they all knew it. Spider tried to guard Lefty, but the crafty playmaker was too quick. He was one of those talents with physical gifts, more dynamic in his thinking of the game, anticipating plays. Lefty just thought out of the box; he saw the game differently, as if he were in a blimp over the court looking down, capable of predicting the movements of all the participants, anticipating moves ahead of everyone else. In fact, if you played with Lefty and weren't paying attention, he could hit you so perfectly with a hard pass that it could embarrass you, even hit you in the face with the ball if you weren't paying proper attention.

The next time down the court on defense, Spider dug in deep again and guarded Lefty even more aggressively, but now he tried a new technique—backing off Lefty to give himself more room to adjust for Lefty's lightning-quick change of direction. Lefty attacked, closing the gap between him and Spider. Lefty dribbled the ball like it was on a yoyo string. When he was arm's length away from Spider, he pushed the ball out away from his hip to his left, dribbling with his left hand; then he crossed over to his right on the dribble drive. He blew by Spider again, like a roadrunner, scoring on a layup with his right hand.

It was a move that Spider would remember. It was at that moment he realized that there were always better players out there and he'd somehow have to adjust to compensate and close the gap. He'd have to work harder if he wanted to compete with players like Lefty.

Making a good number of his long shots and some sharp passes, Spider had a nice game. He sat down with Genie after the game, having lost, waiting to play again. The garrulous Genie asked, "Hey, what's your name again?"

"Solly. Solly Cohen, what's yours again?"

"Genie, Eugene Wallach. You live around here?"

"Not far, we just moved to Grand Avenue. They play here often?" asked the newcomer.

"Yes, every Monday, Tuesday, and Wednesdays and sometimes Thursdays between 6:00 p.m. and 9:00 p.m. Why don't you come tomorrow? You know Lucio Rossini said he's coming tomorrow," Genie insisted.

"That's great! I'll try and make it," Spider replied.

"You know, he doesn't live far from here, just down the way on Creston Avenue," said Genie.

Before Spider could get a word in to respond, Eugene, in his own inimitable way continued, "Sol, this is Lenny Lesser."

"Hello Sol, nice to meet you," said the dark-haired Lesser, who had a flashy look, like that of a young Errol Flynn.

"Nice to meet you, Lenny," said Solly.

"And that's Wally Sencer and David Polansky. They just won, and they're staying on the court. We'll wait to play them again if they win."

"Wait," the black-haired olive-skinned Polansky said. "Three of the guys are leaving. It's just me and Lefty. You guys play with us, OK?" he asked pointing to Lenny, Genie, and Spider. "I am going to hit the water fountain," said Polansky, the youngster with the muscular calves of a track star.

"Nice to meet you, Sol," said Dave.

"Yes, hello, Solomon," said Wally Sencer, impishly twisting Solly's name. "Nice to meet you as well. I'm Wally...Wally Sencer."

The night center was a great spot to play ball in the evenings, and Spider promised his mom that he would go to temple on Friday nights in exchange for her letting him go out during the school week to play night ball. His father did not approve of this ball-playing, preferring that his son start working a job to earn for the family. Spider had different ideas. He wanted to play ball.

Lefty Levine had been the dominant player at the night center for as long as anyone could recall. He had the look of a champion athlete. He had thick auburn hair parted on the left side, and his dark eyes looked at you without seeing you; he was that focused. His nose was punctuated with a high bridge and a slight turn to the left, where it might have taken a blow on one of his fearless drives to the basket. His powerful legs gave him the ability to dribble the ball and change direction with incredible traction, like the late great Gayle Sayers.

Four years later, Lefty would team with Ralph Kaplowitz, Sonny Younger, Billy Giles, Sid Carson, Benny Auerbach, Mel Glover, Leo Gottlieb, and Spider. They were part of DeWitt Clinton's 1937 team which beat defending champion Thomas Jefferson High School in the semifinals and Seward Park High School in the New York City Championship.[7]

The 1937 Clinton team consisted of ballplayers who had learned the game playing schoolyard ball at places like Creston. Many continued to play in college, and some went on to play professional basketball. DeWitt Clinton High School profited from this stable of ballplayers and consequently became a basketball powerhouse, winning the City Championship often.

Lefty would play at CCNY on a full scholarship; he was touted to be the next Bill "Red" Holtzman, the City College star.

Not everyone, however, makes the transition from schoolyard to organized ball, and Lefty struggled to make the transition at CCNY. While at Clinton, his individual style of play was so dominant that the coaches were just happy to have him out there. Lefty was ahead of his peers at a young age. He had matured ahead of everyone. He was accustomed to beating his competition, almost spoiled by his early success. When Lefty went to CCNY, he struggled to adapt his game to play with other players who were at his level. The competition got better, and some of the kids he had dominated in the night center or the schoolyard had caught up. Lefty lasted but a year at CCNY. For the first time he dealt with obstacles in his path to success. He would not achieve the greatness that everyone in the schoolyard expected of him.

While drugs were not yet a big problem in the schoolyards and colleges, the popularity of the game and the attraction of large college basketball crowds drew the attention of professional gamblers. Some ballplayers were impacted by gamblers who were associated with organized crime. A point-shaving scandal ultimately led to the demise of the LIU, CCNY, NYU, and other top-notch New York Metropolitan College Basketball programs.

Lefty Levine was a legend of the night center and the schoolyards in the Bronx during the mid-1930s. The kids who saw him play would talk about his ability with reverence for the rest of their lives.

The night center was Spider's engagement with a series of friendships and a crew that would hang together for the remainder of their lives, playing basketball, socializing, commuting on trains together, and even serving in the army in World War II.

On the Wednesday night before Thanksgiving, Wally Sencer asked Lenny, Genie, Spider, and Dave Polansky to come over. The group walked together down Jerome Avenue up to East 184th Street and then hiked up the stairs to Wally's family's fourth-floor walk-up apartment. "Come in, fellas," spouted Wally. "Mom, sorry but a couple of my friends are over. OK?"

"OK, Walter," said Mrs. Sencer. "Dad's not home, but I have some corned beef and cabbage. It's been boiling now for a bit. Would your friends like some?"

"Oh yes, Mom, that's great," replied Mrs. Sencer's son.

The Creston crew entered the apartment while Wally's mom had started cooking dinner. The kitchen aroma was a small cloud of the sweet smell of the corned beef. The boys were truly appreciative of the Sencer family's generosity. Wally's mom had a big heart and was genuinely concerned for the boys. She tried to make sure that they had enough to eat. Everyone knew how hard the times were, and she wanted dearly to be helpful to her son's friends. "How were your games at the night center? Was it crowded? Did you boys have fun?" Wally quickly answered for the group.

"Mom, it was great. We had a great time. Did those books come yet?"

When Wally's mom answered affirmatively that they indeed had, Wally smiled. The loving mother was happy to hear that her son had such nice friends. As they talked with Mrs. Sencer, Spider realized that Wally had vanished. All the boys knew about Harry Houdini, the great magician and showman who was both an escape artist and someone who could make himself appear to disappear. Wally had vanished like Houdini, no longer in the main room of the apartment. The others had not noticed Wally's disappearance, or so it seemed.

Wally was witty and well read, and his rapier-sharp brain induced you to match wits. Spider wanted to engage more with his new acquaintance, but Wally had disappeared. It was surreal. Had he imagined that Wally had entered the house with him and the others, or was this some kind of alien kidnapping like "Buck Rogers" in the radio show? "Excuse me, Mrs. Sencer," inquired Spider, "is Wally OK?"

"Oh yes," replied Mrs. Sencer. "Wally is in his room reading. He always reads about science. His uncle just sent him some biology books. He wants desperately to be a medical doctor. He reads all the time. We are used to it. He throws himself into study or reads without regard to anything or anyone, but he doesn't mean anything by it. That's just Walter. You boys sit down and grab a plate. You're gonna love this corned beef and cabbage. We'll be lucky if we see Walter for a while, so relax and enjoy the food as he studies. I'll put the radio on in the living room so you boys can listen to some music."

Spider was dumbfounded. He wondered why Wally had invited the boys over if he was going to his room to read. He saw that Dave, Genie, and Lester were not disturbed at all by Wally's behavior. "Yeah, Wally does this all the time. It's normal for him. He'll be out in forty minutes or so or whenever he's done reading. He's a whiz, you know. He's just like that. Man, he knows everything about everything," said Genie Wallach. Spider acquitted his new friend of his idiosyncrasy and waited with the others. They listened to the radio, chatted with each other, and enjoyed the stellar meal. After an hour, Wally came out of his room and gave his mom a big hug. He was happy for whatever he had learned.

By the time Wally emerged, Dave Polansky and Lennie Lesser had departed, so it was just Genie and Spider remaining. Wally was the genius in the group. He was brilliant and constantly distracted by the myriad of thoughts that his active mind generated.

Wally was a great friend to many, compassionate to all. He enjoyed subtle humor and a good laugh. His friends were very important to him, and if you could tolerate his peculiarities such as his obsession with study, he was enamored of you. He appreciated your respect, patience, and friendship.

After he had emerged from his room, Wally greeted Spider and Genie. "Sorry, fellas, I lost track of time." Wally spent another twenty minutes talking to Genie and Spider about his interests in biology, and they exchanged thoughts and pleasantries. Wally's knowledge of all subjects—science, literature, politics, and world events—was greater than most. Everyone was interested to hear what Wally had to say about all subjects. He was a liberal bon vivant. He loved to live and let live. He did not filter anything or anyone, and he accepted people for who they were and for what they thought. He did not try and change their thoughts or their passions. In return, he respected you if you accepted him as he was. He was not overly outgoing, but when you got to know him, you wanted to hear what he had to say. He was entertaining and someone who was always learning new things and expanding his horizons.

The time went quickly, but they had been at Wally's for two hours or so, and it was time for them to go home. They thanked Wally and his mom for the great meal and headed home.

Genie lived nearby on the Grand Concourse, which was considered a more comfortable and upscale address. Spider lived on Grand Avenue, which was a bit further of a walk from Wally's family apartment. Genie and Spider walked home together.

"Yeah, that Wally is something," Genie said.

"Yeah," said Spider, "he's really sharp!" The two youngsters walked a little further talking about the night center, the schoolyard, Lefty, Wally, Dave, and Lennie. "Thanks for getting me in the game, Genie. It looked like I would never get in with all the kids waiting to play. Thank you. Are there always games like that?"

"Yep. Yeah, we play all the time, almost every day except Fridays during the week and the center is closed on weekends."

"That's great, Genie, I'll start coming. Do you always play here?"

"Yeah, Solly, what else am I gonna do? I gotta play and get in shape to play at Columbia Grammar next year," Genie replied.

The boys' route took them by Genie's home, and Genie went up to the Grand Concourse apartment. "See you next Monday," Genie said.

"Great, see you then, or maybe at Creston over the weekend?" said Spider, who turned away and headed home. Spider passed Burnside Avenue and walked back to his apartment on Grand Avenue. It had been a great night. He had met a whole new world of friends and had played some great ball at a fantastic new place. Life was good.

After the brief holiday respite from play, Spider walked to the night center the following Monday. He ran into a couple of familiar faces on the way. Dave and Lenny were hanging around the neighborhood newsstand, and Spider reached out to them.

"Hi," said Spider, turning to greet his new pals. "You going over to the night center?"

"Yeah, we sure are, in a couple of minutes. How ya dooin?"

"Good," said Spider. "Heading over there myself right now." The three boys joined up and walked over together. They talked about the night center and how those low-lying ceiling pipes made it hard to shoot there. Lenny and Dave complimented Spider on his shooting the last time and talked about Lefty Levine.

"Lefty is phenomenal, isn't he?" Dave said.

"Yes, he is. I had a rough time guarding him!" said Spider sheepishly.

Dave replied, "You know, he's really good, and it's very rare to see anyone stop him. But when you are guarding Lefty, he's quick, and the only thing you can do really is when he crosses over you may be able to slap at the ball and deflect it. It's not easy, but once you let him get going to his left, he's almost impossible to stop."

"Thanks, Dave," said Spider. It was the first time that Dave would teach Spider something, but not the last.

As they approached the night center, the boys had a good heartfelt talk. "We are gonna play ring-a-levio on Sunday, over at my building, Solly. There are a lot of good spots to hide, in the stairwells especially. So, if you wanna com'on by around two on Sunday afternoon. We usually get a milkshake over at the candy store after. Com'on over, we go by my building on the way back from the night center, an' I'll show you where to go Sunday." Spider felt delighted by his new friendship. Good things were starting to happen for him.

Spider looked forward to the weekend to meet up with Dave, Lenny, Genie, and Wally. Dave was a couple of inches shorter than Spider, but his strong core and legs rippled of muscle, and made him one of the fastest runners around. His muscular calves, in particular, enabled him to accelerate in a sprint with lightning speed. His tightly cropped dark hair and keen brown eyes distinguished him and gave him a striking appearance. He had a presence about him when he was in a room. He was intense, serious, but could enjoy a good chuckle with his pals. He was focused on success. He spoke glowingly of Wally Sencer as the boys walked to the night center. "Wally is the smartest guy I've ever met," said Dave.

"You're no slouch, Dave, you're pretty sharp yourself," uttered Lenny. Lenny was quiet but accommodating. His deep-brown eyes had a bit of mystery to them. His neatly combed black hair and pallid complexion resembled more Robert Cummings, the star of the late '50s TV show *Love That Bob*, but Lenny was a good schoolyard ballplayer. Reserved, polite, and unassuming, he was content to groupify with Dave, Spider, and other pals. Soon, they entered the night center. It was going to be another good night of basketball.

The first game was full court 5 on 5 ball on the night center court, the only court for games. The teams were divided so that once again Lefty and Spider were on opposing sides. Lefty got the ball off the first possession, and taking Dave's advice in guarding Lefty, Spider tried to anticipate Lefty's crossover dribble from left to right, but Lefty was too quick. When Spider slapped downward to steal the ball, Lefty hesitated in anticipation, raised up for a nanosecond, and rocked back in the same very direction to speed by his opponent and lay the ball in. "That's OK," Dave said, "nice try, Solly. Keep working, you'll get him." But Lefty was too tough. It was another evening of fun ball, and the boys looked forward to the weekend.

Sunday came and Spider joined Dave, Lenny, Wally, Genie, and Lucio Rossini to play ring-a-levio. Lester Mintz came with Lucio and Artie. Dave organized the game. "We'll divide up into two teams: Wally, me, Lenny, and Solly against Genie, Lester, and Lucio. It's 4 on 3 because I asked Lester Hirschfield to come, but he didn't show," said Dave, continuing, "You guys go first to hide, and we will count to hundred and then track you down."

Dave counted out and after he got to hundred, he shouted out the words, "Ring-a-levio 1, 2, 3, here we come!" Then they were off, and the thrill of the hunt was on. There were all kinds of hiding spots around and under Dave's apartment building. In its stairwells, hallways, and nooks and crannies, the kids could remain in hiding spots that could go unnoticed. There were small entryway foyers and vestibules which tucked under the stairwells on each floor. These hiding spots were plentiful and allowed the game to perpetuate. Dave's building had six stories and two different stairwells. There were spaces under the stairwells where bicycles, strollers, and other large pieces of equipment were secured, and which also provided cover and opportunities to hide as well.

It was a great afternoon, and as the day welcomed its cousin, dusk, the boys grew weary of ring-a-levio. Each team had found all of their opponents once, and there was nothing further to play for. It was too late to get a milkshake; they had played too hard and too long. Fatigued, they said goodbye and headed home. It was the first such group union of the crew, and they found that they were genuinely interested in each other. They enjoyed hearing what the others had to say, and they wanted to listen to each other's views of everything from basketball to analysis of every kid in the schoolyard. Most importantly, they all liked ice cream, milkshakes, and, of course, egg creams. In their own way, they were all different, with diverse talents; yet in a way, they were alike, joined by their passion for ball.

Eugene Wallach had introduced Spider to this great crew, and Spider appreciated it. Genie was friendly to all, and everyone liked him. He was charming and loved and lived the game of basketball.

As Spider got to know Genie, he appreciated that his new pal could light up a room with his pleasing personality. Spider also learned that much of what Genie said had to be taken lightly. He was a kind soul and loved his friends. He had a way of talking to try and elicit a response. "Hey, Polansky, Rossini scored more than you. What do you think about that?" Or, "Hey, Solly, Lesser says he's got a full scholarship to college and you don't." The bold and sudden bursts of the outrageous belied the quiet and shy inner Genie Wallach personality.

Genie was so shy he struggled to meet girls. In the balance of things, Spider returned Eugene's favor of the night center, ten years later, as it was indeed Spider who introduced Genie to his wife Harriet. Harriet was a petite and attractive redhead who had a twin sister Charlotte. Genie, in a burst of newfound courage, gathered the nerve to ask Charlotte on a date, but Charlotte already had a boyfriend. Spider knew that Charlotte had a twin sister and arranged for Genie to meet her. Charlotte's sister Harriet and Genie ultimately got married. Genie and Harriet remained happily married for over sixty-five years. Harriet was the perfect wife for Genie. They had a wonderful life together raising two handsome and successful children, Michael and Barbara. Genie never changed being outrageous, but Harriet knew how to handle him. When Genie made one of his off-the-wall comments, Harriet simply smiled and said, "Oh, Genie, come on." Genie would acquiesce at Harriet's suggestion and stop, changing the direction of the conversation into more innocuous commentary.

As lifelong pals, the schoolyard crew helped each other out. They rooted for each other. They became lawyers, Certified Public Accountants (CPAs), salesmen, and doctors and rarely charged each other for their respective services and were happy to share their learned skills with their boyhood pals. They were from the schoolyard, a bond which lasted a lifetime.

Dave Polansky, discreet and polished when he spoke, chose his words wisely. With Genie, if he hadn't thought it, he hadn't said it. Dave was different. He was studious and serious. His words were purposeful and reflected his deliberate thoughts. He treated everyone he met with dignity and respect, and no words left his mouth without careful consideration.

Like Genie, Dave loved his friends. When you listened to Dave talk about basketball, you were listening to one of the most intelligent basketball minds.

After school hours, the boys played every game they could think of in the schoolyard. Basketball, stickball, hand ball, and a little baseball were most frequently played. Sometimes they played stickball in the occasionally trafficked side streets outside the schoolyard, or they played a game of frenetic ring-a-levio in and out of the neighborhood apartment buildings.

On some days, they would go to the Mullaly Playground adjacent to the old Yankee Stadium to run on the track. The track encircled a football field, which hosted high school and neighborhood pickup football games. Dave was an elite 440- and 880-yard runner. He trained and prepared his pal Spider for the physical exam for entry into the local Bronx Police Department precinct. Dave had a legitimate chance for All-Metropolitan Track Honors at CCNY until he was struck in the back of his calf muscle by an errant javelin thrown during a track and field competition. Dave recuperated, but it set back his track career and he never quite regained full form after the injury.

The crew of boys from Creston grew up together and stayed engaged in each other's lives. As they matured and stopped playing ball in the schoolyard, they continued to help each other as they began their careers, each contributing in their own unique way. Wally was the science and medicine man. Spider was the lawyer; Mintzy and Genie, the salesmen; Artie, the artist and philosopher; Dave, the professor and coach; Lucio, the coach and gifted speaker; Flicky, the contractor; and Lester Hirschfield, the CPA. They each had their own perspective and opinion on basketball and lifestyle.

Mel Fields was tall for his age and proved himself to be a rugged schoolyard ballplayer. Younger than most of the Creston crew, he was mature for his young age, but he started playing with his pals three to four years older because he was good enough to play with the older players. They called him "Flicky" because it was easier to pronounce than his Austrian family name of Flichtenfeld. The family name would be legally shortened to the name "Fields." Mel never liked the nickname "Flicky' but tolerated it from his pals. He grew up with three sisters and his father Louis, who was thirty-four years old when Mel was born. Mel would grow to be tall and strong, 6 foot three, and 180 pounds when he was discharged from the army in 1946. His mother Anna passed away, and his dad remarried. His stepmother, Ethel, welcomed Mel back after World War II, his dad having passed away. He was an intense player, a solid rebounder, and his elbows were seemingly sharpened daily, giving him a reputation for physical board play. He was not a great shooter nor skilled from the free throw line. He could, however, grab rebounds and make quick outlet passes. He could rifle the basketball, vacuuming it off the boards and then passing it with pinpoint accuracy. He was unselfish, embraced his rebounding role, and was skilled at getting the ball to the shooters at the perimeter. Flicky was wiry, with tanned olive skin, brownish-blond hair, and powerful shoulders. Hc backed down to no one and was best battling for 50–50 balls under the boards. Mel would play against the legendary Bob Cousy at the famous Nevele Country Club. Everyone was excited to see if Mel could contain the much-heralded Cousy. Mel was really up for the game and was one of the best defenders in the schoolyard. Mel guarded Bob Cousy, but while Mel was an excellent high school player, Cousy was one of the best ballplayers of his time. Mel did his best and played Cousy tough, but Cousy scored 20 points...in the first half! Cousy was that great.

Mel joined the Seabees in the Pacific Theater during World War II, helping to build pontoon bridges among other projects. Mel became wealthy from both his contracting business as well as hard moneylending. He would lend money on a handshake, taking interests in enterprises which needed capital. When the company hit big he would share in the upside of the company, yielding him exponential profits on his loans. If the loan went bad, which it rarely did, he was a good sport about it and moved on. He loved his buddies, but he was more of a lone wolf. He moved to Manhattan when most of the Creston boys went to Bronx high schools, but he loved coming back to the Bronx on weekends to play at Creston.

Rebounding is such a critical component of any game, and the rebounders sometimes are overlooked as scorers are flashier and grab more acclaim. But if you don't get the ball off the boards you can't get anything going, and in the schoolyards that skill was appreciated. The kids always wanted to play with rebounders like Mel when picking teams.

Rebounding amounted to winning. Usually if you outrebounded your opponent in the schoolyard games, you won. If you won, you stayed on to play more games against the myriad of boys waiting to play. Everyone wanted to stay on the court, if possible to play all day without having to wait on the sidelines.

The Creston Schoolyard crews were so close that they wanted their children to know each other. Many of their children knew each other and interacted. As they garnered adulthood and all of the crew had children, Dave Polansky became a teacher to many of their children and developed several camps which became a platform for his teaching of sports to those children.

Dave loved to expatiate on the game of basketball. Looking forever distinguished, Dave liked to smoke his pipe, loading it and lighting it, all the while reflecting and speaking about basketball. There were many Creston crew group informal roundtable discussions with Spider, Dave, Genie Wallach, Lou Rossini, Lester Mintz, Artie Reichner, and sometimes Lenny Lesser. Dave would do most of the talking, lecturing as a de facto professor of the game. He was a great coach and teacher. Loved by his players, he furthered his knowledge of the game by hobnobbing with other metropolitan area coaches. One of Dave's associates was the great Red Sarachek, the then Yeshiva Men's College basketball coach, who was an advisor to many NBA coaches. The high-profile professional coaches looked to Red for behind-the-scenes offensive and defensive strategies. He was widely considered a genius of the game. Dave and Red both had the same issue. They were both great coaches with very limited university money to recruit blue-chip players. After the CCNY point-shaving scandal, City College was banned from playing in Madison Square Garden, and basketball was de-emphasized as no longer being a big-time sport. The CCNY team that had won both the NIT and the NCAA Tournaments in the same year (the only team to ever do so) would no longer remain at the pinnacle of college basketball. Dave Polansky picked up the pieces of the CCNY Basketball Program after the scandal, taking over from the legendary Nat Holman. The program continued under Dave's masterful guidance, but CCNY would never return to the national stage as a top nationally ranked NCAA team.

Everyone admired Dave for his knowledge and ingenious approach to the game. He gained his knowledge from the schoolyards when he was a preteenager and continued afterward in his journey as an assistant coach and ultimately as a head coach. He developed a theory in coaching. He saw the game as a series of lanes and alleys that had to be recognized and taken advantage of on offense and defended on defense.

Like the whole of the Creston crew, Lester Mintz played in both the schoolyard at Creston as well as in the night center. Mintz went on to play at New York University and later in the pros in the American Basketball League, one of the indirect predecessors to the NBA. Beyond being a very good basketball player, Lester was funny, warm, and charming. You always felt that Mintzy was great fun to hang around with to enjoy an evening out on the town or at a party. At reunions of the Creston boys, Lester was the life of the party, laughing heartily and making those around him share in his laughter. One time, Lester went to one of the reunions at the Brown's Resort in the Catskill Mountains. Everyone else showed up with their wives. Lester had everyone in stiches as, having recently been divorced, he showed up at the dinner dance with his new girlfriend, a stunning Swedish blonde, but who happened to be six months pregnant. None of the Creston crew had ever heard Lester mention the girl, and it was a big surprise to see Lester dance the whole night with his gorgeous and very pregnant friend from Stockholm. She was a nurse at Mount Sinai Hospital, and Wally Sencer had introduced him to her that very day. They danced every dance. They were enamored with each other and danced cheek to cheek for the duration. If you knew Lester you just had to get a kick out watching him put on a show dancing with his Swedish friend. He was the free spirit among his schoolyard pals.

Wally Sencer met Mintzy first in the schoolyard, and the two of them became good friends playing ball. Wally was not nearly as good of a player, but Mintzy respected Wally greatly and Wally became one of the biggest winners ever to come out of the schoolyard. A top neurologist in New York City, Wally also was a scholar and became a renowned professor at the Cornell Medical School in Downtown Manhattan.

After he became a doctor, his friends affectionately referred to Wally as Dr. Fiddlefoos. A serious professor of medicine and a physician, Wally was a Santa Claus-type figure—jovial, affable, loving, and caring toward friends, particularly his schoolyard pals. He had thin brown hair and an infectious smile when greeting friends. He was all in on anything he did. When he studied he surpassed most in focus, blocking everything out but his work. When he played, he was in the moment, concentrating on nothing but basketball, and when he socialized, he was the master of the gathering. He thought only of the task at hand to the exclusion of all else. If he was playing ball, he didn't worry about his studies. If he was socializing he was the best friend and the most charming character imaginable, never giving his studies or playing ball a thought.

Kind and giving to his friends and family, Wally could nevertheless show an acerbic wit and sarcastic sense of intellectual humor. His mind was so sharp that many didn't understand him, and if they did, they were concerned about getting shown up in a match of wits. His barbs were multidimensional, and just as you thought you understood what he was saying he would come back with a remark that would convince you that you had missed the point completely and did not understand what he was talking about. It made you feel inferior, but just at that moment Wally would smile and give you an affectionate avuncular hug.

Wally was also a great teacher. He taught his friend Spider how to focus on his work and exclude all else from his mind. A prodigious reader, Wally read and studied ravenously. He could go for weeks without speaking to any of his friends, often skipping the schoolyard and night center pickup games when his studies proved more important to him. He was singular in this unwavering intensity to make himself the most well read and knowledgeable person he could be.

After Wally became a medical doctor and Spider returned from the war in Europe, Spider enrolled at NYU Law School. At the same time, Spider played pro basketball in the ABL, hustling back and forth from the various out of town arenas to NYU Law School, often taking trains and taxis in the early-morning hours to alight at school, sleep-deprived but ready for class. At the time Wally and Spider both lived in different small single-room-occupancy dwellings near Gramercy Park in Manhattan. They became best friends. They double-dated with some of the girls that they met in bars, at the hospital, or in the summer at the beaches. They went to New York Giants' football games at Yankee Stadium, New York Knick games, and college basketball games at Madison Square Garden.

After the war, it seemed like everyone was celebrating the war's end. It was summer. These were good times, and people were having fun. The two Creston Schoolyard young men would create secret identities, pseudonyms, sometimes introducing themselves as movie characters to impress. They could take on roles of fictitious characters like "Gus Langley," an actor going out to Hollywood soon for a big movie screen test. If their character was unsuccessful in impressing, they would change tactics. At 11:00 p.m. they would say the word "Blimey." This meant that they would double up on their socializing in search of the most fun. They would fondly recall their shenanigans for the rest of their lives, reflecting on their postwar meanderings in Manhattan, which was alive and a fun place to be.

Artie Reichner became a distinctive personality in the Creston crew. As a ballplayer, he was a fast dribbler, who used his dribble to set up an accurate one-handed running shot. Artie started playing ball in the schoolyard a little before Spider. He met Spider when he helped him shovel snow off the court at Creston one Sunday morning. "Thanks. I was getting tired," said Spider. They soon found themselves in a 3-on-3 game. They both knew how to pass to each other, waiting until a defender turned his head or "fell asleep" on a play. When that happened, one of them would instinctively cut to the basket, receive the pass, and lay the ball up off the backboard. Artie liked to play ball with Spider. They worked well together because they read each other's moves on the court. Artie had other interests besides basketball as well; he loved art and literature. He analyzed works of art and liked to frequent museums. Ironically, he would end up owning a piece of a building right behind the Museum of Natural History in Manhattan.

When World War II began, Artie and Spider found each other in the army. In basic training camp, in 1943, they trained for war in Europe. The world was in a state of apprehension and chaos. One day during the year's hottest summer day, Spider led the calisthenics at his division's basic training camp at Frenchmen's Creek near Miami Beach. There were about 1,000 or more soldiers that Spider directed in the exercise. They were doing conditioning, doing jumping jacks, push-ups, sit-ups, leg lifts, and then they ran in place for several minutes at various intervals. It was over 100 degrees and extremely humid. All of a sudden some screaming and yelling emanated from the center of the giant group of exercising army soldiers. As the leader of the calisthenics, Spider was responsible for the safety and welfare of the group and started to panic. Had someone died? Was someone passed out and in a coma? He rushed toward the source of the ruckus. Knifing through the rows of soldiers, amid the great buzz of chatter and gasps of scores of exhausted men, Spider could see that one of the soldiers lay prone and motionless on the asphalt parking lot of the adjacent hotel. The desiccated young man appeared pale and was immediately attended to by the medics.

Spider entered the area of the fallen soldier and stood looking at the face belonging to the listless body. He recognized the face but wasn't sure of the soldier's identity. He panicked because he had never seen death before and didn't know if the man was still alive. Spider tried to get a closer look and moved to the other side of the body in pursuit of a clear perspective. After he made his maneuver, Spider could clearly see. "Holy mackerel," he thought, "I don't believe it! It's Arthur!" It was his old pal from the neighborhood, Artie Reichner. He had passed out from dehydration and was comatose. If Spider wasn't so worried about Artie's health, he would have smiled, if not laughed. What a coincidence! "What are the odds of this," he pondered. Fortunately, Artie was given some smelling salts under the nose, and he quickly regained his wits.

"Solly," he said. "What are you doing here?" Then he realized his error. "Oh, man, I forgot where I was. Sorry," Arthur said with a slight smile. Arthur was polite, apologetic, and exhausted. The two school-yard pals would remember the experience affectionately for the rest of their lives, retelling it with a good belly laugh each time.

The schoolyard was the hub of their lives. It gave them the wonderful experience of getting to see each other almost every day. They didn't need cellphones or even house phones to communicate. They knew where they would be each day, and they hung out. Their immigrant parents were delighted at their sons and their progress in school and in meeting new ambitious friends. These boys would have better lives than their parents who had sacrificed everything to come to this new beautiful, rich America. They envisioned a brighter tomorrow for their youth. Martin Luther King's dream that one day his children would not be judged by the color of their skin but rather by the nature of their character was three decades in the future, but the immigrants of the Creston crew wanted something similar for their children. They didn't want them to be judged by their ethnic background, their religion, or where they came from, but rather by their own character, work ethic, and achievements. America was the land of opportunity and everything was possible.

Youth goes by in a minute, an ephemeral divine gift. Never appreciated by youth itself, it is a marvel that allows one to run, jump, and play all day, seemingly without fatigue or failure. The schoolyards were full of youths flexing muscles on its playing surfaces. The playing surfaces were gathering places to play and socialize, try out new ideas, and realize new associations. The schoolyards were wonderful places for these immigrant adolescents to grow up. These youth would grow up to be called "The Great Generation." They were, indeed, a generation rich with long-time associations and friendships built with a deep foundation, developed over time with friends deliberating with each other and taking the time to get to know, respect, and appreciate each other. Schoolyards, a cultural phenomenon, were contained areas, learning grounds for a great generation of youth.

CHAPTER 5
Big Brother Benny

THEY PLAYED ALL THROUGH THE summers on the hot asphalt-and-concrete courts. The days of constant ball-playing became weeks, then months, and time went by so quickly. Each year different kids developed, some advanced ahead of others from one fall to the next. Each kid grew and developed in their own unique way.

Ralph Kaplowitz and his brother Danny were outstanding Creston Schoolyard ballplayers who went to DeWitt Clinton High School. When the Kaplowitz brothers took the court, the schoolyard games were high energy and competitive.

Ralph Kaplowitz had become a star of the DeWitt Clinton High School varsity basketball team. Ralph, several years younger than Danny, followed his brother to DeWitt Clinton. Ralph was always picked first in the games at Creston, even if he came late and there were kids waiting to play ahead of him. You could say that Ralph was the "King" of the schoolyard, and when he showed up, everyone perked up. Polite yet competitive, Ralph rarely lost a pickup game at Creston. During 1936–1937, he captained DeWitt Clinton High School, leading them to the New York City High School Basketball Championship. He played college ball at NYU where he was an All-American. Ralph played professionally, a starter on the first New York Knickerbockers' 1946 BAA (NBA team).[8] His teammates on the Knicks were Ossie Schectman, Sonny Hertzberg, Jake Weber, and Leo Gottlieb.

Danny Kaplowitz played at Long Island University, where his 1939 team won the NIT and were deemed the national champions of collegiate basketball, going undefeated, winning 25 games without a loss. Danny played pro basketball in the American Basketball League, known as the ABL.

Ralph was a tall, slender figure and had thick brown hair, parted on his left side and combed neatly. His fiery dark-brown eyes could disarm an opponent. He used his wiry frame in the pivot to body up and position defenders using his sharp coat-hanger shoulders and solid torso. He had long arms, which belonged to a man 4 inches taller. He had the long, strong legs to play a power game. He was strong under the boards and was surprisingly speedy for a man 6 foot 4 inches in high school. His fine set shot and accurate hook shot allowed him to move swiftly to the basket if the defense guarded him close, and like a greyhound, he was graceful, organized, and well balanced, running the court with incredible stamina, seemingly never tiring.

On one Monday, Clinton was off from practice, and the schoolyard was crowded. Danny and Ralph came to play at Creston in the afternoon. Benny Cohen was nine years older than his brother Spider and the oldest boy in his family. Benny left home when he married Gertrude. He began to work, moving into a small one-bedroom apartment in the Bronx. He did not go to college. Instead, he went to work at the local US Post Office. The post office was a desirable position with great job security and benefits. The entrance exam sought to weed out the many and choose the few, so it was a tough and challenging examination. Benny passed the exam, securing a position at the post office. The Bronx, and for that matter the entire United States, still suffered from the poor job market and the poor economic conditions of the Depression. Any job was good, especially one that was with an established company or government agency. The post office, unlike some other employers, did not host oppressive work conditions, and, most importantly, the post office usually did not lay off employees and was known for excellent benefits and good treatment of its staff.

Benny excelled at the post office and was often called upon for advice. He was a sage analyst of postal operations. Well read, and intelligent even beyond his book knowledge, Benny also excelled in his knowledge of languages.

Postal work was tedious and exasperating. Benny was only twenty-one and would have been a junior in college had he continued his studies. Still a very good athlete, he longed to free himself from the shackles of work to play basketball. The problem was finding time to do so. He had played at the Creston Schoolyard until he graduated high school. Benny was also a well-known, outstanding, and formidable stickball player. He could hit mammoth drives of the little rubber ball used in the schoolyard stickball contests. Once a week, Benny went back to his parents' apartment to visit. His brothers Spider and Murray were younger, still living at home with their parents. Benny liked to visit them but also liked to go to his secret hiding place in their apartment.

On the top shelf of the deep hallway closet, Benny hid his treasure trove. Toward the back of the top closet shelf, two shoeboxes lay hidden behind hats and scarfs. Inside the shoeboxes classic baseball cards appreciated in virtually perfect condition. Benny had been keeping these baseball cards as long as he could remember. Benny's cards included Babe Ruth, Lou Gehrig, Pie Traynor, Jimmy Foxx, Al Simmons, Chuck Klein, Tony Lazzeri, Frankie Crosetti, Home Run Baker, and others. One special card was of Shoeless Joe Jackson, which Benny figured would be worth a pretty penny one day. Benny kept these cards in little sheaths of a soft translucent paper, which protected the cards and preserved their excellent condition. He organized the cards meticulously, in alphabetical order.

Every time he went back to see his parents and brothers, he would sort his baseball cards. He told Gertrude, his wife, about the cards meaning to take them to his marital apartment. For some reason, however, he had not done so. He had accumulated the baseball cards hoping one day they would become incredibly valuable. He loved to collect baseball cards, and he loved the game of baseball. He knew the teams and the players. He had hoped one day to be a pro baseball player. Hank Greenberg and Babe Ruth were his favorites. He excelled in stickball in the schoolyard and in the street just outside the schoolyard on Creston Avenue. He was one of the very few kids who could hit a ball "3 sewers," considered a giant blast marking the length in between the sanitation sewer covers. Benny could hit both right- and left-handed pitching equally well. His blasts were line drives, and he would pound down on the ball and rocket shots that seemed to rise in stages majestically skyward. Kids would talk about him in the schoolyard, fascinated with his batting prowess. "Shots fired, shots fired," they would say jokingly, when the crack of Benny's stickball bat rocked a ball with a sound that ripped through the yard.

The long day of work at his Bronx Post Office was an endless parade of people rushing to get their correspondence and packages off to loved ones and friends. Many of the Jewish customers sent packages of every necessity imaginable, including gold coins, important documents, and cash to family in Europe. They were worried about the well-being of these relatives, and people were tense. Sisters and their brothers in America were concerned for their sisters and brothers in Germany, France, England, Belgium, Holland, Roumania, Hungary, Austria, and Poland. Reports and eyewitnesses of German Nazi atrocities were already widely known in the Bronx Jewish community.

Benny was not normally even tempered by nature, but today he was irritated. Today the waves of complaining customers descending upon him had him aggravated. The folks coming into his post office expected everything and lacked simple manners.

Benny had not planned to play ball at Creston; he usually didn't even pass by the schoolyard to get to his parents' apartment. He usually went straight there. For some reason, today he wanted a diversion, so he passed by the courts. Benny saw the courts and the kids playing and realized that he missed playing ball himself. "How did this happen?" Bennie questioned himself as he stood. "It feels like I haven't played in so long. I should play more often!" He was on the side of the court, merely observing Spider, his brother, who was shooting around with a couple of other kids. He had just come from the post office and was still in his post office work shoes. He had intended to stop off at his family's Grand Avenue apartment to visit his family and check out his baseball cards, but once he entered the schoolyard, Spider spotted him on the sidelines and pleaded with him to play some ball.

"I can't, Solly. I just came from work. I can't play in these," Benny said, pointing to his rubber-soled post office work shoes.

"That's OK, Benny, come on, please play. We need you. These guys are good," Spider implored.

"All right," Benny said reluctantly, welling up with fraternal pride.

So Benny took off his post office jacket, threw it just outside the court's boundaries, and remained in his blue Bronx Post Office pants with the white stripes down each side. His lonely white shirt and hidden tank top undershirt felt a bit chilly at first. He would soon warm from the heat of his body working hard while running up and down the court. Benny had long since stopped playing organized basketball. "I hope I can last out here," Bennie thought as he jogged onto the court, feeling stiff. "Man, I'm really stiff! I need to loosen up a bit," Benny mused as he readied to play. Spider passed Benny the ball, and he warmed up taking a couple of shots and a couple of layups; his body began to feel comfortable on the court. He barely realized that he was on the court in his work shoes. Everyone else had on shorts, T-shirts, or basketball practice jerseys and sweatpants. Importantly, everyone else on the court was getting ready to play in good sneakers and not work shoes.

Benny was stronger than his 5-foot-10 frame suggested. He had a low center of gravity and used his strong lower body and arm strength to ward off taller players under the basket for rebounds. He could move his opponent away from the hoop, forcing him out from his comfort range, away from the bucket, making it more difficult for his opponent to score. Benny was not easily impressed. So when he saw Ralph Kaplowitz, he was not intimidated in spite of Ralph's stellar reputation. Besides, he had other things on his mind. He was still thinking about work and was still bothered by his workday.

Ralph Kaplowitz was a sophomore at DeWitt Clinton, just having finished a banner year there and already a star on the varsity basketball team. The courts were not quite as chilly as they had been, and the weather at the schoolyard was moderate. In any event, the boys were accustomed to playing in the twilight of winter. Everyone was excited about the imminent spring. The Kaplowitz boys were brimming with confidence. They expected to "stand the court," anticipating a run of wins to keep their place on the court as winners. No one could remember the last time Ralph's team had lost in schoolyard pickup games. It was assumed that his team would win even before the game even started. It was a given. His brother Danny was really good as well, so anybody who could keep the score close would achieve at least a moral victory.

Benny joined his brother Spider and Lou Simon as they started shooting baskets. The rules in 3-on-3 and 5-on-5 games were that the winner was the first team to make seven baskets. You had to win by two baskets, or the game extended until one of the teams won by two baskets. Benny, nine years older than Spider, hadn't played any ball in a while. His job at the post office kept him from hitting the courts. His principal exercise now was to haul packages back to the holding area after they had been dropped off at the post office counter. Benny was stationed there daily to deal with the many customers. He directed their letters and packages and provided stamps and other postal materials and information.

They started to play half-court 3 on 3 and did so until the score was tied 4–4. More kids wanted to play, and they added two a side and transitioned to play full court. "Goodness," thought Benny, "I don't know if I have a full court game in me." But he was still jazzed about his day at the post office, and he wanted to release some of the angry energy from the day's frustration at the post office by playing with his brother. He acceded to the 5-on-5 whole-court game. The postal officer's stamina would be tested, as they wiped the slate clean and the score started at 0–0.

From the very start, Ralph wanted the basketball, and once he got it, he backed down in the low post on Benny. With his DeWitt Clinton practice sweatshirt flapping with the wind as he moved quickly, he went to work. Ralph got a quick pass from his brother Danny, turned in the pivot, and laid it up easily on Benny. Benny untucked his shirt to free his arms.

The next time down the court on offense, Ralph, the best ballplayer in the schoolyard, backed in on Benny again. Benny bent his elbow and rested it on Ralph's lower back using his free hand as a rudder to steer the Clinton star away from the basket. He arched his body and flexed his muscles to defend. His entire body and strong arms now moved in unison. This time, when Ralph tried to back in again on him, Benny forced him out away from the basket. Ralph shot falling away from the basket, off-balance and out of his range. He missed. The next time on defense, Benny stayed fierce. Ralph couldn't get a good position on his next shot either and let it go from the foul line. He missed again and the ball rang off the rim where Benny grabbed the rebound. He fired the outlet pass to Spider and then followed him downcourt. Benny hustled up court just in time to get a return bounce pass from his brother to beat the younger Kaplowitz back for the layup. The following time down, he set a pick for Spider and rolled off Ralph, getting a pass back for a little lefty hook shot—good for another basket. Ralph didn't expect the shot from the left side, but Benny could shoot with either hand. On defense, Ralph tried to take Benny to the hoop backing in one time and then turning and facing to drive the next, each time underestimating the power and grit of the post officer. Inspired by his unexpected success in the game, Benny felt a swell of energy, feeling powerful and fully engaged. He wasn't thinking that running up and down the court would have a consequence, and he did not worry about running out of gas. He hadn't run and played this hard in a long, long time and didn't concern himself about whether he would ultimately tire. He just let it all go and played as hard as he could for as long as he could like it was a championship game.

With the score tied at 5, Benny moved out to the left corner and Lou Simon hit him with a pass. Benny launched a beautiful two-handed set shot from the far corner. As Ralph came up on him, Benny fearlessly shot the ball right through Ralph's outstretched arms, and the ball went in the basket for a score. The next time down with the score once again tied at 6, Benny got a pass from Spider and drove on Ralph to the basket. As Benny beat Ralph, his brother Danny came over from the weak side to block Benny's shot. Benny extended his left hand to ward off his defender and laid the ball in off the board to give his team a one-point lead. With the game on the line, and for his grand finale, Benny hit a set shot about 5 feet beyond the free throw arc to win the game. Ralph, who would soon be an NBA champion, was shocked. The game was over, and Benny had made six of his team's eight points in leading his team to a big surprise schoolyard win. Ralph and Danny had made all six of their team's points. "That guy was pretty darn good," thought Ralph. In fact, the Clinton star knew he had been handled by Benny. "Nice game, Benny, now I remember you from a couple of years ago. You used to play more regularly here. You were pretty good then. Too bad you didn't keep playing. You could have been one of the really good ones. We'll have to play again soon. I'll get you next time!" But on this day, Benny proved up to the task, thwarting the soon-to-be College All-American's advances to the rim, and putting Ralph away with a postal worker's demonstration of rebounding, passing, running the floor, and shooting.

In an organized game with officials and referees, Benny might have been called for a foul or two on defense, but in the schoolyard, it was a tougher game and that was not the way the game was played. It could be more physical than games with referees. Kids didn't go out of their way to call fouls, and rarely did. Benny's tenacious style of defensive play neutralized Kaplowitz. That was quite an accomplishment as Ralph was very competitive and didn't like getting beat. In fact he rarely did. He was a winner and a champion going on to win the BAA/NBA Championship in 1947 with the Philadelphia Warriors besting Max Zaslofsky and the Chicago Stags in the finals.[8]

Spider was proud of his older brother, who ruined his pants that day in the fervor of the competition. Benny, the hero of the schoolyard, and his brothers would have a hearty family meal of noodles and chicken soup, pumpernickel bread, and borscht as they regaled the family with the events of the day and of Benny the hero. It was a good family day, and the boys were delighted to spend time with each other. Murray and Spider liked having their older brother around and very much looked up to him.

When Benny retreated to his apartment that night, his wife Gertrude chastised him. "Ben, you can't play ball like that and ruin your work pants! What are you going to wear to work tomorrow? Let me wash them for you. There's a nice breeze blowing. I'll leave the window open in the kitchen and hang them out on the line off the fire escape so the wind can dry them. Maybe they'll dry by morning," Gertrude uttered. She would become an Iowa State Representative and was adept at handling almost any difficult crisis with aplomb. Benny quickly showered and got to bed soon after returning from his banner day at the schoolyard. He had given it more than his all, and he was completely wiped out from his day at the post office and from playing ball.

While his wife was not happy, Benny felt that her ire was a small price to pay for the great feeling that he had from the wonderful game, his performance, and the great workout and sleep that were a consequence. Soon Benny and Gertrude moved out to Iowa, leaving New York City. Benny became an egg farmer in Waterloo. The legend of the off-duty postal worker and his successful combat with the All-American lingered like a hidden spiderweb at Creston Junior High School. Benny, while born a New Yorker, was modest and more Midwestern and was never impressed by the admiration shown to him in the schoolyard for his athletic prowess in either stickball or basketball. Humble, never arrogant, he was an extraordinary athlete.

Like many others at the time, he would not be able to fulfill his dream to play college basketball. He had to work. He had to earn. He was mostly a mellow man of mild temperament, but on this one day, his competitive spirit had been perked, and in the end, he took quiet satisfaction of the knowledge that he could be really good. He was the best ballplayer in the schoolyard that later winter's day, and his family's All-American.

CHAPTER 6
The Creston Crew

THE SCHOOLYARD WAS THE BEST classroom. Its kids learned from each other, from the trials of competition, and from the players who returned there to mentor the schoolyard kids with their passion for the sport. Many of these players had gone on to college or the pros to play, and some just loved to coach and mentor. The Creston Schoolyard was a free flow of ideas, and players.

Dave Polansky profited and learned from the experiences of these schoolyard returners. He really listened and absorbed. From the composite of techniques and basketball philosophies, he formulated his own. A physical conditioning expert, he knew from athletic experience that the ballplayer who developed endurance through training would be rewarded later in the games. Moses Malone made this notion famous. In 1983, Moses led the Philadelphia 76ers to the NBA Championship with a sweep over the Los Angeles Lakers. His quote, "I'm a greyhound in the fourth quarter,"[9] reflected his confidence in his endurance. Malone was a natural and reached the pinnacle of the NBA through his excellent stamina and dominant skill.

Dave Polansky embraced conditioning in his own training and in coaching and training players. He worked his players into better condition so as to outperform. The conditioning regime paid off and the players benefited, often winning games against equal or more talented opponents.

Dave finished high school and went to CCNY. He graduated there and became a well-known CCNY professor and basketball coach. Dave's play designs anticipated movement with and without the basketball through "lanes and alleys." Vince Lombardi drew up rushing plays with blocking schemes aimed to seal off the defense and create open lanes to spring his running backs to advance the football. Dave had a similar concept in basketball. He envisioned lanes and alleys on the basketball court which could be used in tandem with screens to seal off defenders, creating open space for players cutting off those screens and getting to the rim for baskets.

In the schoolyard, Dave designed innovative plays that captivated his Creston pals. Dave's imagination inspired confidence and trust, and he was a leader looked up to by his mates in the schoolyard. He was a scientist of the game. He studied it. He wrote papers as a professor at CCNY on the game of basketball. He was impressed in the early 1950s with the athleticism of the great African American basketball players in college and pro basketball. He wanted to coach the best players and get the most out of them. He took over for the great Nat Holman in the early '50s. After the point-shaving scandal, CCNY could no longer sign blue-chip recruits. It was the sad end of a great program that is still famous for being the only college team to win both the NCAA and NIT tournaments in the same year. In spite of these limiting factors, Dave's teams played disciplined and aggressive basketball. Dave always gave his team a great chance to win. Dave was a natural-born coach and disciplined athlete, and as a coach, Dave's knowledge and focus was second to none.

Lou Rossini loved to kid around but was always ready to play ball. Lou had a great sense of humor. One time he walked up to Genie Wallach in the Creston Schoolyard and playfully said, "Genie, you know what I really like about you? It's perhaps what makes you so extraordinary. . ." Then Lucio remained silent, as Genie waited and waited in great anticipation of a wonderful compliment from his friend Lucio. But Lucio was just playing around and never finished his sentence, leaving Genie hanging. Finally Lucio smiled. Genie finally realized the gag and started to laugh along. Lucio and Genie both got a kick out of it. Like Dave Polansky, Lucio showed leadership and coaching instincts at an early age. Lucio joined Genie Wallach and attended Columbia Grammar High School. They played there and continued to play ball together at St. John's University. Genie Wallach could reciprocate the gags and needles with the likes of Lucio and his other schoolyard pals. Genie really liked to needle his more serious friends to make sure that they didn't take themselves too seriously. He could say something like, "Polansky, I heard Shike Godhouffer (then a pro basketball player who originally played at Creston) is coming back from the pros today to teach you a lesson!" This was an absolute tall tale, and Dave, amused, would just laugh it off. Genie would smile along, and they would share in the humor of the moment.

The most intelligent of the crew was Wally Sencer, but Wally's academic pursuits cut short his days of playing ball at the schoolyard. While he didn't intend to miss hanging out and playing ball, Wally was preoccupied with his schoolwork, his reading, and his exploration of all things science. Wally became a prominent and successful neurologist at Mount Sinai Hospital and the great medical and psychological friend of his schoolyard buddies, tirelessly helping them in their medical needs for the rest of their lives. He was a valued friend and resource.

Wally enjoyed his Italian food and dining out in Manhattan. He grew to be a cherubic and charming man with a wonderful smile. His sparkling smile and sharp wit distinguished him as a unique character and friend. He adored Spider for his athleticism, and Spider admired Wally for his knowledge and his character. Their friendship ran deep, and they grew to rely on each other for their complementary skills.

In the schoolyard, Arthur Reichner had a good running one-handed shot and was a streak shooter, inexplicably getting hot shooting the basketball, capable of making six or seven shots in a row without missing at times. Had he been more consistent, he might have advanced to play in college. Like many, he played in the schoolyard and loved it.

In 1946, after they had served in World War II, Spider joined a group of his schoolyard pals as they played together in the summer as members of the recreational counselor staff at the Nevele Country Club. It was a reunion of sorts for some of the Creston Schoolyard kids. Spider had just finished his rookie year playing for the New York/Brooklyn Gothams in the ABL. He was joined by Dolph Schayes, then a freshman at NYU, Mel "Flicky" Fields, Milty "Whitey" Gries, and Lester Mintz. Dolph, Lester, and Whitey were NYU players. The resort took their staff basketball teams seriously, carefully recruiting the team for every summer's competitions against rival country clubs and resorts. They competed against other Catskill resorts, and the stakes were high. Spider told the Nevele manager about his old pal from Creston, Arthur Reichner. Wanting to get some of the Creston crew back together, Spider raved to the Nevele owner about Arthur's shooting. "He's a deadly one-handed shot, I tell ya!" The Nevele was a legendary Catskill mountain resort for the greater New York metropolitan area. The Nevele was proud of its competitive adult basketball team and provided room and board to the players to play on its team.

One of the owners dealt with the players and was their number one fan. He knew Spider, Dolph, Lester Mintz, and Milty Gries from their collegiate and pro ball reputations. Spider realized that the Nevele had to approve Artie to play as he, unlike the others, did not play college or pro ball. Spider sought to help his friend who wanted to join Spider and his schoolyard buddies at the resort in the summer. Spider, like his other schoolyard pals, was always looking to help out a fellow schoolyard mate. He told the ownership of the marvelous shooting ability of his pal Artie. He approached the owner Mr. Slutsky, as the boss entered the player bungalow. "This Reichner kid can really shoot and help the team," said

Spider. Mr. Slutsky did not react immediately; he remained silent and departed. Later that evening, however, as most of the players were resting or sleeping in their bunks, Slutsky once again came into the player's bungalow.

The owner approached Spider and asked, "Where's that deadeye shooter?" Spider pointed to the bunk where Artie was resting, and said, "He's over there, Mr. Slutsky." The owner approached Artie and said in an audible whisper, "How you feeling? Hey, are you a right-handed shooter?" Artie nodded in the affirmative, half asleep. Spider was listening intently and could barely believe what he next heard. Slutsky continued in a further whisper to Artie, "Why don't you sleep on your left side so you protect that good shooting arm for tomorrow's game, OK?" Artie simply nodded his head and didn't say a word. Spider was content that his spiel had worked, but he and Artie would share a good laugh about this fabulous moment for years to come. He thought how much fun it was to be there at the Nevele with all the boys he had grown up with, away from the Bronx, in the fresh air of the mountains and this beautiful farm country and landscape. "When this ends," he thought, "I will savor the time up here and remember it." "Thanks, Solly," Artie told Spider, "can't wait to play tomorrow!" Artie fell asleep shortly after the exchange. It had been a great day, and he had a great sleep. The Creston crew would laugh about the Nevele owner wanting to protect Artie's shooting arm for decades, retelling the story countless times. Artie and Spider would remain good friends for the rest of their lives.

In the Catskills, at the Nevele, the reunited Creston crew had fun. They were lifeguards and counselors, ate well, and played good basketball. Dolph Schayes was the star of their Nevele team, and everyone enjoyed playing with him, because he made his teammates better. The Nevele would be the home of great summer basketball with superior competition versus surrounding resorts. Games between resorts were well attended. These outdoor basketball games in the backdrop of the

Catskills hosted great summer ball for many years. Besides the Nevele, there was the Brown's Hotel and Resort, Kutsher's Hotel and Country Club, Grossingers, the Concord Hotel, the Granit Hotel, and Brickman's, among others. The Catskills were so popular people called them the Borscht Belt or the "Jewish Alps."[10]

Kutsher's Resort hosted the "Maurice Stokes Benefit" game where some of the best NBA All-Stars would come to help raise money for the incapacitated former NBA Rookie of the Year for the Cincinnati Royals, Maurice Stokes. His teammate Jack Twyman put on the event and the proceeds went to the benefit of the fallen athlete. After being the Rookie of the Year in 1956, Stokes played three years in the NBA becoming an All-Star, before being stricken down by his illness, which he incurred playing in the NBA. In a game in 1958, Stokes was knocked unconscious after driving to the hoop. In a subsequent game, soon after, Stokes suffered a stroke during the game and was paralyzed. The Maurice Stokes benefit game would be held for years afterward at Kutshers, and Stoke's benevolent and kind teammate Jack Twyman became his legal guardian and took care of him. Stars like Wilt Chamberlain, Bill Russell, Oscar Robertson, and the like would play in the benefit year after year. In 1965, you could get there two hours early to watch the game, and it was truly unique to see all these great pro stars playing and giving back for a fallen comrade. You could watch the game up close, sitting on the grass encircling the court. It was better than courtside seats at official NBA games, a real treat.

Spider and Lester Mintz horsing around in the Catskills at the Nevele.

Left to Right: Arty Reichner, Saul Cohen, Lester Mintz, and Milty Griese

The beautiful Bernice Rosenthal, soon to be Mrs. Bernice Cohen, my mother.

They were married August 18, 1951, after courting for 2 years.

Photos from: Barry Cohen's Family Album

SCHOOLYARD FRIENDS FOREVER

Photo from: Barry Cohen's Family Album

Center front clockwise: Dolph Schayes, Milty Griese, Unknown,
Saul Cohen, Unknown, Flicky Fields, Unknown, Lester Mintz,
last 4 persons unknown

SMART SET

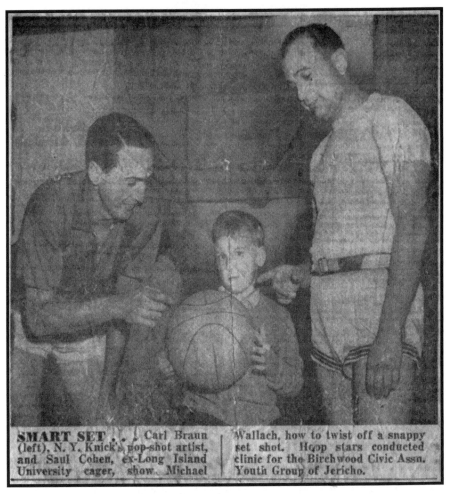

SMART SET . . Carl Braun (left), N.Y. Knick's pop-shot artist, and Saul Cohen, ex-Long Island University cager, show Michael Wallach, how to twist off a snappy set shot. Hoop stars conducted clinic for the Birchwood Civic Assn. Youth Group of Jericho.

Photo: New York Journal American

Carl Braun, NY Knicks Star, April 17, 1959, at Jericho Country with Genie Wallach's Son Michael center with the ball and Saul Cohen to his right. The crew never stopped caring about each other and their families.

CHAPTER 7

Coach Regan: Lineup Dewitt Clinton

* * *

"I DON'T VONT U TRY out basketball!" shouted the gray-headed Russian father to Spider. "You should be voyking mit me! Or you just get a job like Benny. Vus es dus? Mama, u tell!"

Spider's mom, Jennie, didn't speak. She wanted the best for her son and wanted him to go to school and be happy. "Abrahm, luz em gayen! He's still young. Let him get an education."

With that Spider's father, Abraham, began to yell at him in a mixture of broken English and Yiddish, "I voudn't givya a nickl mit yer futah, vistach, ni eine nickl." Abraham was mad at his son. He wanted help in his business, and he wanted Spider to work there.

He was getting older and needed help. When Spider left the house that day he felt like he had let his dad down, and he was sad. Had it not been for his mom's words of support, he might have actually run away from home. He felt worthless, but he had to overcome his melancholy. He had basketball try-outs in the afternoon. He had long awaited this day. He thought only about basketball for the rest of the day, trying to block out his father's angry rant.

The gym at DeWitt Clinton High School was the home of some great high school basketball. An all-boys school at the time, Clinton was having its junior varsity basketball tryouts. Spider looked at the many champion-ship banners on the walls and could plainly see what he already knew—namely, DeWitt Clinton was a perennial New York City High School Boys Basketball Champion.

"OK, boys, line up, line up, line up, line up. One at a time, make a layup, get back in line, miss, you're done, head for the locker room." It was January 1935, and the skinny youngster from the Creston Schoolyard was tryout nervous. The ninth-grader was apprehensive, if not intimi-dated. There was Lefty Levine from the night center also trying out. Everyone looked bigger, stronger, and faster.

"The top twelve of you make the team," Coach Regan said, firing words at the young Bronx boys, adrenaline running through their bodies, nervous, fre-netic. The boys lined up at the foul line. To make the team you had to catch a pass from the coach, dribble to the basket, and make the layup. Moving deliberately upon receiving the coach's crisp passes, the boys hustled to make their layups, and so they went: make, miss, make, make, miss, miss, make, miss, make, miss, make, make, miss, miss, miss. After seven boys had made their layups, they were all thrilled to have made the team. The twenty boys remaining were now ready to compete for the team's last five spots.

Then like a rogue wave, the moment overwhelmed him. It was his turn, and he was at the foul line, waiting. Coach Regan had the ball and readied the pass. Spider had thought about this moment all day and every day for the past two weeks. He could think of nothing else. He had practiced rigor-ously in the schoolyard. Genie and Lucio had already made their teams at Columbia Grammar. They were already showing off their junior varsity team practice jerseys with their school name and emblem printed on the front.

The wild-haired Spider stood at the foul line, anticipating the pass from Coach Regan. For some reason, he lost his concentration and began thinking of the tongue-lashing his father had given him that morning. It threw him off-balance as the ball was passed to him. He moved to receive the ball but moved too soon to catch it. The ball hit him in the finger, and he muffed the pass. The basketball rolled out of bounds. A student assistant retrieved the ball, and Spider headed toward the locker room in ignominious defeat. What an embarrassment! "I missed the pass. I didn't even get off a shot," thought Spider. "I'm done," he thought. "It's over! How can I go on?" How can I face my friends in the schoolyard?" He could barely breathe and started to panic.

Sometimes when all seems lost, without a sliver of hope, opportunity presents itself. So, like a clandestine operative, Spider feigned his departure to the locker room and turned back surreptitiously to the court. With a quick shuffle of his feet, he slid over to the end of the tryout line. The action of the shooters and layups continued unabated, and it didn't seem like anyone noticed. The next two boys made their shots leaving three spots with six boys remaining. Spider was nervous, exposed, and apprehensive, standing at the very end of the line. He felt sure that he would be called out for his transgression. The following two boys missed their layups, and the next two boys made them. Now there was only one spot left. The next boy missed his layup and went behind Spider. They were now the last two boys left in the line.

Out of the corner of his eye the man in the gray cotton sweatshirt with COACH REGAN stenciled in bold black letters took note as the youngster toed the foul line, waiting for his pass. The square-jawed red-haired coach pretended to ignore the youngster's violation. Sometimes the universe reconciles itself with a paradox. A right can be a wrong and a wrong can be right. Here as he readied for the trial, Spider thought, "This time no mistakes." He thought of Starlight Park, the Bronx Coliseum, and how his father had shown him the toughness and craftiness of Benny Leonard. He was a winner, a champion. Spider knew he could do better than his first attempt. His perseverance was his asset, and he concentrated hard to catch the pass and make the shot.

The fair-skinned coach did not look much older than many of the Clinton varsity players. He was savvy beyond his age, and while he admired Spider's grit, he knew that he had broken the rules in attempting a second chance to make the layup. If this kid was going to make the team, Coach Regan wanted him to earn it. "OK, let's see what this kid can do here. I heard he was pretty good, but I'm gonna make it hard for him, and if he still makes it so be it," thought the coach as he ripped an errant baseball pass over Spider's head, destined for Moshulu Parkway. There was no way that Spider could catch it, let alone grab it and make a shot thereafter. In that instant, Spider thought of his doubting father. "I can't catch it. I won't make the team. I'm done," thought Spider in that fleeting moment. The ball was at least 6 inches above Spider's head. His father's words, "I vudn't give you a nickl for my son's fuuutr," flashed through his mind and motivated his body into the Clinton gym air higher than he ever imagined. He stretched his outstretched arms, and the good Lord helped him grasp the basketball with his right hand, extending himself like a wide receiver leaping for a winning pass in the end zone amid defenders. In one smooth rounded motion, without landing, Spider caught the ball and shot it while in the air. Before his descent Spider released the basketball, throwing it in a singular motion toward the basket. It wasn't a layup by any means, nor a set shot, but something in between the two. He shot it as a heave, without control, without any technique. It was a shot of survival, a moment he would never forget. He could never have practiced the shot, nor duplicate it, but somehow, the ball alighted off the backboard and through the long net chords for a basket. "Wow!" thought the boy. "I wonder if that counts, or if they knew that this was my second shot. Could he disqualify me?" He began to sweat more than usual. His heart beat like a tom-tom drum at Little Bighorn. He could hardly breathe.

Spider was so nervous he was shaking like a precarious tectonic plate in an earthquake. Was this the end of all of his dreams? At least had he left the court after his initial miss, he might have had a chance at the intramural team, but now he was done. There simply was no way out and nowhere to hide. Thoughts rushed through his mind like seagulls flocking to the ocean in search of fish to eat. His brain was consumed and overloaded.

While he was contrite and the clouds of doubt had descended upon him, he still hoped for the best. He knew he would be good enough to participate if he just got the chance. Had Coach Regan looked at him at that moment directly, the skinny youngster would have likely broken down. The tension was exasperating. Finally after what seemed like an eternity, Coach Regan, shouted, "OK, bring it in, this is our team!" Spider was not a religious man, but he quickly looked up at the heavens in appreciation of the divine. A good fortune had found him, and the young boy made the team! It was only the junior varsity team at DeWitt Clinton, but it put him on track to ultimately make its varsity.

DEWITT CLINTON PSAL NYC CHAMPS

Photo from: Barry Cohen's Family Album

DeWitt Clinton New York City Champs 1936-1937 Photo

Front Row: (Left to Right) Leo Gottlieb, Mel Glover,
Ben Auerbach, Ralph Kaplowitz, Billy Giles.
Back Row: (Left to Right) Coach Regan, Red Friedman, Lefty Levine,
Sid Karson, Saul "Spider" Cohen, Sonny Younger, and Manager Red Barlin

Spider got his practice DeWitt Clinton sweat suit and started to wear it when playing pickup games in the schoolyard. He was very proud of his near team gear and washed it meticulously by hand after each time that he wore it. He was now a member of the Clinton junior varsity team. The season started, and he excelled, quickly becoming the team's leading scorer in its first two games. Things were starting to look bright for Spider. In the third game of the year an unfortunate accident took place, which curtailed his junior varsity career.

On the third game of the year, Clinton entertained the Columbia Grammar School JV at the Clinton gym. The game started out fine, and Spider made his first three shots as Clinton took a ten-point lead with a minute to go in the first half. Genie and Lucio, his two schoolyard pals, played for Columbia Grammar. Lucio was number 8 and Genie was number 3 for Columbia Grammar, one of the City's finer academic high schools. Then Spider stole the ball off of his pal Genie and drove quickly to the basket, crossing over on the dribble drive, keeping the ball in his right hand as he dribbled. Approaching the left side of the basket, he leaped fearlessly toward the hoop, switching the ball to his left hand for the layup, but was hit on his right side by Lucio, who had come over to help Genie. While the hit wasn't malicious, Spider hit the hardwood floor, landing on his right hand, bending it backward in an awkward position. He was in severe pain. He tried to hold back tears but couldn't fully control them. They poured down his cheeks involuntarily. He had broken two bones in his right hand. He was done for the junior varsity season. He would have to wait until next year to show his talents to Coach Regan, who would ultimately take over the Clinton varsity club.

Undeterred by his injury and the cast he had to wear, Spider could not keep himself from the lure of the Creston Schoolyard. After a week, he began to practice in the schoolyard. The schoolyard in winter was empty, but Spider found sections of the asphalt yard void of snow, and he targeted his practice there. He decided to make the most of his injury and turn his time off the court playing games into a positive thing. He set a goal for himself. He wanted to be able to shoot as good with his left hand as he did with his right. If he could perfect his left hand, he could create a weapon to make it tougher to guard him. The defense could not anticipate which hand he was going to shoot with, and that would be hard to stop. His true talent remained his deadly two-handed set shot, but that would have to wait four weeks, enough time to give his strong right hand a chance to recuperate and regain its strength.

After a couple of days, the snow started to fall again. He knew that if the snow couldn't be removed from the courts, he couldn't practice. So he found a way to shovel the snow off the court using his left hand with the shovel left outside the janitor's room. He cleared the court daily, giving himself just enough of a lane about 3 feet wide to shoot from the foul line, retrieve his own rebound from the basket, and return to the foul line. He practiced almost every day and developed his left hand, which grew strong and effective in shooting layups and short shots. Spider's hand was broken and in a cast, but it did not impede his shooting. He worked not only on his lefty layups but short lefty hook shots and one-handed short-distance lefty shots as well.

At DeWitt Clinton, when his classmates saw his cast, they reached out to Spider and gave him words of encouragement, which inspired him. As he stopped by the student lounge waiting for classes or in the lunch-room, his classmates would sign his cast to try and cheer him up. His Creston classmate, now at DeWitt Clinton, Edith Deutsch offered Spider words of encouragement. "Best wishes, Solly, hope you get better soon!" Then his pal Artie Reichner proffered a witty remark, "Climb the ladder of success but remember to fall in the arms of happiness! Get better soon, and we shall see you back on the courts playing again!" It made Spider feel good to hear the kind words of his classmates, but it seemed like an eternity to have to wait to play again. He hadn't received the same compassion at home, where he had been ridiculed by his dad for his injury and his pursuit of the childish game of basketball that his dad called into question. "You vill get job now, you can voyk after school but you must vork," his father barked at him in broken English. Once again, Spider's mom came to his rescue and the onslaught from his father abated. He was free to get his education and in the meantime work on his game.

In the early spring, his cast removed, Spider once again continued his shooting practice. Now that he had mastered shooting with his left hand close to the basket, he moved out deeper and deeper until he could make 20 free throws in a row with his left hand. He struggled to convert lefty hook shots as he had difficulty angling his body correctly to take a left-handed hook shot. He practiced religiously for the rest of the spring to get as good around the basket with his left hand as he was with his right, but finally, he did it. His surefire lefty shots opened up the court so that he had more options and more ability to get his shot off in traffic. The left-hand shot allowed him to shield the basketball from bigger players with longer reaches, who did not anticipate him shooting from the left side. He found that this shot could not be blocked easily.

A hook shot felt more natural with his left hand than that with his right hand. After all, he and his brothers, Benny, Israel, and Murray all shot pool with their left hand. Now it began to feel natural to shoot a ball with his left hand. He grew confident with this newly found advantage, using it against defenders to score when he resumed playing pickup games at the schoolyard and night center later that spring.

The days flew by, and Mondays became Fridays and then merged unceremoniously with weekends. The weeks became months, and after a while it was summer. The schoolyard became the boys' home for many hours each day. The asphalt teemed with young boys playing basketball, handball, and stickball and pitching pennies in the alleyways just off the courts by the streets. They didn't care how hot it was even as sneakers burned from the hot asphalt's radiating heat, which seemed to penetrate their soles.

By the end of the summer, Spider was both accurate and confident using either hand to shoot driving to the basket. He would make the varsity the next year and begin to show promise.

Dewitt Clinton High School was one of the most handsome high schools in New York City, and its boys' basketball team won the City Championship in 1905, 1913, 1914, 1916, 1918, 1919, 1925, 1926, 1934, and 1937, prior to World War II, ultimately winning eighteen New York City Championships and being the City runner-up ten times.

The Mosholu Parkway boys, as they were called, were a dynasty. Their DeWitt Clinton teams featured players who came from the many nearby schoolyards—Bronx boys who had started to play ball at an early age, developing their skills and gamesmanship. In 1936–1937, DeWitt Clinton, playing with Lefty Levine and Spider, won the New York City High School Basketball Championship.

After graduating from DeWitt Clinton at age sixteen, Spider enrolled at CCNY, in its night school. Legendary New York Knicks' coach, William "Red" Holzman, was the star of the CCNY varsity team, and Spider was relegated to playing on the night school team, the City College Night Owls. While he had graduated from DeWitt Clinton, he found that his slight physique needed to be developed, so he sought to get stronger and train to get more muscle to compete with the best college players.

Spider played hard and led the Night Owls in scoring an average 17 points per game. Nat Holman, the coach, watched him play but did not select him for the varsity. Disappointed and melancholy, Spider felt all was lost. Dave Polansky also attended City College at that time. Sensing Spider's frustration, he wanted to help his schoolyard pal. One day, he told Spider to meet him at the track at the Mullaly playground. Dave convinced Spider that he needed to engage in an ambitious training regimen designed to make Spider stronger and more competitive. Dave's intention all along was to make Spider stronger, increase his stamina, and help him become a better, tougher ballplayer. Eager to improve, Spider turned to Dave and followed Dave's regimen of strength development and training. "Saul, why don't you try out for the police force. It's a good salary and good benefits, and I will train you to get strong to pass the difficult physical exam." The exam involved doing twenty-five chin-ups, hundred perfect push-ups, two-hundred perfect sit-ups, a one-mile run in under six minutes, and complete an obstacle course in under four minutes. Spider replied, "OK, Dave, I got nothing to lose. If I get stronger, it will help my basketball as well, so let's do it."

Acting like a drill sergeant, Dave ran Spider up and down the football field at the Mullaly playground. They were training at Mullaly so often that they learned to identify the sound of the crowd roar whenever the Yankees played and the Bronx Bombers hit a homerun. Dave was a good trainer and physical education expert, and he trained Spider to get in the best shape of his life that summer. Spider began to curl 80 pounds with each arm individually, got significantly stronger, and felt much better about himself. He took the police exam and passed it with ease.

Lucio Rossini

Photo from: Barry Cohen's Family Album

CHAPTER 8

Dolph

* * *

IN THE FALL OF 1938, Mel "Flicky" Fields brought a young friend to Creston. He looked big enough to be in college. The tall boy didn't talk much, and he was five or more years younger than most of the kids playing. He came from 181st Street and University Avenue, near the uptown NYU campus and the northern Morris Heights section of the Bronx. His name was Dolph. "Flicky, what's with the kid? He's a baby. Can he play?"

"Oh yeah, he can play, watch him. He's only eleven but he can play with us right now!" Flicky replied. Genie, Spider Lucio, Lester, Dave, and Phil Rick were shocked. They were all in high school, and here was this kid in grammar school that Flicky said could play in their games. Why, there were college kids that played as well. Was Flicky gone mad, they wondered.

Dolph Schayes was already 6 foot, 5 inches tall. The boys got Dolph into a game. Nobody expected him to hold his own. They put him against Lester Mintz, who was already playing ball at NYU. The game began, and Dolph didn't wait long to show off his skills. Lester Mintz played on the freshman team at NYU. Flicky set it up so that Lester guarded Dolph. On the third play of the pickup game, Dolph surprised Mintzy and everyone else. Schayes drove to the basket to score on a 5-foot hook shot, going by the somewhat cocky Mintz as if Mintz was standing still. Maybe Mintz was overconfident, so he quickly began to try harder working against Dolph. He was able to block one of Dolph's shots the next time the precocious youngster drove the lane, but Dolph held his own, scoring on some outside shots and once again on a layup. Mintz's team won, but Dolph's team was very happy with the way he played. He had held his own against a college player. Mintz was very impressed by the poise of the youngster. "Hey, that kid can really play. Eleven years old? Wow, he's incredible," said Mintz and confronted Genie and Philly Rick. They all agreed. They had seen greatness, albeit young greatness.

Dolph would go on to play at DeWitt Clinton High School. He continued to grow and progress, becoming a basketball star at DeWitt Clinton High School, then at NYU, and later in the NBA. He went on to be voted as one of the top fifty best players in the history of the NBA.[11]

Dolph Schayes ultimately grew to the height of 6 feet, eight inches. He could shoot like a small guard and dribble the ball effectively as well. His outside shot demanded respect, and if a defender came up to press him, he had a knack of beating anyone driving to the hoop. Early in his NBA career Dolph suffered a broken hand. The team trainer put a cast on his right shooting hand and wrapped it with a rubber protective soft cushion. Tough as nails, Dolph continued playing with his broken right hand. He developed his left hand during this time and became skilled at using his left hand to shoot. When he got the cast off, he found that he could, in fact, shoot equally well with either hand. Dolph went on to win an NBA Championship in 1955 with the Syracuse Nationals. He played in 760 straight NBA games and was a perennial NBA All-Star, making the first or second All-NBA Team for nine consecutive years. He became skilled at the "up and under" move. This move involved Dolph ball faking, deftly enticing the defender to leave his feet to block the shot. With the defender in the air, unable to adjust, Dolph would explode by him with a power dribble drive to the hoop. He was an excellent outside shooter and equally adept at driving to the basket, able to shoot virtually any shot with either hand effectively. Dolph was also a pinpoint passer, always looking for and hitting the open man.

Dolph understood how to move well without the basketball to get to open spots on the floor, receipt passes, and score. After he starred as a player with the Syracuse Nationals, he took over the reins as coach once the Syracuse team moved to Philadelphia and changed their name to the 76ers. He was named the NBA Coach of the Year in 1966. In 2015, the Bronx would celebrate his life and name a street after him called "Dolph Schayes Street."[11]

Dolph was the classic case of a good player, who kept getting better and better, working harder and harder. He was good in high school and improved as a player at NYU, becoming an All-American, but he really didn't reach his peak until he turned pro. He was even better and tougher in the pros than he was at NYU.

Dolph Schayes played fifteen years in the NBA. He loved his NBA career but would always relish his memories of the schoolyard and the fun he had playing there. He enjoyed the great ball movement, spacing, cutting to the basket, and on-court camaraderie in those crafty Creston Schoolyard games.

Over the years, Spider would enjoy hearing Dolph speak as the keynote speaker in the yearly South Florida Basketball Association Luncheon at the Polo Club in Boca Raton, Florida. Dolph would exchange greetings with Spider and the rest of the Creston crew who attended the event with him. Spider enjoyed seeing Dolph, and when they reminisced, Spider would perk up with newfound energy, like he was going back in time to the schoolyard and reliving the moments playing here. Dolph—albeit younger that the Creston crew—became a folk hero of the schoolyard, being the best player ever to come out of there.

Flicky, Genie Wallach, Dave Polansky, Lester Mintz, Lennie Lesser, and Artie Reichner were part of the Creston crew that attended the South Florida Basektball Luncheon. Often, Dolph would be asked to speak, and his Creston crew loved to listen to his stories. He had reached the top level of pro ball. They were all from the Creston schoolyard, and while no one from there had gotten to the pinnacle of the sport like Dolph, the fellow Creston Schoolyard crew all enjoyed Dolph's success and were proud of him. He represented the schoolyard, and they all felt that he represented them as well.

Dolph had a wonderful sense of humor and would delight the attendees at the basketball luncheons. He had so many wonderful stories to share.

He told the story of the NBA in the early 1950s. At that time, the league was mainly an East Coast league with a few teams based in the Midwest. The players would play on the same team for many years, and they got to know the other players and coaches in the league. One of the coaches Dolph associated with was Lester Harrison, the coach of the Rochester Royals. Lester loved guards from New York City. There were many good city guards such as Red Holtzman of CCNY, Ossie Schectman of LIU, and Bobby Wanzer from Seton Hall. They all became standout NBA players. Wanzer played for the Royals at the time. Harrison, through Wanzer, heard about this guard from St. Johns, "Andrew Levine." Well, Andrew's last name was actually Levane, not Levine, but there were no scouts and no videos of the games at the time. Lester decided to have Andrew up for a workout in Rochester for the Royals. Lester was Jewish, and he really loved the thought of having a great guard from New York who was also Jewish.

After the workout, Lester went into the locker room to see Andrew "Fuzzy" Levane. Andrew came out of the shower unclothed, and as Lester approached, he was surprised and couldn't help but notice Levane's anatomy. He exclaimed, "Andrew, you're not Jewish!" When Dolph told that story, in his own charming way, the luncheon attendees got a big chuckle.

Dolph enjoyed telling the story about Bob Cousy Day in Boston. Dolph was a fierce competitor, and when he played for the Syracuse Nationals they were in Boston fighting for a playoff spot in 1963. There was a sold-out partisan Boston Garden, 13,909 fans in attendance to honor Bob Cousy. Cooz', as he was called, had taken the Celtics out of the cellar in the NBA standings to make them a six-time NBA champion. The Celtic organization was paying homage to Cousy hosting "Bob Cousy Day." The team gave Cousy a nice new car, a boat, and a chandelier from its owner Walter Brown—a present for Cousy's wife. The Syracuse team, for its part, gave Cousy a set of its well-known signature Syracuse China as a gift. The pageantry and ceremony for Bob Cousy Day was significant in Boston sports history.

Before the game began, Dolph spoke at the pregame ceremony and told the audience what a great player Cousy was, foisting accolades on the Celtic great. The Syracuse All-Star hoped to curry favor with Celtic crowd, and to create some positive energy and try and win the game. The Nationals were fighting for the last NBA playoff spot, and it was getting late in the season.

Cousy got the microphone. What was he going to say? The crowd grew silent in anticipation. What was the "Cooz" going to say? Would there be an emotional hug with Bill Russell or with Red Auerbach? The anticipation was intense. Robert Cousy had earned a reputation as the gold standard of guards in the NBA. He had a storied career at Andrew Jackson High School in Queens, then went on to greatness at Holy Cross College, and then led the Celtics to six straight NBA Championships, becoming one of the most loved sports personalities in Boston history. Everyone who knew Boston Celtics basketball knew his name. As he got ready to speak, the tension was overwhelming. Just then, a passionate Celtic fan shouted down from way up in the balcony, "We love you, Cooz." The entire arena went wild after the shrieking fan's plaintiff cry, and every fan in the arena began to chant the same thing over and over again: "We love you Cooz, we love you Cooz, we love you Cooz." The chant became a deafening roar, the way only the old Boston Garden fans could roar. It was a rhythmic Celtic incantation. "We love you Cooz, we love you Cooz!"

Dolph looked over at the Celtics. Bill Russell was crying, Red Auerbach was weeping and had his hands over his eyes, Cousy couldn't control himself; tears were pouring down his face as he was also crying. Then Dolph looked over, and he knew Syracuse was going to lose when he saw all three referees crying![12] The Nationals, in fact, lost the game jeopardizing their playoff hopes!

Another story Dolph liked to tell involved an incident that took place after he stopped playing pro ball. When Dolph stopped playing, he coached the Philadelphia 76ers for three years and left right before the 76ers won the NBA Championship with Wilt Chamberlain. Bill Russell was the star of the Boston Celtics at the time and was the best team ballplayer in NBA history. He was the game changer and Hall of Famer for those great Celtics teams. Red Auerbach was the legendary Hall of Fame coach of those teams, and Bob Cousy was their outstanding playmaker and future Hall of Famer. The Celtics were champions of the NBA every single year from 1957 to 1963. The owner of the Celtics during that time was Walter Brown.

Dolph became the NBA Head of Referees for several years after he stopped coaching. He knew almost every player in the NBA, every administrative person in the league office, and all the NBA coaches as well. Dolph often talked with Red Auerbach, the coach of the Celtics. Red Auerbach was a tough, competitive coach. His Celtics team and Dolph's Syracuse Nationals team were rivals and hated each other. But when Red retired, he took Dolph aside to give him some fatherly advice.

Red recalled a story that he wanted Dolph to hear about his success. "Dolph, sometime after the 1964 Celtics' NBA Championship season, Walter Brown sat down with me to negotiate my salary for the upcoming season. It was sometime around July 1964. Walter said, 'Red, you know things are tight, and we are not making much money. But you are doing a fantastic job. I want to give you a raise for the next season. What do you want?' Dolph, I had thought about this for quite some time leading up to the discussion, and I didn't hesitate responding immediately to him. 'You know, Walter, first I wanted to be a basketball player and then a coach. I played at George Washington University, and now here I am the coach of the Boston Celtics. But, Walter, I always dreamed of owning a professional basketball team. So as part of my compensation, I'd like a piece of the ownership of the team.' When I got here, the Celtics were the worst team in professional sports. Now they are one of the best, and we have won six NBA Championships in a row. Today, the Boston Celtics are the most valuable team in the league and a source of enormous pride in the Boston community. So I thought I would have to wait for a response, but Walter didn't hesitate. He told me that we had a great relationship, and he added, 'OK, Red, you have my word. You have 10% of the team ownership, congratulations!' I had dealt with Walter for quite some time, and we both trusted each other. Walter's word was good for me, and I thought that was that and we had a deal. It was not written down, no signed contract, but our handshake and verbal deal was enough for both of us. I was content, and I went home relieved, optimistic about the Celtics and my future."

"Just a couple of months later on September 7, 1964, however, Walter Brown unexpectedly suffered a massive heart attack and suddenly passed away at the young age of fifty-nine. Dolph, I didn't know his wife as well as I knew him. His widow Marjorie called me after Walter passed and surprised me. 'We're selling the team, Red,' she said. I told her something that I was not sure she knew. 'Marjorie, Walter promised me 10% of the team.' 'Yes, I have heard something about that, but there is nothing in writing.' I was concerned, Dolph, really nervous. Marjorie was nice but noncommittal. She said, 'Red, come to the closing, and we'll work it out.' Well, I found out that the Celtics were being sold for $3,000,000, a whopping sum in 1964. So I called around and found the best Boston business law firm that I could. I paid them a retainer which drained all of my savings to fight any possible legal challenge to my claim. I brought three lawyers from this big-time law firm with me to the closing. The Brown family law firm offices hosted the meeting. When

I showed up at the closing, I asserted my claim to the Brown heirs, and said, 'Walter promised me ten percent of the team.' Marjorie responded, telling me, 'All right, Red, let me step out of the room and talk it over with my sons.' Several minutes later Marjorie Brown returned to the room and said, 'Red, I talked it over with my boys, and we are in agreement. You got your ten percent ownership of the Celtics. Walter Brown's word is good.' I practically jumped up and kicked my heels together, but I walked out of the closing with a three hundred thousand dollars check representing my ten percent share of the Celtic's sale proceeds."

After Red told this story to Dolph, he said, "You know the morale of this story, right, Dolph? If you don't ask you won't get!"[12] Dolph thought about that and realized the great Celtic coach's wisdom. He would remember the lesson and incorporate it into his thinking.

Dolph loved to tell the story of the great Bill Russell. Dolph became friends with Russell, perhaps the greatest team player in NBA history, winning eleven of thirteen NBA Championships ending in 1969. The Celtics started winning when Russell began playing for them. Prior to the Celtics, Russell won two NCAA Championships with the University of San Francisco winning 56 games in a row. In 1956, Russell led the United States to an Olympic gold medal as well. He was a winner all the way.

Forty-plus years after retiring from the NBA, Dolph and Russell played golf together. They talked about the big salaries being paid to current NBA players. Dolph mentioned the disparity in salaries of the current-day players compared to the salaries when they both played, saying, "Russ, you won eleven NBA Championships in thirteen years. Can you imagine how much you would make today?"

"Wouldn't have made a difference, Dolph," said Russell. Dolph continued, "Russ, in my sixteen NBA years, the total amount of salary that I made was $275,000! There are guys today that make $4 million dollars a year with no stats, like 3 points, 2 rebounds, a game. Can you even imagine the piles of money you could make now?"

Russell listened carefully. He was nonplussed and responded, "Wouldn't have mattered, Dolph." Dolph was curious about the Celtic star's seemingly cavalier response.

"Russ," Dolph, now animated, said, "Shaq makes $21,000,000 a year, and he has won only three titles. That's a quarter a million dollars a game, Russ! You won eleven titles. You could have made $30,000,000 or more in today's NBA!"

Russ replied again, "Wouldn't have changed a thing, Dolph!" Now Dolph was dumbfounded. How could this be? No difference with that kind of big money? What did he mean? This was a staggering amount of money; it just didn't add up. It didn't make any sense to him. Russell's ability was incredible. What was Russell thinking? How could he not see the benefit? So Dolph asked candidly, "Why wouldn't it have mattered, Russ? How can you say that? The disparity is unbelievable. We were born too early!" After a deep sigh,

Russ replied, "It wouldn't have mattered, Dolph. My first would have gotten it all anyways!"[12] The two men smiled and then laughed a hearty laugh.

As great as Dolph was, his NYU coach, Howard Kann, told his pro coach Al Servi at Syracuse, "Dolph will never make it in the pros. He's not tough enough!" Dolph, however, proved Kann wrong, in part because his pro coach, Al Servi, made him tougher and better by Dolph's own admission. Dolph was selected to the NBA Hall of Fame, validating his lifetime achievement in the game of basketball. He was further honored and voted one of the fifty best NBA basketball players of all time, in 1996. He was tall and talented, but his hard work ethic made him an all-time NBA great.

Dolph Schayes at the Nevele Country Club

Photo from: Barry Cohen's Family Album

Dolph Schayes Top 50 NBA All Time Players

Photo: Barry Cohen's Family Album given by Dolph Schayes to Saul Cohen

AT THE NEVELE

Photo from: Barry Cohen's Family Album

Left to Right:
Dolph Schayes, Unknown player, Lester Mintz, Mel "Flicky" Fields,
Saul "Spider" Cohen, Milty "Whitey" Griese, Arthur Reichner.

Dolph Schayes autographed 50 years after the fact, at the Anniversary of the
Nevele Country Club's 50th Anniversary.

CHAPTER 9

Long Island University Basketball

✳ ✳ ✳

SPIDER PASSED THE POLICE EXAM in July 1938 and was set to take a job with the local law enforcement agency at a nearby Bronx Police Precinct. It was a good job with solid pay and benefits. If he decided to work with the police, it would make his parents happy. He was ready to embrace his new destiny. To celebrate the occasion, Spider and Dave Polansky went out to a tavern on Jerome Avenue not far from East 163rd Street. Genie, Lester, Philly, Lenny, Flicky, Lucio, Artie Reichner, and Wally Sencer joined them, and they reminisced about some of the games in the schoolyard, talking basketball, their schools, and their future plans. Then they tried to decide who was the greatest ballplayer ever to come out of the schoolyard. Everyone agreed that it would be Ralph Kaplowitz, except Flicky who said that Dolph would be the best.

There were a lot of good players that came out of the schoolyard like Shike Godhofer, Barney Sedran, Lefty Levine, and others but Ralph won out as the consensus. It had been a long evening of basketball talk and libations. Slowly, everyone went home, except Dave and Spider. The two pals remained and continued to have a few more drinks. They talked about the police exam and its difficulties. Spider thanked Dave for his strength and conditioning program. They congratulated each other; Spider thanked Dave for his training, and Dave appreciated

Spider for his discipline, perseverance, and hard work. It was a nice moment for both, and they savored it. The minutes raced by, and soon the bar closed. It was 1:30 a.m. They left the tavern, finding the temperature outside hotter and more humid than expected. The usual night breeze off the river had deserted them. There was a heat wave in the city, and neither young man was used to drinking as much as they had to boot. Normally, they would have left with their other pals, but this was a night of celebration for them. They were putting an exclamation point on their hard efforts, which had borne fruit for both friends. The night crept up on them and got the better of them. They didn't realize it but the heat and liquor were making them happier and more carefree than usual.

As they walked home they passed Creston Junior High School and entered the schoolyard. The night was magic, and the two good friends in the darkness of the moonless sky were seemingly in a dream. The night was a fantasy, a joyous once-in-a-lifetime night for the two young men. It was a moment not like any other they had ever had before.

Dave, free of inhibition, started to sing inside the schoolyard. Spider had never seen the usually studious and pensive David so jovial and free. Dave was fascinated with the echo of his voice in the schoolyard canyon, which surrendered to the mountains of buildings. The surrounding buildings hovered like sleeping nonjudgmental giants. Satisfied, exhilarated at his friend's passing of the police exam, Dave began to sing rhythmically in appreciation and in a staccato voice, "Soll-ee Cone..., Soll-ee Cone..., Soll-ee Cone...." Dave the composer sang his own Solly Cohen song, first chanting, then singing, then chanting again. Spider could hardly believe what he was hearing; it was so much out of character for the soon-to-be Professor Polansky. With Dave singing those words over and over again, the boys began to smile and then laugh. It was now 2:00 a.m. The streets and schoolyard were quiet and empty but for the light of the lonely lampposts. They left the yard and the magnificent moment they would forever share. It was a moment born of the school-yard, and the enduring friendship they had developed there.

Spider struggled with his decision but did not sign up to work for the police precinct. In the fall, he went to CCNY and played for the night school team. During one of the early season games at CCNY night school, Spider spotted someone in the stands. He found out after the game that it was Coach "Pic" Picarello, the assistant basketball coach of Long Island University. "Hello, Saul, I'm Coach Pic, LIU Basketball. How you doin'? I watched you play tonight. You have a deadeye shot. You should be a starting guard on the varsity at CCNY, but they seem to be all set at that position. Too bad for CCNY, but at Long Island University, you have a chance to play right away, sophomore season. You'll have to earn it, but we feel that you have what it takes. We need guards like you, and uh, you know, we are going to play in the Madison Square Garden six times this year and we'll make the NIT there as well. If you're not scheduled to start for the City varsity next year, we'd like you to come and play for us at LIU. We have a full scholarship for you, all expenses paid. You know LIU is not far away in Brooklyn; it's an easy subway ride from your family in the Bronx. What do you say?"

Spider couldn't believe what he was hearing. "Yes, sir, I'd like that a lot." "Great, Saul, I'll be your coach next year on the freshman team. The best of luck. We'll see you soon. By the way, I got your address from the Night Owls coach, Mr. Wells, and we'll send all the paperwork in the mail. Please sign it, have your parents sign it, and send it back."

Spider remembered the short, stout dark-haired man with the gray fedora and black band around the brim, with a matching gray suit. He had come to the early CCNY night school game against NYU Dental School. Spider had 22 points and did not miss a shot. Coach Pic would come to several more games, and each time Spider had an impressive game for the night school team.

Spider signed to play at LIU in the fall of 1939 and was the leading scorer on the freshman team, averaging 15 points a game. After the season, there were games and practices for the LIU varsity during the summer. It was here that Spider really made his mark, starring on the LIU varsity at Manhattan Beach and in Saratoga, playing with many of the returning LIU lettermen. He got to know them all. Ossie Schectman was fast, tenacious, and a great point guard and defender. Sol "Butch" Schwartz could speedily run the court and was a good shot and tough attacker of the basket on his drives. The 6-foot-4 captain, Sy Lobello, was tall, fast, strong, and a great competitor. He was also the most approachable and generous of spirit. Dolly King was an Adonis of a man, built like a young Jack Johnson, almost as fast as Jackie Robinson's brother Rey, and as strong as Bronco Nagurski, the football player. He excelled at both football and basketball. His performances in summer basketball tournaments and exhibition games drew appreciative crowds, eager to see him play and get his autograph.

Frank Fucarino came to LIU with Spider, and they played on the freshman team together. That summer and the following year, they both played for the varsity. In World War II, Fucarino served in the army with Spider. Fucarino proved to be an extraordinary athlete with great stamina that impressed all.

One day in basic training, Fucarino and Spider were training with their army group at Hunter's Field in Georgia. It was a blazing hot day, and the drill sergeant was grilling the troops, trying to get them battle ready. The drill field was hotter than the air temperature, which was already over 105 degrees. It was oppressively humid, and most of the soldiers in training could barely breathe. Someone said that the temperature on the field in the sun was over 125 degrees! The men wore full gear and full army backpacks loaded to the gills. After all of the marching drills and calisthenics, the drill sergeant shouted out to an incredulous group of conscripted soldiers, "Men, this field is two miles around the perimeter. Now you need to circle the entire field once." The men were all exasperated from what had already been a heavy workout of calisthenics, marching, and the obstacle course. The thought of a subsequent two-mile run was almost overwhelming. They all thought about telling the sergeant that it was too hot to run, but no one dared talk back to the tough Arkansas-born drill sergeant, who called out to the tired troops, "And don't even think about lightening your packs. They are only 50 pounds, and in combat you'll need to carry all your gear. You may also have to carry another soldier, plus your pack, so get ready and listen up: one time around, full pack."

The troops began to trot slowly around the field. The sergeant said "once around," but didn't specify a required time needed to finish. They were on their own to figure that out. The men just wanted to get through it any way they could. Frank Fucarino started the two-mile trek seemingly in an all-out sprint, knifing through a crowd of fellow soldiers to the front of the group of runners. He was sprinting. Every other member of the group was exhausted before, during, and after the two-mile run. In the end, only Frank Fucarino stood unblemished. He had completed the two-mile course, and he was ahead of all the other soldiers by at least 200 yards. When he finished, he did not bend over, nor fall down from heat exhaustion as many other soldiers did. He did not put his hands on his knees. He finished and began jumping up and down like a college football player running to the sidelines after being introduced in the starting lineup of a big game, bouncing up and down and bouncing off teammates. Bounce and bounce on the balls of his feet went Fucarino. His fellow infantrymen couldn't believe what they saw. They were exhausted. They were looking to get a cold shower and take a nap. Fucarino couldn't stop bouncing.

"Sarge, Sarge," Fucarino cried out.

"What is it, Private Fucarino, you all right? Sunstroke?"

"No, Sarge, no, Sarge. Can I do it again, do it again please?"

"What do you mean?" said the Razorback Sarge in disbelief.

"Can I run the course again, right now?"

The sergeant waved his hands at Fucarino and said, "Fucarino, you're crazy! Get in and get a shower!" That was the talent and endurance of Frank Fucarino.

Besides Fucarino and Spider, Hank Beenders and Dick Holub, both 6 feet, 5 inches, joined as newcomers at LIU for the 1940–1941 season. The team was a solid blend of largely experienced players who were seniors and the incoming sophomores—many of whom had experience as stars of the freshman team. The task at hand was for the coaches to have the players mesh and make them work well together and be the best team they could be.

The coach, Clair Bee, was a dapper, well-respected man who had earned his stripes already having been to every NIT from its inception, and who had already won the 1939 NIT Championship. He was a disciplinarian, a teacher of basketball fundamentals, and a master strategist and psychologist, always analyzing his players and getting the most out of them through motivation. He was also the athletic director at LIU and had been the football coach as well. He believed in repetition in practice of the fundamentals of the game of basketball and in long practices. Players played virtually all year with only a partial respite from the grind in the summers. Bee arranged jobs for the players at the Manhattan Beach Parks department during summer, and the players got to practice and play ball at night under the lights.

LIU did not lose a game in the summer and fall exhibitions of 1940, and things were looking up for the LIU basketball team heading into the 1940–1941 season. Spider was a sophomore, along with Holub and Furarino, and Beenders was a junior. They would join Schectman, Schwartz, Lobello, and King on the LIU varsity.

Saul "Spider" Cohen vs Orgeon at Madison Square Garden

Saul Takes Off!

(News foto by Payne)

Saul Cohen, LIU, leaps high for ball in front of Oregon basket. While still in air, he turns to pass ball to teammate. LIU won, 43-21.

Spider vs West Virginia

...heartbreaking first round NIT loss his Junior Year.

OUCH -- Form wasn't the only thing upset when West Virginia defeated L.I.U. at Garden. The athletes took numerous tumbles. Saul Cohen of L.I.U. suffered this particular spill when he collided with Lou Kalmar. Saul scrambled to his feet immediately and in mixup over rebound retrieved ball, shot and made basket.

Photo: Article appeared in the Brooklyn Eagle

Duquesne vs. LIU at Madison Square Garden February 8, 1941

Dukes Win Thriller—Before 18,000 Fans

The last game LIU would lose before reeling off 11 straight to win the National Intercollegiate Men's Basketball Championship, Ossie Schectman #24, Saul Cohen #29, Hank Beenders #30 for LIU, Paul Widowitz #12 and #5 Moe Becker for Duquesne.

Becker hit a half court shot at the buzzer for the 36-34 Duquesne victory.

By Acme Telephoto

Duquesne University's basketball team scored its most impressive victory of the season last night, defeating Long Island University, 36-34, for the second straight year, before 18,000 fans in Madison Square Garden.
Telephoto shows Paul Widowitz (No. 12), Duquesne star, going into the air with Oscar Schetchman, LIU, for a rebound. No 29 is Saul Cohen and No. 30 is Harry Beenders, both Long Island, while Moe Becker can be seen standing next to Beenders.

Spider vs Selmen of Rice

Photo: ACME NEWSPICTURES INC

LIU vs Rice, Madison Square Garden, December 30,1941

LIU vs Rice Institute, December 30, 1941, Madison Square Garden

IT'S MAGIC—It really is magic, the way the Speed-Ray camera freezes tense expressions and fast motion of these basketball players in New York Garden game. Chester Palmer, 14, of Rice, dribbles down center court as Saul Cohen, 20, of Long Island U., tries to grab the leather. L. I. U. won, 61-57. Speed Ray 100,000th-second photography was introduced to newspaper world early this year by Boston American-Record-Sunday Advertiser. And Speed-Ray finishes 1940 winner and going away from news photo world with this topflight shot.

Photo: Article appeared in the Brooklyn Eagle

Spider at Work

LIU vs USC Garden Dec 28, 1942

Spider scored 19 vs USC in the Garden. Bee called him "simply the best". LIU scored 40 points as a team.

Photo: ACME NEWSPICTURES INC

Saul "Spider" Cohen

Photo from: Barry Cohen's Family Album

LONG ISLAND UNIVERSITY BASKETBALL 1940-1943

CHAPTER 10

Coach Clair Bee

✳ ✳ ✳

CLAIR BEE WAS ARGUABLY THE greatest college basketball coach of all time. He, along with Joe Lapchick, Nat Holman, and Phog Allen were the best college basketball coaches of the 1930s and 1940s.

Bee won three national championships, according to the Premo Porretta Power Poll.[13] This poll ranked the top collegiate teams by collecting data based on their competitive strengths. The poll included the top 25 college teams' competition against all opponents.

Bee's LIU team sported elite winning records when they won the Premo Porretta Poll highest ranking in 1936 (26–0), 1939 (24–0), and in 1941 (25–2). The last two championship teams were winners of the nation's then most prestigious college basketball tournament, the National Invitation Tournament (the NIT).

The NIT was founded in 1938, when Ned Irish invited six teams to compete in a new tournament.[14] The following year the NCAA would promulgate its own tournament, but it did not surpass the NIT as the premier collegiate post-season tournament until the 1950s. Originally a 6-team field, the NIT grew to 8 teams by 1941. These teams included teams from the New York metropolitan area, and the best teams selected from other regions of the United States.

The NIT was a new concept and fascinated spectators intrigued to see the best teams play one another in a tournament in one venue. Basketball enthusiasts from the New York metropolitan area and beyond packed Madison Square Garden for the NIT. The 18,500 fans attending the games gave an unprecedented cash gate in college basketball and greatly exceeded the crowds of the then pro basketball games.

Every tournament game was a big event, covered by the large media newspapers, radio, and newsreels.

Clair Francis Bee, known as the "Innovator," impressed and influenced his players. His practices were calculated to detail different drills each minute each day to get his team better each practice.

Bee believed that the team who made the fewest mistakes would win, and his practices were designed to enable his players to execute moving the ball rapidly, employing a menacing defense and limiting turnovers. There were correct ways to play defense and press. His teams worked on combining passing, cutting, picking correctly, moving without the basketball, and limiting mistakes. Repetition promulgated good habits in his players, and free throws were emphasized by Bee with his players practicing them over and over.

Bee wrote a series of books, called the Chip Hilton series, which emphasized many of the ideals that he taught his players in real life and the values he tried to instill in them. He had great players and pedestrian players, but he went on to have the second-highest NCAA College Basketball (Division 1) winning percentage post-1934 of all time. He had been the number one ranked winning percentage college coach for this period until a recent run by Gonzaga coach, Mark Few, who surpassed him.

Bee influenced great college coaches as Bobby Knight, Dean Smith, and others. Bee was admitted into the Basketball Hall of Fame in

Springfield, Massachusetts, in 1968. He designed the 1-3-1 wheel zone, created the three-second rule, and later came up with the 24-second clock in the NBA. He was a bridge from basketball's roots, interacting with the game's founder, Dr. James Naismith. He chose the best competition for his teams, chartering the first private plane in history to play an intercollegiate game. Looking for a challenging away schedule, Long Island University flew to play Michigan State, DePaul, and the University of Baltimore in 1941. Bee wanted his team to look its best, and he provisioned handsome silver uniforms with white trim and silky sailor warm-up suits, which his players were proud to wear. The uniforms had a white sailor flap at the neckline in the back, with the silver-colored warm-up suit.

Bee's teams won forty-three games in a row, a record streak at the time, before losing to Hank Luisetti's Stanford team in Madison Square Garden. Luisetti was the first to perfect the one-handed jump shot. Ironically, LIU would stop a 43-game streak by Seton Hall a couple of years later in the semifinals of the NIT. Bee named Luisetti to his all-opponent team and would also name another great player to that team. Petar "Press" Maravich," the father of Pistol Pete Maravich, scored 27 points against LIU one night, for his small West Virginia College, Davis-Elkins. The next night he poured in 31 more against another tough opponent. Bee named Maravich to his all-opponent team along with Bob Davies and Hank Luisetti, among others.

An admirer of talent that reflected the best of the best players, including opponents, Bee would model the character of Chip Hilton in his fictional series of sports books on the real-life superstar of Seton Hall, Bob Davies.

LIU played their home games in a bandbox court on the fifth floor of the LIU College of Pharmacy. The games would become a big draw on campus and the 1,000 or so fans who crammed the place each game lined up for tickets hours before the start. LIU very rarely lost on the Pharmacy court, losing only 3 games at home in a span of 150 home appearances.

Clair Bee's Long Island University basketball teams won 95 percent of their games from 1931 to 1951.[15] A great teacher of pivot play and movement without the basketball, Bee was a media favorite. He often played to the beat writers who followed his team to inspire and charge up his players. He used criticism and praise in the press to get his team ready to play their best. A player was either "in the plans" or "out of the plans." If you were out of the plans, you had to work hard in practice to get back in the mix.

Bee espoused hard work, compassion, leadership, and good sportsmanship. His Chip Hilton books reflect the values he learned early in life in his small hometown of Grafton, West Virginia. While Bee fashioned the central character of his books, Chip Hilton, on Bob Davies of Seton Hall, he dedicated his book *Championship Ball* to Simon "Sy" Lobello, the captain on his 1941 LIU NIT Championship team.

Coach Bee loved his players, who came from diverse backgrounds. At LIU, on the 1940–1941 team, Sol Cohen, Ossie Schectman, Butch Schwartz, and Al Simon were Jewish; Hank Beenders, Frank Fucarino, Dick Holub, Dolly King, and Sy Lobello came from different denominations of both the Catholic and Protestant church. The team Bee put together that year was singular of purpose. They all wanted to win for their school and Coach Bee. For his part, Bee cared for them uniquely and treated them all fairly like they were his second family.

There are awards that are named after Clair Bee and the heroic Chip Hilton character in his books. The Clair Bee Coach of the Year Award is awarded every year to a coach who makes an outstanding contribution to the game of college basketball. The Chip Hilton Player of the Year

Award is awarded to a men's college basketball player who is a senior and who demonstrates strong and personal character both on and off the court.[16]

Clair Bee, an extraordinary teacher, shared an attention to detail teaching the game of basketball to his players, coaches, and his readers in his many sports books. He would continue his teachings of the game to young campers as the founder of the Kutsher's Basketball Summer Camp.

Bee demanded strict attention to every aspect of the game to inspire great effort, communication, and team play. Following this winning dynamic, Bee owned a career record of 413 wins and 88 losses.

Bee's 1941 team won the NIT, then widely accepted[16] as the college basketball national championship. While winning was very important to Bee, sportsmanship was paramount in the accomplishment of victory.

On his Long Island University Basketball teams, Clair Bee was the alchemist who put the pieces of the team together one by one through recruiting and intense training. As for the 1940–1941 LIU team, all the pieces were in place to have an outstanding season. They had experience, rebounding, shooting, and speed. Their mid-season challenge would be to replace the extraordinary William "Dolly" King,[16] a once-in-a-lifetime athlete who would graduate midway through the season and who was a great rebounder, defender, and dominator of the backboards.

The 1940–1941 LIU team had big shoes to fill. Clair Bee's 1935–1936 team was his gold standard for excellence. That team won all of its games in a single season, going undefeated and winning all games by an average of 23 points. The team was determined to be the best team in the country, although the NIT did not exist at the time, so there was no tournament following the season.[16]

The Olympic Committee voted for basketball to be an Olympic sport for the 1936 Games. Taking place in Berlin, Germany, the Games sought for all countries to bring their best players. Within the United States, basketball was dominated by the East Coast teams and specifically the powerful New York college teams. Long Island University was the best of the best and the overwhelming favorite to win the pre-Olympic tournament in Madison Square Garden, and thereafter to comprise the US Olympic Basketball team.[17] Most if not all of the entire Long Island University team was destined to be selected for the Berlin Olympics to represent the United States.

The Long Island University Basketball team, however, decided to boycott the 1936 Olympics. They did not show up for the Madison Square Garden Pre-Olympic Tournament. LIU President Tristram Metcalfe announced that the LIU players were not playing "in protest of the Olympic Games being held in Germany, and the political and social changes therein."[17] The LIU President said that the players and the school "did not believe that any United States players or teams should participate in the games, because of Germany's Fascist regime, oppression of minorities, religious persecution, and its racist politics."

The LIU basketball players were not without substantial reasons to forego this great "once-in-a-lifetime" honor to represent their country. In April 1933, the Civil Service Law in Germany was established, creating the ability of the Nazi-led German Government to legally remove "undesirables" from the civil service profession including professionals like lawyers and doctors.[18] That same year, the Dachau Concentration Camp was opened to house 5,000 prisoners. The religious "ethnic" cleansing of the Jews of Germany and the "death camps" such as Dachau were considered to be immoral, as well as the inhuman treatment of the Jews and other minorities, such as the Romani and even priests.[18]

At their annual party rally in September 1935, the German Nazi party passed the "Nuremberg Laws" further excluding Jews from German society and served as the legal justification for the arrests and violence against Jews that followed.[18] While many of the players on Long Island University's basketball team were United States residents or citizens, all of their parents were European immigrants. Many of the players were Jewish, and brutal rumors about German treatment of Jews permeated the mindset of those players whose families had relatives still trapped in Europe, living in fear of the German Nazis and their ethnic cleansing. The LIU players were chastised by sportswriters for not playing in the games from a sports perspective. The LIU players that participated in the boycott were Ben Kramer, Marius Russo, Jules Bender, Ken Norton, Leo Merson, Arthur Hillhouse, Bill Schwartz, and Harvey Grant.[19] Some of the players were Jewish, as was the manager of the LIU team.

The boycotting of the games came with great personal sacrifice to the LIU players and the school, as the team surely would have garnered the glory and fame of winning Olympic gold, because the United States won every basketball men's gold medal until 1972. The Olympic gold medal would have been great for LIU basketball, but it was not to be. The 1935–1936 team was led by All-Americans Jules Bender and Art Hillhouse, both extraordinary players. Bender was called by Coach Bee "the best shooter on the move that I ever coached."[19]

Undefeated LIU Team in 1936 boycotted the Berlin Olympics

Photo: International Jewish Sports Hall of Fame

Left to Right: Coach Clair Bee, Willie Schwartz, Julie Bender, Ben Kramer, Ken Norton,
Leo Merson, Marius Russo, Arthur Hillhouse.
Schwartz, Bender, Kramer and Merson were Jewish.

LONG ISLAND 1940-1941 TEAM PRIOR TO DOLLY KING DEPARTURE

LONG ISLAND U. SQUAD
Photo: 1941 NIT Championship Game Program

Clair Bee Showing LIU Basketball Fundamentals

Fundamentals of Good Basketball

Few high school basketball players graduating into college ranks are skilled in the fundamentals of the game but have merely fallen into it. Faced with this problem most college coaches undertake the laborious task of breaking their players' bad habits and teaching them the fine points of pivoting, shooting and ball handling. Coach Clair Bee, who produces outstanding teams at Long Island University, shows you here some of the things every good player should know.

The set foul shot can mean points. Coach Bee spends lots of time teaching his players how to execute it.

Flexibility of fingers and wrists are important assets. L. I. U. players acquire this by tossing medicine balls.   Wide World

One of the most important plays in basketball is the recovery ball from the bankboard. Bee teaches his players to get to the position and use a spread eagle of their legs to prevent an opp from getting the ball. Average fan doesn't realize how intricate ketball plays are set up.

Photo: Barry Cohen's Family Album

Saul Cohen and Moe Becker
LIU vs Duquesne

Saul Cohen's aggressiveness seems to astonish Moe Becker in L. I. U.-Duquesne game in Garden. International News Photo.

Photo: Article appeared in the *Brooklyn Eagle*

LIU vs. Oregon

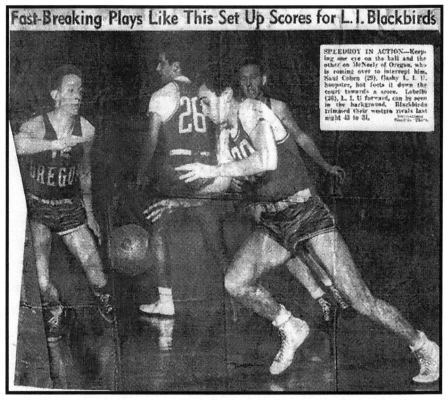

Photo: Article appeared in the *Brooklyn Eagle*
Saul Cohen #29, Sy Lobello #26 for LIU and McNeely of Oregon
Madison Square Garden, December 14, 1940

Clair Bee

Born: March 2, 1896
Alma Mater: Waynesburg (1925)
Career Record (major schools): 21 Years, 413-88, .824 W-L%
Schools: Rider (53-8) and Long Island University (360-80)
Conference Champion: 3 Times (Reg. Seas.), 0 Times (Tourn.)
NCAA Tournament: 0 Years

Record includes games as coach of major schools, and does not reflect forfeits or vacated games.

Coaching Record

Season	School	Conf	G	W	L	W-L%	SRS	SOS	AP Pre	AP High	AP Final
1928-29	Rider	Ind	22	19	3	.864					
1929-30	Rider	Ind	20	17	3	.850					
1930-31	Rider	Ind	19	17	2	.895					
1931-32	Long Island University	Ind	20	16	4	.800					
1932-33	Long Island University	Ind	17	6	11	.353					
1933-34	Long Island University	Metro NY	27	26	1	.963					
1934-35	Long Island University	Ind	26	24	2	.923					
1935-36	Long Island University	Metro NY	25	25	0	1.000					
1936-37	Long Island University	Metro NY	31	28	3	.903					
1937-38	Long Island University	Metro NY	28	23	5	.821					
1938-39	Long Island University	Metro NY	24	24	0	1.000					
1939-40	Long Island University	Ind	23	19	4	.826					
1940-41	Long Island University	Ind	27	25	2	.926					
1941-42	Long Island University	Ind	28	25	3	.893					
1942-43	Long Island University	Ind	19	13	6	.684					
1945-46	Long Island University	Ind	23	14	9	.609					
1946-47	Long Island University	Ind	22	17	5	.773					
1947-48	Long Island University	Ind	21	17	4	.810					
1948-49	Long Island University	Ind	30	18	12	.600					
1949-50	Long Island University	Ind	25	20	5	.800	11.16	6.96		3	13
1950-51	Long Island University	Ind	24	20	4	.833	12.55	5.92		2	
Career	Overall		501	413	88	.824	11.85	6.44			
	Rider		61	53	8	.869					
	Long Island University		440	360	80	.818	11.85	6.44			

Appearances on Leaderboards, Awards, and Honors

Consensus All-Americans	Games	Wins	Win-Loss Percentage
		1934-35 LIU 24 (1st)	1935-36 LIU 1.000 (1st)
		1936-37 LIU 28 (1st)	1938-39 LIU 1.000 (1st)
			1940-41 LIU .926 (1st)
			Career .824 (3rd)

All Time Best Men's College Basketball Coaching Win Percentage (01/07/21)

1.	Sam Burton	.8333		36.	Tony Bennett	.7288
2.	Mark Few	.8308		37.	Henry Lannigan	.7278
3.	Clair Bee	.8244		38.	Jim Boeheim	.7276
4.	Adolph Rupp	.8218		39.	Dana Kirk	.7264
5.	John Wooden	.8039		40.	Lew Andreas	.7262
6.	John Kresse	.8012		41.	Lou Carnesecca	.7245
7.	Thomas Kibler	.7962		42.	Larry Brown	.7238
8.	Ralph Jones	.7918		43.	Tom Izzo	.7227
9.	Jerry Tarkanian	.7902		44.	James Usilton	.7218
10.	Al McGuire	.7867		45.	Joe B. Hall	.7214
11.	James Freeman	.7830		46.	Dave Rose	.7205
12.	Francis Schmidt	.7818			Fred Schaus	.7205
13.	John Calipari	.7772		48.	Gregg Marshall	.7202
14.	Roy Williams	.7763		49.	Cam Henderson	.7201
15.	Dean Smith	.7758		50.	Joe Lapchick	.7198
16.	Bill Self	.7685		51.	Edmund Dollard	.7190
17.	Mike Krzyzewski	.7673		52.	Dudey Moore	.7162
18.	Jack Ramsay	.7647		53.	E.A. Diddle	.7154
19.	Frank Keaney	.7638		54.	Bo Ryan	.7151
20.	Walter Livingston	.7627		55.	Tom Blackburn	.7140
21.	George Keogan	.7618		56.	John Thompson	.7138
22.	Vic Bubas	.7607		57.	Hec Edmundson	.7135
23.	Harry Fisher	.7590		58.	Pat Page	.7131
24.	Fred Bennion	.7559		59.	Ray Mears	.7128
25.	Chick Davies	.7476		60.	Arthur Schabinger	.7118
26.	Edward McNichol	.7470		61.	Nolan Richardson	.7109
27.	Thad Matta	.7403		62.	Eddie Sutton	.7101
28.	Rick Pitino	.7388		63.	Edward Kelleher	.7099
29.	Everett Case	.7378		64.	Piggy Lambert	.7094
30.	Sean Miller	.7367		65.	Randy Bennett	.7093
31.	Phog Allen	.7352		66.	Billy Donovan	.7090
32.	Ott Romney	.7351		67.	John Lawther	.7089
33.	Doc Meanwell	.7349		68.	Hugh Greer	.7081
34.	Lute Olson	.7314		69.	Peck Hickman	.7077
35.	Nat Holman	.7297				

70.	Bob Knight	.7062
71.	Rick Majerus	.7053
72.	John Becker	.7025
73.	Edward Hickox	.7019
74.	Bob Huggins	.7003
75.	Frank McGuire	.6994
76.	Bennie Owen	.6975
77.	Jamie Dixon	.6970
78.	Jim Calhoun	.6966
79.	E.C. Hayes	.6966
80.	Tiny Grant	.6962
81.	Denny Crum	.6959
82.	Douglas Mills	.6959
83.	Honey Russell	.6935
84.	Hank Iba	.6931
85.	Eddie Cameron	.6923
86.	Jay Wright	.6920
87.	Larry Weise	.6918
88.	Chris Mack	.6917
89.	Gene Smithson	.6906
90.	Harold Anderson	.6904
91.	John Wilson	.6867
92.	Lee Rose	.6847
93.	Ozzie Cowles	.6837
94.	Herman Stegeman	.6827
95.	George Cooper	.6804
96.	John Oldham	.6804
97.	Mike Montgomery	.6801
98.	Guy Lewis	.6797
99.	W.O. Hamilton	.6793
100.	Mick Cronin	.6788
101.	Stew Morrill	.6783
102.	Harry Combes	.6781
103.	Zora Clevenger	.6771
104.	Digger Phelps	.6769
105.	Branch McCracken	.6766
106.	Bob King	.6762

107.	E.J. Mather	.6749
108.	Herbert W. Buck Read	.6742
109.	Jack Gardner	.6741
110.	Leo Novak	.6738
111.	Roy Skinner	.6731
112.	Alex Severence	.6726
113.	Ray Meyer	.6716
114.	John Chaney	.6710
115.	Don Haskins	.6707
116.	Dutch Hermann	.6697
117.	Matt Painter	.6673
118.	Jack Gray	.6667
119.	Jim Harrick	.6667
120.	Michael White	.6667
121.	Lefty Driesell	.6661
122.	Skip Prosser	.6659
123.	Kelvin Sampson	.6655
124.	Bruce Pearl	.6654
125.	Wimp Sanderson	.6654
126.	Neil Cohalan	.6653
127.	Neil McCarthy	.6652
128.	Hank Crisp	.6650
129.	George King	.6635
130.	Steve Fisher	.6632
131.	Doc Stewart	.6632
132.	Jimmy Ashmore	.6613
133.	Dana Altman	.6611
134.	Gene Bartow	.6599
135.	Dave Gavitt	.6599
136.	Shaka Smart	.6599
137.	Terry Holland	.6593
138.	Harry Litwack	.6590
139.	Pete Carril	.6579
140.	Billy Tubbs	.6577
141.	Harold Bradley	.6576
142.	Harlan Dykes	.6561

143.	Norm Stewart	.6556
144.	Gene Keady	.6555
145.	Pete Newell	.6555
146.	Dick Tarrant	.6548
147.	Louis Cooke	.6544
148.	Rick Barnes	.6542
149.	Steve Alford	.6537
150.	Rick Byrd	.6535
151.	Fred Taylor	.6527
152.	Jack Kraft	.6522
153.	Eddie Hickey	.6521
154.	Leonard Palmer	.6514
155.	Craig Ruby	.6511
156.	Steve Prohm	.6505
157.	Scott Nagy	.6495
158.	Mike Brey	.6494
159.	John O'Reilly	.6493
160.	James Needles	.6492
161.	Frank Kerns	.6489
162.	Charles Spoonhour	.6487
163.	Lou Henson	.6485
164.	Albert McClellan	.6463
165.	Archie Miller	.6463
166.	Ralph Miller	.6456
167.	Anthony Grant	.6453
168.	Blaine Taylor	.6441
169.	Ben Carnevale	.6438
170.	Joe Meyer	.6438
171.	Ben Howland	.6437
172	Tubby Smith	.6437
173.	Pat Foster	.6432
174.	E.L. Roberts	.6423
175.	John Thompson	.6419
176.	Red Manning	.6416
177.	Keith Dambrot	.6415
178.	Bob Nichols	.6412
179.	Fran Dunphy	.6409

180.	Mike Anderson	.6405
181.	Taps Gallagher	.6405
182.	Pete Gillen	.6395
183.	Frank Hill	.6385
184.	Howard Cann	.6381
185.	Bruce Weber	.6378
186.	Moose Krause	.6374
187.	Gary Williams	.6374
188.	John Beilein	.6373
189.	Johnny Dee	.6367
190.	Don Corbett	.6366
191.	Mark Turgeon	.6362
192.	Hugh McDermott	.6357
193.	Gale Catlett	.6348
194.	Carroll Reilly	.6346
195.	Leonard Sachs	.6346
196.	Rick Stansbury	.6341
197.	Everett Dean	.6334
198.	J.W. Pollard	.6333
199.	Jack Leaman	.6327
200.	Ladell Andersen	.6322
201.	Murray Arnold	.6305
202.	Charles Moir	.6302
203.	Ted Owens	.6297
204.	Babe McCarthy	.6295
205.	William Anderson	.6290
206.	Larry Finch	.6286
207.	Alfred Robertson	.6282
208.	Jack Hartman	.6280
209.	Jim Valvano	.6276
210.	Paul Evans	.6274
211.	Jim Dutcher	.6271
212.	Sam Barry	.6265
213.	Tom Davis	.6264
214.	Vadal Peterson	.6260
215.	Scott Drew	.6254
216.	Tippy Dye	.6250

217	Luke Urban	.6250
218.	Josh Pastner	.6247
219.	Tim Floyd	.6242
220.	Kermit Davis	.6210
221.	Abe Lemons	.6201
222.	Everett Shelton	.6200
223.	Bob McKillop	.6198
224.	Bill Frieder	.6197
225.	Joseph Mullaney	.6194
226.	Tom Young	.6190
227.	Ben Jacobson	.6181
228.	Glen Rose	.6179
229.	Mike Lonergan	.6177
230.	Andy Kennedy	.6163
231.	Darrin Horn	.6161
232.	Leon Rice	.6161
233.	Mitch Henderson	.6160
234.	Dave Bliss	.6159
235.	Randy Rahe	.6157
236.	Carl Tacy	.6156
237.	Buzz Williams	.6152
238.	Jimmy Earle	.6142
239.	Austin Johnson	.6139
240.	Don Donoher	.6138
241.	Brad Brownell	.6129
242.	Brick Breeden	.6127
243.	Bob Dukiet	.6127
244.	George Flint	.6127
245.	Lon Jourdet	.6125
246.	Steve Lavin	.6124
247.	Frank Haith	.6119
248.	Eugene Lambert	.6107
249.	Arthur Powell	.6105
250.	Lon Kruger	.610

CLAIR BEE

Photo: Wikipedia

CHAPTER 11

Puerto Rico, the
SS Borinquen

* * *

SS BORINQUEN

Photo: Postcard Barry Cohen's Family Album

The Long Island University players boarded the ship the SS *Borinquen* in New York Harbor. The ship was a retrofitted military transport turned passenger cruise ship.

Top Side Aboard the SS *Borinquen*

Photo from: Barry Cohen's Family Album

September, 1940 From San Juan Returning to Brooklyn

Left to Right Long Island University Basketball Players:
Saul "Spider" Cohen, Hank Beenders, Dolly King, Simon Lobello
& Frank Fucarino.

The LIU Team went undefeated in all Preseason Exhibition.

Saul Cohen and Dolly King

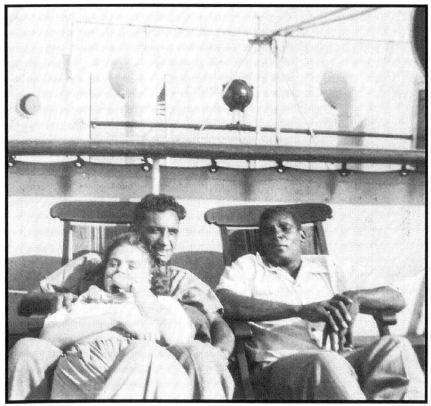

Photo from: Barry Cohen's Family Album
August, 1940

On the SS *Borinquen* with unknown passenger in tow on the way to San Juan from Brooklyn Harbor. King would graduate and play Pro Basketball on a number of teams leaving LIU in late January, 1941 Prior to LIU's National Invitational

The SS *Borinquen* was a passenger liner built in the United States in 1931. Originally designed to move troops as a transport service for the army, it had capacity for 1250 troops and was 400 feet long. After being converted to a passenger ship, it transported the LIU basketball team from Brooklyn Harbor to San Juan in early September 1941, taking three days to make the voyage.

The LIU basketball players and coaches were assigned second-class berths, which allowed the boys to sleep in their own bunk bed with two per cabin. The seas were rough, and several of the boys got seasick. The team sailed to Puerto Rico for seven exhibition games in fifteen days with practices and basketball drills on their non-game days. The coaches for the LIU club on the trip were Head Coach Clair Bee and Assistant Coach Pic Picarello.[20]

Upon its arrival on the island, the team checked into to the El San Juan Hotel. The lobby sofas and chairs of the plush destination resort were made of a deep, rich mahogany framework, and the reception and front desk had walls of oak paneling and ornate design depicting people sailing just off the hotel's private beach. There were photos of mountains northeast of San Juan and some of the island's multicolored and beautiful wild parrots flitting from one tall tree to another.

The players waited patiently in the lobby. Many of them had already bought postcards and were writing home to their parents or girlfriends. Spider forgot to write his parents but bought one postcard to send to each of his schoolyard pals: Lucio, Wally, Genie, Dave, Lester, Philly, Arthur, Lenny, and Flicky. In a few moments the team bus would pull up in the back of the hotel to transport the players to the outdoor basketball court on the bay hugging the Caribbean. The first scrimmage versus the Puerto Rico Athletics basketball team was highly anticipated by the incoming sophomores, eager to show off their skills. The distinguished slender man in the white linen suit and silver tie was the head coach, Clair Bee, slightly gray at the temples, with his distinguished dark-brown hair parted in the middle. The coach had a powerful voice and an austere penetrating aura that captivated his players. While he played baseball, tennis, and football in high school, he had gravitated to the game of basketball. He stood in the lobby of the hotel amid his players, who were buzzing about the sights and sounds of Puerto Rico. Many were on their first trip of any kind. It was elegant and unusual for a college team to travel in style like this, and the players were excited. Seniors Sol Schwartz, Ossie Schectman, Captain Simon Lobello, William "Dolly" King, and Lou Simon were making their second trip to Puerto Rico, and having been to the hotel before, they helped the newcomers to the team by explaining the location of the various hotel amenities. The highlight of the amenities was the hotel pool, sauna, and whirlpool bath.

"OK," said Coach Bee, "let's get started. I hope all of you are enjoying the nice hospitality and the excellent food at this fine hotel. Mr. Luis Jorge Garrido-Gonzales is the general manager. You'll see him in the front row of all our games down here, a real big fan of ours every time we visit. If you need anything he'll direct you to the right person. You can ask for him at the front desk. We've been here before as you seniors remember, and it was a great experience. So while we want you to work hard, execute and play well, enjoy yourselves as well. We'll be playing seven games here on the Island. After our scrimmage against the Athletics team tomorrow, we have a game the next day against the Puerto Rico Olympic team. Next week we have two games against the San German club team, the team that our own Victor Mario Perez played with. The following weekend we play the Santurce club team, two games back to back, and finally we play two games the following week against an Island All-Star team that has a couple of players from Venezuela and Mexico. Remember, we are also ambassadors of the game here, and we did not lose a game last trip. So let's play well and show good sportsmanship. We will be playing on outdoor courts, which is nothing new for you all as you have been practicing all summer outdoors on the courts at Manhattan Beach. The courts here might get a bit wet from the afternoon rains, so be careful practicing on them. They have a tradition here that the winning team gives the losers their jerseys after the games. We have brought extra jerseys for this reason. This is the beginning of what we hope will be another championship season."

"We have a tough schedule with seven games at Madison Square Garden, and a grueling road schedule including games in Michigan at Michigan State, in Chicago at DePaul, in Baltimore at the University of Baltimore, and in Philly at LaSalle. I consider the present squad one of the best that I have ever coached. If we are not a great team, the responsibility will be mine. All the requirements for a great team are present: height, speed, shooting ability, weight, desire to play, and desire to win. We need to work on our defense, but I believe you are mentally alert and ready to learn. We can and we will overcome our weaknesses by placing a greater value on the ball, by concentrating individually on our personal defensive measures, and by thoroughly mastering all the types of defenses we will employ. I suggest all of you become familiar with my book that Coach Pic just handed out so that the basic principles of our offense and defense will be mastered. Naturally, I have many new ideas and personal plans which are not written in the book, but the material in the text lays the foundation. By now you know your weaknesses. I suggest you try to correct them in our practice games and in your own personal practices. Thinking about the various game situations when you are alone here in the hotel or back in New York when you are on the subway commuting to school, when you go to bed, and at other non-playing times will greatly help you to progress. If each of you work hard and master the plans that we have prepared, we will be a championship team."

"Team spirit is most important. Everyone cannot start the game. Those who do start must be supported by every man on the bench. I expect the same kind of enthusiasm on this squad, which has prevailed with our great championship teams of the past. There has never been one boy on any of our teams who did not cheer his teammates on. Cliques will not be tolerated, nor animosities. We must work together as one. As your coach and leader, there will be times when I must correct you. Such criticism will be constructive, and you will be expected to receive it in the spirit in which it is given. We seek to point out your mistakes so not only you but the other players may benefit. Enjoy your time here and learn. When you get back to school in Brooklyn, let us not overlook our studies, as it is important to keep up our schoolwork so that the team may not be weakened by ineligibility. Remember: Anyone can be a contender! Let's be the champion!"

The elegant forty-four-year-old coach then left the room. The players were all impressed by his comments, even the seniors who had listened to him for the past two years. They marveled at the coach's ability to communicate effectively—rarely, if ever, repeating the same speech. Each time he spoke, he had a profound impact on his players. He was revered by all who played for him. The players were inspired by their coach and ready to play some ball. The talk was done, and the team headed to the bus for a practice and a scrimmage. The ocean breeze felt rich with sea air, and the boys enjoyed their transport with bus windows open. The LIU players were a talented group and expected to win all of their games in Puerto Rico. It was a challenge playing outdoors in the rain, and several of the games were delayed due to wetness on the courts. A native of Puerto Rico, playing for LIU, Victor Perez took the LIU players on a tour of the sites of the city of San Juan and the old "El Morro" Fort overlooking the ocean. Several of the players tried the delicious fruity rum drinks of the island. They had a blast. The most unique game came when over two-hundred green iguanas decided to occupy the outdoor court about an hour before game time and could not easily be persuaded to leave by any of the local basketball officials. It could have been easy to remove them from the court, but apparently there was a dominant male iguana that had cordoned off the corner of the court near a tree. It was apparently his romantic period, and there were no less than eight females who were battling it out for his affections. After an hour with no luck removing the creatures, an animal handler was called in, just in time to enable the game to proceed.

The Long Island University team did, in fact, win all seven of their exhibition games in Puerto Rico and the local townspeople appreciated their expert display of good ball handling, passing, shooting, and excellent defense. The only problem they had was that each time they won they had to furnish their opponent with their winning jerseys. With ten men on each opponent, it made seventy jerseys that the LIU club had to give away!

The LIU basketball team had a great trip, and the incoming sophomores learned Coach Bee's systems and began to blend with the experienced seniors. The team packed up from the hotel, and while they readied to leave Puerto Rico, Coach Picarello got on a boat to Cuba to scout players and to arrange travel accommodations and scheduling for the next year's preseason exhibition games in Havana.

On September 19, 1940, feeling optimistic about the upcoming season, Coach Bee and the LIU team headed back to Brooklyn, once again on the SS *Borinquen*. The boys awoke the next morning to bright sunshine and a glorious day at sea. The seas were stable, and the boys took to the deck of the ship. Spider found a comfortable reclining wood-framed, canvas-backed chair on the top deck of the ship. He secured a chair and heard the stomping and rumbling of the feet of his three teammates heading up the stairs. It was Dolly King, Frank Fucarino, and Hank Beenders. The rush was on for the lone open lounge chair on deck. Dolly King rushed on the scene and secured the chair to the chagrin of his two teammates. He now sat next to Spider, and they started a conversation. It was the first time outside of a practice or exhibition game that the two engaged in a dialogue.

"Good for you, Dolly," said Spider.

"Yeah, I got it first (the chair), too bad for you guys," said Dolly, flashing a smile at Beenders and Fucarino.

Dolly had a wonderful smile that made everyone around him smile. Like the sun rising in the east over the ocean, his laugh radiated from his muscular midsection and rippled the smooth skin of his distinguished face. When Dolly laughed it was a bubbling brook of sheer liberation and joy. Perhaps it was the freedom that he had learned growing up in Brooklyn, or perhaps it was his defense to cover up the pain he felt from the racial injustice and unfair treatment that he felt in breaking the color barrier playing college ball. He had almost left LIU because of it.

Joining Dolly in laughter was an inevitable consequence of being with him. To be with Dolly was to smile, to laugh, and to be free of pretense. He laughed from both the stomach and his soul.

"Dolly, I saw you play football last year at Ebbet's Field. That's pretty swell that you play both sports in college. Not many fellas can do that. Are you going to play both sports again this year?" Spider asked the chiseled 6-foot-3, 220-pound William King.

"Sure am," said Dolly. "We are going to have a good team this year. Do you remember Robert Trocolar, from Virginia?"

Spider shrugged his shoulders, replying with his gesture that he didn't remember the name.

"You know, he's that kid that transferred in from the University of Alabama last year. He's about my same size. He runs offense from the wingback position, but he can play every skill position on offense as well as safety on defense. He's on the basketball team too, and he'll probably join the team after football season. He's supposed to have a tryout next year with a couple of teams in the pro National Football League. I'm sure you'll meet him soon enough. He's a real nice kid. He hit me with some touchdown passes last year. He throws a nice spiral, pretty accurate too. Football's OK, I guess. I'll be ready for football season when we get back. But I love basketball, probably even more than football."

"That's good for LIU football. I always wanted to play football, just wasn't very good at it and never could afford the equipment," said Spider. Dolly apparently was not stimulated to respond, and Spider thought that he might be bored with the conversation. He turned to look at Dolly to verify his concern. When Spider turned around to see why Dolly wasn't answering, he saw that Dolly had nodded off and was asleep. "Well, that explains why he wasn't answering," thought a relieved Spider who leaned back and relaxed in his chair. The delicious sun kissed his face, and he loved the feel of its embrace and the smell of the ocean that infused oxygen into his Bronx lungs. He had never been so relaxed and soon nodded off for an eternity it seemed. Taking a nap was something he had never done before, but the refreshing ocean air put him to sleep. He awoke invigorated and felt the wonderful tinge of his bronzed skin chilled by the wind-carried ocean spray.

Dolly, awake now, was reading the paper and asked, "Good nap?"

"Wow, yes, excellent!" responded a renewed Spider.

Dolly looked at Spider and asked, "Solly, when is lunch? I'm getting hungry, man, they better feed me good. I am starved!" But before Spider could answer, a petit young girl approached. She had light-brownish-blonde hair, straight as spaghetti, that flopped down on all sides except for her forehead, which had short bangs that stopped just above her almond-shaped eyes and pencil-thin eyebrows. As she walked toward Dolly and Spider, her hair hung straight down on all sides and vaulted up and down with each step as she strode closer. As she moved toward the two LIU players, they noticed that she had a baggy dress on with a bright blue-and-yellow floral pattern. She looked very young to be by herself on the boat, perhaps sixteen or seventeen, but she acted older. She wore no makeup and did not exude any sensuality; in fact she looked more like a tomboy than the girls the LIU players would expect to meet in Brooklyn. She looked at the boys and thought, "Whew, these boys are handsome!" She was a "pistol," full of energy and loaded with questions for the boys. She had an air about her that seemed interesting. She was full of confidence and carried herself gracefully. She strode toward the boys with her feet pointed outward with a bounce in every step, like a ballerina. She was plain looking yet somehow captivating. Dolly and Spider introduced themselves by name to her.

"Hi, I'm Solly."

"I'm Bill, Bill King, what's your name?" said Dolly, expecting a serious answer.

The mysterious young girl replied, "Hello, I'm Carmen Miranda!"

"Wait a minute," replied Spider. "So where is your hat with the fruit in it?" Spider said jokingly.

Carmen Miranda was a movie star, singer, and dancer also known as the "Brazilian Bombshell," and everyone knew what she looked like and that she was around thirtyish, so everyone knew that this girl couldn't be the real Carmen Miranda.

"Come on," said Dolly, "what's your real name?"

The unknown mystery girl simply smiled and did not respond. Then, the diminutive young girl questioned Spider and Dolly, "Where are you guys from? Oh, Long Island University! That's great. Basketball, you play basketball. Why were you in Puerto Rico? Did you like it? Where did you stay? How was your food? I'm going to Hunter College this upcoming fall."

In about two minutes the girl had peppered the boys with a barrage of questions and commentary the likes of which they had never heard. They found her charming and refreshing. She was garrulous and bold, a pleasant change from most of the more reserved girls they met in college.

The conversation ended, and it was time for lunch. The boys went back to their cabins and washed up for lunch, which was served in the dining area below the main deck. It was a lavish feast, and the offering of potatoes au gratin, mixed vegetables, roasted chicken, and barbecued beef was complimented by hearty helpings of various types of dark and light bread and butter. Dessert was a rich chocolate cake with chocolate frosting. Dolly had two full helpings and was happy with the lunch. The boys were happy after a great meal and some of them went back to their bunks for a nap, but Spider and Dolly couldn't wait to get back to the top deck and enjoy the salt sea air. Spider was tanned from playing and walking around in Puerto Rico with the strong sun doing its work on his face, bronzing his arms, shoulders, and legs. Wearing an argyle sweater that kept him from feeling chilled in the shade and the moist afternoon winds on the top deck, Spider took a deep breath and languished in the warm embrace of the sun at sea. Dolly came up and joined Spider, and they secured the two canvas deck chairs once again.

After a half hour, the shade gave way to the sun, which soon covered the boys lounging on the deck. The heat of the day disarmed Spider of his sweater, and he laid it on the deck under his chair. The refreshing ocean air was a soothing curative to the hectic and grueling training schedule for the LIU team in San Juan. It was relax time, and the boys made the most of it. Most had never been on a boat, and many would next board a ship not for a cruise to and from a resort hotel to play ball, but rather to be transported by sea for the war.

Dolly, powerfully built, wore a soft white cotton polo shirt with short sleeves that stopped just above his rippled biceps. He was relaxing and trying to fall asleep when the fair-skinned young girl from their morning encounter arrived alone on deck.

"Buenas dias," said the girl.

"Bonjour," said Spider, not knowing Spanish and replying in the French, which he had learned in grammar school. He didn't know Spanish, but he knew Latin and could figure out many words in Spanish from their Latin roots.

Realizing that Spider didn't speak Spanish, she replied, "Oh hello," in fluent English with a cute little Spanish accent. "Would one of 'ustedes' (you) like 'darme' (to give me) your chair?"

"Well, these chairs are really comfortable, but you can join me and share the chair with me!" said Spider, not expecting the girl to manipulate her body so quickly onto his lap, binding herself to him in the chair.

"OK, that's fine!" said the girl, as she climbed up and joined Spider on the canvas deck chair. When she landed in Spider's lap, Dolly woke up. He opened his eyes but couldn't quite believe that Spider had the young girl lying in his lap on the chair.

Just then Frank Fucarino pulled up with a camera. "Wait, let me get a photo of you all!"

Dolly said, "Nah, man, don't, Frank!" But Dolly didn't know Frank Fucarino. Frank snapped a photo that captured Dolly on one chair and Spider with "Carmen Miranda" on the other. Relaxing and wanting to nod off, Dolly merely replied, "OK, Frank, I am going to remember this!" But that was Frank. The slim spunky girl soon left the top deck. She had a way of carrying herself that was tantalizing as she carried herself away from the boys with a sprightly and athletic gait.

The group of LIU players got a kick out of the mysterious girl. The whole trip from San Juan to Brooklyn took three days, and they didn't see "Carmen Miranda" the next day. The captain invited all passengers to a dance party to celebrate the last night of the trip onboard. While the coaches didn't like the boys partying as a rule, it had been a long trip and they promulgated no objection to the boys having a little fun before returning the next day to school in Brooklyn.

Entering the dance hall, the boys gathered at the bar just off the dance floor. Some drank cokes, and some drank beer. The entire team was there, and they were laughing it up reliving the Puerto Rico trip and telling the story of the hundreds of green iguanas and the male Casanova of the species that had the females fighting over him only to delay the start of one of the exhibition games there.

"Hey, Victor, you're like that male iguana, aren't you," said Hank Beenders playfully to Victor Mario Perez, who was joining the team on the trip back to school. No one, besides Victor, had ever seen an iguana before the trip.

Then Frankie Fucarino said, "You know, they cut off the tail of the iguanas and eat them down there because supposedly the meat of the tail is an aphrodisiac!"

"Come on, Frank," said Sy Lobello.

"No, Simon, it's true. I spoke to the animal handler down there, and they told me that it is sad because they have a lot of the iguanas that are walking around with no tails because of this."

"Frank, I don't know where you get this stuff, truly amazing," said Hank Beenders. The boys were laughing it up and having a great time. There were a bunch of older couples dancing on the dance floor, and they were playing salsa and merengue music, popular in Puerto Rico and other parts of the Caribbean.

Soon, Spider left with Dick Holub to go up to the top deck at night and look at the night sky. When they arrived there were dozens of bright stars visible. They saw a shooting star flash through the night sky and then two others. They thought it was good luck. Then they saw some lights off in the distance coming from some cargo ships, which they eventually passed by in the night. Just then they heard some footsteps and the elegant figure of a shapely woman in a lavender Taffeta dress, which, tightly wrapped, clung snugly to her body. Her matching belt secured the top part of the dress which had a plunging neckline highlighting her soft, fair, slightly freckled skin. She wore dark mascara and eye shadow and tastefully applied rouge, which pointed to her green eyes that sparkled like stars in the moonlight. She smelled like evergreen as her scent wafted over her secret admirers, Spider and Dick. She looked over the railing of the ship down at the ocean for several minutes. She listened to the waves caressing the ship and welcoming it homeward to the north. She wore a white cashmere shawl to keep her exposed shoulders warm. The two boys were fascinated by her but could not identify her face as she quickly left the deck. Dick Holub retired to the cabin he shared with Spider, but Spider decided to follow the graceful figure.

The mystery woman was heading back to the dance. Spider entered the ballroom in pursuit of this dream girl. As he entered the room, he spotted Frank Fucarino and Dolly King at the bar drinking a couple of Coca Colas. Frank looked at Spider and said, "Solly, look!" He was pointing at the dream girl whom Spider had followed from the deck. She had just come onto the dance floor to dance with some stranger she seemed to know. "That's her! That's Carmen Miranda," said Frank.

"Who?" replied Spider.

"That brick house that just walked in. I wonder if she has a Chesterfield?" joked the irrepressible Fucarino, making a play on words. The Chesterfield was a brand of cigarettes, and Frank was referring to the mysterious lady's ample bosom in making his jeu de mots.

Spider now looked closely, and he could see for himself what Frankie was referring to. It was indeed the girl from the top deck two days prior. "My goodness," said Spider. "That's incredible. She was all over me, and I was wondering whether she was attractive enough. She didn't even look like a girl, and I thought she was so young. She looks at least twenty-two. She's prettier than the real Carmen Miranda."

"Wow, she's gorgeous," said Dolly.

"Well, it's too late now," replied Spider. "She's with that guy, and they're cutting a rug," said Spider complimenting the dancing couple.

"I guess you can't judge a book by its cover, especially if the cover changes," joked Frankie. Spider and Dolly agreed, and the boys headed to their cabins to retire for the evening.

The next day, the boys exited the boat at the Port of Brooklyn, with the fond memories of the great trip and their fall adventure. They disembarked and carried their gear off the ship. Coach Bee was finishing up a couple of letters in his cabin and was late getting off the boat. The team went ahead and were already on the bus headed for the LIU campus. The coach had a lot on this mind. As he headed to disembark, Carmen Miranda spotted the coach and somehow realized that he was the coach of the boys she had spoken with on the top deck. "You are the coach of this Long Island basketball team, right?"

"Why yes," replied Coach Bee proudly. The pretty girl was dressed to the nines and made quite an impression. While Carmen Miranda spoke to the coach, he was trying to organize his papers and files as he carried one of his suitcases as well. The wind was blowing, and it made it difficult to keep track of his papers which were trying to waft away.

"Coach, this is my real name and the phone number of where I am staying in Manhattan. Would you please give this paper to the boy they call Solly? He is very funny. Please tell him to call me. Thank you. And please tell him that I'd like to give him some lessons in Spanish!" The coach assured the girl that he would be sure to give Solly the information. As luck would have it, as the coach descended off the boat, on the sloping metal plank, a gust of wind jostled the small sheet of paper containing Carmen Miranda's information, dislodging it from the coach's stack of papers and out of his hands. The mysterious girl's information floated into the harbor and was lost, unbeknownst to the coach. The coach was preoccupied and soon forgot about the interaction with Carmen Miranda and the paper. The coach was distracted further when another gust of wind tried to disarm him of the bulk of his working papers which detailed the coaching strategies and notes from the trip to Puerto Rico as well as the scouting reports for LIU's opposition for the upcoming season.

Later in the year, when the weather turned cold at college, the LIU players who were on the boat would all warm to the recollection of the mystery girl who called herself Carmen Miranda. They relished the experience and her photo with Dolly and Spider, and her glamorous change of appearance on that last night when she got all "dolled up." They never learned her name, but they would distinctly remember "Carmen Miranda!"

The team returned to the LIU campus in Brooklyn. The coach's offices were located inside the Brooklyn Pharmacy gym where the varsity basketball team played their home games. The gym and locker rooms were located on the fifth floor and the coaches' offices were on the fourth floor. Coach Bee had a large office with a cherry walnut desk and a dark black leather chair. In front of his office, there was another office half the size of Coach Bee's but which housed a gray metal secretarial desk. Coach Bee's primary secretary was a pretty blonde-haired young woman, with pale-blue eyes. Everyone called her Kathy, but her real name was

Kathleen Peters. She was studying to be an actress and had just celebrated her twenty-fifth birthday when the team returned from Puerto Rico.

Her athletic physique stood out as she walked to and from the gym to the coaches' offices running various errands for the team. When she could, she modeled bras and posed for artists in Greenwich Village on weekends. At a studio a bit further east in "the Village," she attended an acting class on Fridays. She worked in the coach's office three days a week. On the other two days, Thursday and Friday, a vivacious and vibrant redheaded young lady named Nancy Gibson filled in typing letters for Coach Bee and helping with recruiting. Nancy could take short-hand and type hundred words per minute flawlessly. Her skills were so developed that she didn't have to look at her fingers as she typed. She was aided by the team student manager, Irving Marcus, who together with Kathy, helped to arrange team travel, hotels, meals, and accommodating the needs of any visiting teams.

Nancy studied singing as diligently as Kathy did acting. Nancy lived at home with her parents in Queens and enjoyed reading romance novels and *Photoplay* magazine while taking the subway, then the bus to get to the Brooklyn LIU campus. She had just finished the *Photoplay*, dated January 1940, which featured Carole Lombard on the cover.

Many of the players asked Kathy and Nancy out for a date. Often, as was the style of the day, the ladies wore tightly fit sweaters, the kind that Lana Turner would soon make famous when she was discovered in Hollywood. The sweater accented the beautiful figures of both of the classy looking secretaries. Over the course of the year, the players would find a way to linger in Coach Bee's office trying to pursue Kathy or Nancy in search of a date with either of the splendid ladies. None of the players had much money; commuted from the Bronx, Brooklyn, Queens, Manhattan, or New Jersey; and made little progress with any girls, let alone the two attractive coach's secretaries.

The ladies working in the coach's office had an air of sophistication, which intimidated the young players as well. The boys did not know how to approach these winsome girls, who always seemed too busy or disinterested.

The boys did try hard to get a date with either of the girls, but they always seemed to stumble. They could not find the right words, and each time one of the players would ask to go out with either of them, the ladies would reply, "Sorry, Coach Bee says it is an absolute rule, we cannot go out with any of the ballplayers!"

In 1940, Xavier Cugat, the Spanish Cuban bandleader and movie actor, led an influx of Latin music, musicians, and actors into the United States. Latin music and dancing became popular, and the salsa, the merengue, the tango, and the rumba were all the rage.

To Coach Bee's two secretaries, Xavier Cugat, Gilbert Roland, and Cesar Romero were their idea of the attractive and interesting Latin man. Romero, a heartthrob from Cuba, was the son of the biological daughter of Cuban national hero Jose Marti. The young secretaries dreamed of becoming famous movie stars, fascinated by and hoping to engage with these tall, dark, and handsome Latin men, such as the 6-foot-3 Cesar Romero.

Victor Mario Perez was on the Puerto Rican Olympic team that played a series of exhibition games against Clair Bee's LIU team in San Juan in 1938. Bee loved Perez's speed and stamina, and he offered him a scholarship for the next season. Victor Mario committed to LIU, and Coach Bee made all the arrangements for Perez to join the team. After his freshman year at LIU, he returned to his family home in San Juan. Since LIU was playing in San Juan again the following fall, he stayed in San Juan in summer and joined the team there for the 1940 San Juan Fall Exhibition season.

Victor was from a well-to-do family that owned a very profitable insurance agency in San Juan. He was punctilious and knowledgeable. Like Cesar Romero, Victor was 6 feet, three inches tall and dressed elegantly every day in shirts, ties, and jackets that distinguished him. He looked more like a lawyer than a basketball player. When he was not wearing suits for class or before games, he wore pressed wool trousers and a white collared button-down shirt. When he wore a suit he always had a pearl-colored silk handkerchief in his left breast pocket, given to him by his mother for good luck. He was reputed to be a world-class dancer, but he never mentioned this to his stolid LIU teammates.

Like the other LIU players, Victor noticed Kathy and Nancy when he met with Coach Bee. He was told by his teammates to "stay away from them." The word was that if Coach Bee found out that a player even asked any of these young women out, they would be in big trouble. Of course, that prohibition made it more daring and more exciting for the boys to fathom getting a date with the girls. In fact, the rule was widely known by the team's players, but it had not prevented most of them from living dangerously and trying to date the pretty girls. No one had been successful up to this point, so the boys were resigned to the fact that these ladies were unapproachable. All except for Victor Mario Perez.

Victor did not live near the school; he chose instead to take an apartment near NYU on Washington Square at the Hotel Earl. The place was inexpensive, with Spartan conditions. A common washroom, shower, and single toilet on each of the 8 floors were shared by the hotel's occupants. Inside his hundred-square-foot sleeping room, a sink was the primary amenity. There was a comfortable single bed, and Victor Mario was content with all of this because he was happy to have his own room where he could come and go as he liked.

One day in October, Spider noticed Victor leaving Coach Bee's office. Like a spy in pursuit of his subject, Spider walked secretly down the avenue in front of the Brooklyn Pharmacy building. Victor Mario hiked briskly around the corner with Spider stealthily following him. Turning onto the avenue, he saw Kathy Peters. Spider had never seen her look so pretty. She had touched up her makeup and lipstick, and she looked like a charlotte russe on a dessert tray! Spider could not believe his eyes. There was Victor Mario Perez holding hands with Kathy, walking toward the subway line to Manhattan. Spider envied his Latin friend. "What a charmer," he thought.

The next week Spider asked Victor the burning question as the two players and their teammates left the coach's office after practice. The team headed to the dining room. Spider and Victor walked down the stairs alone to the dining area. "Did I see you with Coach Bee's secretary last week headed toward the Manhattan line on the subway?"

"Yes, Solly, I have been taking Kathy and her friend Nancy dancing at this spot in Greenwich Village. They both go crazy for this song 'Perfidia.' Have you heard it? Xavier Cugat does it best, I think. We have a great time dancing to that. I like to dance and have fun. My mother was a ballroom dancer, and she taught me well. I didn't like it much when I was young. But it does have its advantages, 'la verdad' (the truth). They are … pincushion, muy bonitas. You guys are so serious. Live a little, that's what we say in Puerto Rico. It's more relaxed. You know what I mean. The girls like the Village, and they like to dance. I am teaching them a little Spanish too. They really like that!"

"Wait a minute, Victor, I don't think you mean to say 'pincushion.' You should say, 'They are very pretty,' instead, that's what you mean, right?"

"Yes, Solly, you are right!"

"In English, 'pincushion' is not a nice thing to say!"

"Oh, sorry, thank you for explaining that to me, Solly!"

"Don't worry about that, Victor Mario. I can't speak Spanish, and it's great that you speak several languages. I wish I could. Well, I think it's just great that you are a good enough dancer to teach and that you are having a good time in New York. You are a better man than all of us. Did you say both of them? You are seeing them both?"

"Si senor, cierto" (Yes sir, sure enough), replied Victor Mario affirmatively.

He was a real gentleman with style that the girls went for. Spider marveled at the smooth and graceful way that Victor handled himself in conversation and social situations. He was suave and sophisticated, and Spider admired him as much as Victor admired Spider. Victor had good taste in music, and Latin music would become extremely popular. Two years later, Xavier Cugat's "Perfidia" would become renowned for the famous dance scene in the classic movie *Casablanca* with Ingrid Bergman and Humphrey Bogart. The romantic scene displayed the type of intimate music and dancing that Kathy and Nancy were attracted to.

Spider became good friends with Victor Mario, often eating out together in Manhattan near the Garden, when they got their meal money for games. Spider started to spend time with Victor, and the next time Victor and Spider went to speak with Coach Bee, Spider went in first to talk with the coach. As he walked from the secretary bay to Coach Bee's office, he looked over his left shoulder and discretely noticed Victor and Nancy holding hands. Victor Mario admired Spider for his set shot, and Spider admired Victor Mario for his panache and his stylish flair in social settings.

Janurary 11, 1939, LIU vs Marquette at Garden

Photo: ACME NEWSPICTURES INC
Foreground Left to Right: George Newman #32 (LIU) ,
Glenn Adams #14 (Marquette)
Background Left to Right: Sy Lobello #26 (LIU), Irving Torgoff (LIU),
Erwin Graf (Marquette)

1939 NIT Undefeated National Champs, sans Sy Lobello

Photo: ACME NEWSPICTURES INC

September 2, 1938, LIU Cagers set sail for Puerto Rico for Exhibitions, At Brooklyn Harbor

Kneeling Left to Right: Oscar Schechtman, Daniel Kaplowitz, Coach Clair Bee, Saul Schwartz, and John Bromberg
Standing Left to Right: Joe Shelly, George Newman, Myron Sewitch, Capt Art Hillhouse, and Irving Torgoff

CHAPTER 12

Up, Up, and Away

* * *

DOLLY KING LEFT LIU BASKETBALL after the Butler game, January 29, 1941. Prior to King's departure, Bee would say that Dolly was "the greatest athlete I ever coached. I don't know what we'd do without him."[21] Dolly King broke racial barriers by entering college basketball, a domain largely closed to African American players at the time. In the late 1930s and early 1940s rampant racial inequality and deep prejudice made it difficult for Dolly and other talented African Americans to play college basketball. Dolly King endured the slurs, slings, and arrows of racial prejudice, yet his outstanding achievements had a profound impact on the game. His career was celebrated, as he was named an honoree of the Black Fives Foundation. The Black Fives is an organization that works to research, preserve, showcase, and teach the pre-1950 history of African Americans in basketball while honoring these pioneers and their descendants.[22]

At the time, many basketball fans, sportswriters, referees, and coaches did not feel that blacks should have the opportunity to play against or with white players. During this period, however, New York City colleges did provide some African American athletes opportunities to participate in organized basketball at the high school and college levels.

"Dolly" King was a muscular 6-foot-3, 210-pound center on Brooklyn's Alexander Hamilton High School basketball team, graduating in 1935. Dolly continued his athletics, developing and enjoying a great career in both basketball and football at Long Island University. King was picked on the fall, 1940 "African American All-American Football Team."

The *Brooklyn Eagle* reported that Dolly once played both offense and defense for the LIU football team at Ebbets Field without missing a play. Dolly then played the majority of the basketball game for the LIU varsity, later that evening.

New York sportswriters watched the abuse and the unnecessary and uncalled fouls by opposing players competing against King. Nevertheless, King tolerated the blind eyes of the referees when mostly white opponents tried to injure or maim him under the boards. King never complained and was an inspiration to his teammates and the African American community. Those who saw him play and who knew him respected his mental toughness and discipline. Like Jackie Robinson—who suffered brutal racial inequality—King did not lose his temper and maintained his self-control, focusing instead on winning, not on retaliation. He got his college degree and went on to play pro basketball. Clair Bee admired his courage and protected him.

In an incident in 1937, LIU traveled to West Point to play the army in a scrimmage at West Point. Dolly was forced to stay behind because of the army's refusal to have its members compete against black athletes. It was a tough time for Dolly; he wanted to quit school and sold some of his school books. That's when Coach Bee stepped in and had a one-hour face-to-face meeting and discussion with Dolly. Essentially, Bee told Dolly that he would "have his back," and that this type of thing would not happen again. King was determined to finish school and continued to get his education and play for LIU.

The next year, prior to a game in the south in 1938, Bee kept his word to Dolly King and refused to stay at a segregated hotel unless King was allowed to stay with the team and not separately. The venue did not want to lose the revenue associated with the cash gate of fans eager to see the popular LIU team, and it eventually capitulated and Dolly stayed with his teammates. This raised Dolly's self-esteem and respect for Coach Clair Bee, and that was just one example of what Bee's players loved about him. He was true to his word.

Considered one of the greatest African American athletes and a hero of the time—akin to the likes of Joe Louis, Jesse Owens, and Henry Armstrong—King won the respect of the sportswriters, the coaches, and the fans for his athletic prowess and his excellent sense of sportsmanship. Under difficult conditions, visiting athletes went out of their way to give King a hard time. Frequently, the more burly opponents would use aggressive tactics to rough King up, but King never lost his cool. Despite the bruises he incurred, he behaved correctly, never using his size or strength to retaliate.

Clair Bee was quoted as saying, "As a basketballer no one can top him (King), and as a footballer, I'd match him against any end in the country." Indicating the type of racial prejudice existing at the time, Bee went on to lament, "If it wasn't for his color he would be a sure bet in pro football."[21] Losing the tremendous talents of King, Bee was looking for a replacement piece to what he hoped would be his third national championship team. He knew they couldn't replace Dolly with any one player. There was no one like Dolly. The replacement would have to be in the form of several players, each contributing a unique and important role. The team chemistry had changed, and it was Bee's job to figure it out to enable his club to win. This was a daunting task for Bee as the team embarked on the toughest road trip in its school basketball history.

The practice after the Butler game was LIU's first of the season without Dolly. As the captain, Sy Lobello felt responsible to make sure that the team moved on quickly in pursuit of its championship goal.

Sy approached everyone on the team to encourage them. He moved toward Spider and started to pass and shoot with him on a side basket of the Pharmacy floor. Spider felt comfortable shooting with Sy, and it reminded him of shooting with his pals Lucio and Philly Rick at the Creston Schoolyard. Spider and Sy took turns shooting and passing, and every turn, they'd finish with a punctuating cut to the basket and a bounce pass to the cutter for a layup, encouraging each other when the layup was made. Spider moved to the free throw line to shoot a couple from the charity stripe. "Solly, I betcha a nickel that you miss!" Spider's eyes lit up, intent on making the shot. Thinking this would be easy, he lost his focus and missed. "You owe me a nickel!" said Lobello. The captain then offered up some kind words of counsel. "Solly, you have the best shot on the team. We need you to score more now. Let's try a little something. During the games, cut off my screen, and I'll toss the ball to you off my hip, like a lateral in football. You step back and take the shot after I plant my screen to free you up. You make a couple of those, and that will really open up everything down low in the post. Got it?"

"I'll make 'em if you get it to me, Sy. You know, some of these guys grab my jersey, and it's tough to shake 'em," offered Spider.

"That's OK, Solly, just follow my lead, and I'll get you your shots," replied the 6-foot-4 Lobello. He had taken a liking to the sophomore.

Sy could identify with him as he had been in a similar position as an inexperienced sophomore on LIU's outstanding senior-laden team two years before. He had been nervous and uncertain, and it was Irving Torghoff, a senior, who took Sy under his wing and guided him. It had really reassured Sy, and he wanted to return the favor to his rookie teammates and pay it forward.

Simon was now the senior with a NIT Championship under his belt with a lot of games' experience. He hobnobbed with Jules Bender and Benny Kramer of the 1936 LIU team and the rest of the LIU alumni during and after the varsity games against the alumni. Sy had been kind enough to introduce Spider around to all of the former LIU greats during the

November 29th alumni game at the Pharmacy court on campus. Spider was impressed by the LIU alum, Marius "Lefty" Russo, who now played baseball for the New York Yankees, the Bronx Bombers. Russo could still play a solid game of basketball at the time and was a tremendous athlete.

Simon and Spider practiced the suggested hip pass play several times, and they executed it well in their practice walk-throughs. Feeling confident, Spider felt like he had an edge with Sy on his team. Sy had an extraordinary, almost saintly energy. They were both full of optimism amid the LIU winning tradition. Spider was motivated to continue the winning spirit and play good basketball. He anticipated that he would get the ball and that his job was to shoot and score. Sy was a good "set up" man, and he would give Spider scoring opportunities.

The boys had some very good practices, and the team seemed to be coming together perhaps with a little chip on their shoulders because everyone was telling them that their season would not be a success because they had lost their great star. Soon it was time for their biggest test of the season, the road trip that started with their flight to Lansing, Michigan. They rode the team bus from the campus to the airport.

The DC-9 cleared its throat slowly reminding the boys of their upcoming charter plane trip to the Midwest. The young basketball players from Long Island University, their coaches, and the staff lined up outside the American Airlines Flagship Service plane at New York's LaGuardia Airport. It was a historic flight as LIU became the nation's first college basketball team to charter a plane to an away game. The name "Long Island University Basketball" was stenciled onto the side of the plane. The team waited in the air terminal prior to posing for the obligatory photo for the press to memorialize their trip. Their opponent would be the Michigan State Spartans who had beaten LIU earlier in the season at Madison Square Garden 31–26. It was a tough loss, and Spider had neglected to tape his ankles prior to the game. He had not heeded

Coach Picarello's advice to do so. He was still contrite about the error in judgment.

As he was dribbling the basketball in the second half of that first Michigan State game, Spider was fouled hard driving to the basket and rolled his ankle. He hobbled off the court and missed the remainder of the game. He watched with chagrin as the Beemen saw the Spartans run out the clock, going into a stall and holding the ball. Time ran out, leaving LIU wishing there had been a shot clock to prevent the Spartans' stall tactic. The LIU players felt that Michigan State had an inferior team, as they clung to and survived a slim lead while stalling. The stall frustrated the LIU players and Coach Bee, who collectively thought, "It was time for a rematch and revenge."

The LIU cagers were headed to Michigan from Queens, New York, using the recently finished Marine Air Terminal at LaGuardia Airport. LaGuardia Airport was named after the former New York City mayor, Fiorello LaGuardia. Mayor LaGuardia, an incessant worker and a man of efficiency, pined to get into Manhattan while flying to Newark Airport, New Jersey. The mayor complained that his ticket said, "Arrival New York" and not "Arrival New Jersey," and he was displeased. The airline agents told him that he couldn't land in New York because the City didn't have an airport. LaGuardia subsequently urged New Yorkers to approve plans to build an airport in New York City, which ultimately led to the building of LaGuardia Airport. The location, close to Manhattan, was more convenient for local residents and business travel. The new airport was constructed in part with landfill from Riker's Island in New York City. The airport, which became known as New York Municipal Airport-LaGuardia Field, was opened and dedicated for commercial travel on October 15, 1939, and the LIU Blackbirds would fly out of LaGuardia on their trip to Michigan, a little over a year later.

The new Marine Air Terminal was a busy place as the LIU team arrived. Painters were at work finishing their art in the terminal. The team waited for the plane and noticed the large bronze bust of Mayor

LaGuardia in the terminal. In the ornately tiled terminal lobby there were merchants selling pretzels, chestnuts, peanuts, and soda; they were interacting with customers, one of whom was attempting to haggle with the merchant on price. The lobby had a 30-foot ceiling with air travel- and airport-themed murals. One of the artists still working on the mural had a handlebar moustache and smoked a cigarette glued to his upper lip while painting. Another working artist was talking to one of the airport patrons who wanted to know more about the work being done. The two artists were hand painting their designs on the high-arcing walls that met the barrel-shaped ceiling.

The terminal lobby had a fresh new smell to it, and the wooden benches with steel propellers embedded on each side still had the fragrance of the woodsy oak trees cut from a forest in the Midwest. The building was designed in Art Deco motif with chic exterior and a bald eagle statue affixed to the upper wall of the exterior terminal entry. Inside the terminal lobby, a giant mural, 12 feet high and 237 feet in length, depicted man's involvement in flight, appropriately named "Flight."

"Hey, Saul," said the energetic Al Schneider, a Creston Schoolyard kid who also played at DeWitt Clinton High School. Al was short, compact, and wiry with dark hair, thick eyebrows, and a perennial suntan. Al continued, "I was going to buy you a coffee, but man, they want 5 cents for a cup of coffee! They only charge 2 cents back in Brooklyn. I'm going over to the water fountain instead. Prices are going bananas on everything. The next thing you know they will be selling water for a nickel!"

Spider looked at Al incredulously and chuckled. The muscular point guard had to be kidding. "That will be the day, Al!" said Spider. "What's next, spaceships to the moon, like in *Buck Rogers*?" They both had a good laugh not realizing how prescient they were.

The most prominent of the 8 scenes in the terminal wall mural, elegantly captured 6 pilots and navigators in the airport control tower, reviewing a series of aviation maps. The aviator group was pictured poring over a drawing table with a Yankee Clipper Pan Am Airlines seaplane in the air, just outside the terminal in the background. The mural's air traffic controller was depicted on a microphone in communication with the plane.

The LIU team was a group of hungry boys, mostly from the New York City boroughs of the Bronx, Brooklyn, Manhattan, and Queens. As they left the terminal and posed for a photo in front of the DC-3 American Airlines silver plane, they reflected on just how far they had come. Everything was at stake on this trip. If they won all their games they would be on track to get back to the NIT in Madison Square Garden. If they lost just one, their season would be over with no post-season tournament and the frustration of having to read the *Brooklyn Eagle* and the *Daily News* and realize that the naysayers had been correct. The players didn't want to hear that this was not one of Bee's better teams. The two losses that the team had suffered had made some of the beat writers skeptical. The players wanted to prove them wrong and return to the NIT.

When the team moved outside it was cold as the boys waited in front of the plane in the elements to finish their photos for the newspapers. Most of the boys wore fedoras on their heads, but some of the heartier souls like Sy Lobello did not need more than his lucky home-knit wool scarf to keep warm.

As the boys boarded the plane for Lansing, they were deep in thought. Most were thinking about losing to the Spartans in Madison Square Garden earlier in the season. Their revenge would be well earned on the road. The defeat in Madison Square Garden was particularly bitter to the Blackbirds because of the Spartans' stall. The LIU club didn't think that tactic was fair, but Coach Bee, like many great coaches, didn't tolerate any excuses. They had lost, and now they had their chance to turn the tables on the Spartans. The stall caused LIU to run out of time, and they were frustrated. It had been their first loss of the season, perhaps due to overconfidence.

"Coach Pic," Sy Lobello remarked, "how's the weather going to be in Lansing?"

Everyone on the team called him Sy, but Coach Picarello always called players by their proper names. So he responded, "Simon, a cold front is coming in, and the wind is going to be tough and the temperature right around zero. With the wind it might even feel colder."

The players made their final pose for the press in front of the plane with the stewardess and other LIU staff joining the team in the photo. Going with the team on the charter along with the players were Pete Riley, a huge LIU basketball fan; Irving Marcus, graduate manager; Dick Isaacs, student manager; Len Boylan, airline representative; Coach Clair Bee; and assistant coach "Pic" Picarello. Irving Marcus and Dick Isaacs did the heavy lifting, organizing and planning the trip. It was the toughest road test that anyone could remember for LIU. After Michigan, they continued the grueling four-day, three-game trip on their schedule. The players were looking forward to this big test, and they knew that the organizers of the NIT would not pick them if they lost any one of these games.

Bee often described Picarello as his secret weapon and head scout of players and opponents. It was a big trip for the university and the faculty; the dean of Long Island University, Tristam Metcalfe, was flying in the next day to join the team. There was a buzz around Lansing as word had gotten out that the LIU graduate manager Irving Marcus planned to throw 150 or so small rubber softball-sized mini-basketballs into the stands for the fans. The balls were designed in the patriotic red-white-and-blue colors to show support for the war effort. Irving Marcus was perhaps the busiest person on the trip, constantly in tireless motion to make everything run smoothly, allowing everyone else to enjoy the trip. Destined for the three-hour flight, the plane took off from LaGuardia. A short time after liftoff, when the plane reached cruising altitude, the stewardess came around with real china plates, white linens, and polished silver utensils, and the LIU team was treated to a nice meal of salad, potatoes, chicken, and green beans almondine. Selzer, soda, and different juices were served but no alcohol per the coaches. Spider took a brief nap after the meal and woke up after about an hour. He looked out the plane's window, and his nerves were temporarily calmed by the tranquil scenes below. The terrain of rectangles and squares of farmland were frozen in winter, blanketed with snow. It was the most beautiful landscape he had ever seen. It was a bucolic wonderland vastly different from the streets of the Bronx.

The opportunity to fly to a game to play basketball on the national stage was as sweet as the apple pie that Janice the stewardess served them. The trip was an adventure, the first-time flying for most of the players. Spider got sick on the flight as he became nauseous and returned much of his meal to the paper bag provided in the seat pocket in front of his seat on the plane. Coach Pic told him that this was normal for a first-time flier. Sy Lobello and Sy Schwartz were reading the paper and discussing the budding war in Europe. There were Nazi U-boats off the coast of New York. They were threatening to enter New York harbor where they could actually steer close to the Brooklyn Seaport, not far from Long Island University itself.

The Nazi advance on Europe was disturbing. It seemed that there was nothing to stop the advance of Hitler and his armies conquering different countries as their troops moved westward. Spider tried to focus on basketball. The boys not only had a basketball game to play for LIU but were bringing New York basketball to the Midwest. They wanted to represent New York City basketball well and prove what New York City basketball was all about. The plane flew west and gradually the snow seemed to be pervasive. The boys took notice. "Hey, Butchie," Ozzie Schectman teased, "if it's that cold in Michigan, I ain't taken my warm-ups off!"

CHAPTER 13

Michigan State University

* * *

THE TEAM ARRIVED AT THE Capital Cities Airport in Lansing, Michigan, after a three-hour-and-five-minute flight from New York. When they deplaned, Irving Marcus and the coaches organized another photo at the airport in Michigan to memorialize the historic air voyage. Michigan was distinctly colder than New York City, and the group was chilled as the photographer took various photos of the team with the plane. The managers and some of the players transported the suitcases and the duffle bags that housed the team's jerseys, the souvenir basketballs for the fans, and the equipment, and they attempted to load the bus's undercarriage storage area.

The excited players headed to the bus as well, but the welcoming bus driver came out to greet them, gesticulating in a way to motion the players to go back to the terminal. He then told the coaches that the team could not board the bus. Everyone was enormously disappointed and frustrated. Despite repeated attempts, the bus couldn't start. The engine had frozen, and it simply would not turn over. The boys crammed into the undersized Capitol Cities Airport terminal, which was heated with several portable floor heaters, but it was still chilly. The heaters were meant for the usual handful of workers and passengers that flew out of the tiny airport. The terminal had no food or drink inside.

Ironically, in spite of the efficiency of the brief three-hour air flight, the boys would be delayed getting to their hotel, as it took two more hours for the team to get a replacement bus to pick them up. When that bus finally came, they took off for their hotel. The boys' eyes were struck by the fascinating sight of farms and the barns that had a flow of cows, horses, and chickens on the country road from the airport.

In spite of their transportation mishap, the boys were primed and ready. LIU was a confident group. The Beemen had come together and had not lost since the heartbreaking last-second loss to Duquesne's Moe Becker in the Garden.

The LIU coaches and team found their downtown hotel and its lobby filled with interesting scenes of farms, the countryside, and the college's football games with the teams' players, past and present. There was a small simple front desk counter, and the team manager Marcus was busy straightening out room and meal arrangements. The lobby was punctuated by its low ceilings, which featured ornate hand-painted designs. The Spartan Inn was undergoing an expansion, and there were groups of tradesmen finishing up their work. The team checked into the hotel, and room assignments were distributed. Coach Bee and Coach Pic each had their own room, but the rest of the group doubled up, two to a room. Coach Bee barked instructions to the players as they waited in the lobby. "OK, boys, we are going to take about an hour or so to get situated. Get up to your rooms, freshen up, and we'll leave here to go for practice in the Michigan State gym at four p.m. We'll meet down in the lobby then and head over. Everyone please be on time."

As the boys went about their business in their rooms, they felt a sense of New York pride. After all, basketball was New York City's game. From the hard asphalt of the schoolyards to the world's most famous arena, Madison Square Garden, New York was the place where hungry talent showed off its skills. Having learnt from the trials and tribulations of the City, its players were crafty, talented, and proudly competitive.

Basketball no longer involved a cage enclosing the court. There were no jump balls after every made basket. Those changes had been made several years prior. While Barney Sedran was the king of the cage and the tactics of its game, he had retired before the new rules allowed players the freedom and creativity enabled by open court play. The game now had new rules designed to speed up the game. The rules allowed a freedom of movement with more spacing on the floor for players to make individual moves, to get open, and to shoot. The new rule changes and the larger court enabled more scoring, which made the game more interesting for the fans.

Coach Clair Bee emphasized movement both with and without the basketball, opening up scoring chances both inside and from the perimeter. Every minute of practice not only taught his players fundamentals and technique but focused on the mentality needed to win and work together. Their practices showed off crisp passing and accurate shooting. The three-man weave warm-up drill created opportunity for each player to touch the ball and get a feel for it. Then after several passes the ball would circulate to the open man who would lay the ball in off the glass or take a short running one-handed shot.

Bee understood that many teams knew how to play offense, but few gave defense the same level of energy or focus. For example, Bee once said, "Wilson, you sprained your ankle? Pic, give him the ball and he'll be cured. But if you ask Wilson to play defense his ankle hurts?" Bee would chuckle, but everyone understood and appreciated the coach's message. Defense was the most important aspect of the game. Coach Bee's 1-3-1 wheel zone started as a frenetic full-court press, which then had the players fall back into a half-court 1-3-1 zone press with relentless and dogged swarming of the basketball and the opponent. When the coach called for the 1-3-1, the team was energized by the tactic, which became its signature weapon, often overwhelming its opponent. Most of the LIU players were skilled at execution of the 1-3-1 wheel zone, and if they didn't play the zone with the requisite intensity and effectiveness, they would sit on the bench, being "out of the plans." Defense came first, and you had to give that your maximum effort regardless of how well you played on offense.

Bee emphasized the importance of making foul shots an easy way to pile up points. To better the distribution of the basketball, Bee used a weighted medicine ball to improve passing strength and accuracy, showing his players how to pass the ball correctly with elbows out and snapping off the two-handed chest or a two-handed bounce pass. He liked the players to practice flexible wrists and fingers on the ball. He taught rebounding by showing his players how to grab the right position under the backboard and use a spread eagle to create space and separation and protect the ball. The rebounder stretched his legs apart after grabbing the ball off the glass, warding off an opponent with his legs at the same time.

Coach Bee's practices were long, detailed events lasting up to three hours, emphasizing precision passing, shooting, and rebounding. The coach never stopped teaching, and even after the season ended, AAU tournaments were played for player skill development and team bonding, where teammates could learn each other's tendencies and skills.

Off-season training, exhibition games, and preseason tournaments developed players and permitted Bee's teams to perform at an elite level when the regular season began. Bee was in constant contact with his players and had staff help him promulgate instructional and motivational communications to them.

Many of the college beat writers and other New York press doubted that LIU could survive their three-game road trip without the skill and grace of King. The Beemen would have to win their last six games to make the NIT. They would also have to win on the road—first, at Michigan State, then the next night in Chicago against a tough DePaul team, and finally the following night at the undefeated University of Baltimore. The remaining games were Canisius at home, LaSalle in the Convention Center in Philly, and then finally against a tough Toledo team in Madison Square Garden. In fact, some newspapers were already reporting that Toledo and the University of Baltimore had been given unofficial invitations to the NIT, making LIU's chances to gain an NIT berth tenuous.

The LIU players and staff relaxed a bit from their plane ride and bus mishap. Spider roomed with Dick Holub, also a sophomore who would go on to be an All-American and excellent pro player. He was 6 feet, 5 inches tall, could jump with the best players, and like Hank Liusetti, Holub could shoot the one-handed jump shot, which had revolutionized the game.

"Hey, Solly," Holub said in their hotel room, "I got a letter before we left New York, and it was titled 'What to expect in an air raid.' Did you get that letter from Dean Metcalfe?"

"Yeah," said Spider, "I got it also, a couple of days ago."

"Well," said the tall, lanky forward, "we are going to beat the heck out of Hitler, no matter how many of those countries he takes over!"

"Yeah, that's right, Dick. Did you see that 102-year-old Civil War veteran that said he wants to return to service in the army if we go to war? He wants to personally defeat Hitler."

"No, I didn't see that, Solly, but that's the idea!" The boys were having a good conversation about just about anything that came to mind, each excited about the road trip and peppy with the spirit of the ball games and the adventure they felt on the road trip.

Spider continued, "Dick, let's go see that next 'Sugar' Ray Robinson fight when he comes back to the Garden. Did you see what he did last time out in October against Joe Escheverria? He knocked him out completely in two rounds! And he's only nineteen! I'm telling you, he is going to be the greatest fighter of all time. He is lightning fast!"

"That's a good idea. I know a great place near the Garden where you can get a nice steak dinner, with salad, potato, and a vegetable and a drink for 75 cents! And the food ain't bad at all!" replied an excited Holub.

"OK, Dick, let's get down to the lobby and get ready to go practice," said Spider. The two sophomores headed to the hotel lobby. When the boys reached the lobby, the coaches were already waiting for the whole team to assemble.

"OK, boys, now we are without Dolly for the rest of the season as you know, and this is a tough Michigan State team that beat us with Dolly in New York. They stalled on us and didn't give us a chance to get back in it. That's why we can't let them get up big on us early and do it to us again!" There was a sense of urgency in the voice of the thin, distinguished coach. "First team: Beenders, Lobello, Cohen, Schwartz, and Ossie. Now let's have a great practice and go get them tomorrow night!" The boys piled onto the bus and went over to the new Spartans' arena.

The LIU players took the floor at 5:00 p.m. There were a dozen or so local sportswriters and hometown boosters that were fascinated by the meticulous and detailed practice session conducted by Coach Bee. Every minute of the practice was calculated and worked for a purpose. The practice demonstrated slick passing and weaving and shooting and sprinting up and down the court.

In one drill, Coach Picarello used a tennis racquet to force the players driving to the hoop to adjust to the height of the opponent's big men.

The drill forced the LIU players to alter their shots for the wingspan of the tall Spartan players. The tactic was helpful and innovative. To the Midwest fans, the New Yorkers were looked upon as a phenomenon. The local sportswriters hurried to meet deadlines for tomorrow's edition detailing the New Yorker's appearance and tantalizing practice. Neither the Spartans' fans nor their players liked the team from Brooklyn. The LIU players and coaches were resolute, determined, and confident. They were just short of cocky and that bothered the fifty or so hometown fans who watched the Beeman hustle through their ninety-minute practice.

Sy Lobello was normally mild mannered, but he took exception to one of the more vituperative fans yelling slurs at his teammates. He was angry and wanted to yell back at the crazy man in the stands. The harsh words were the worst slurs about New Yorkers that Sy had ever heard. The man made loud comments ridiculing the LIU players as they ran through their drills. Normally, a tough and competitive guy on the court but calm and quiet by nature, Sy had a burning desire to bop the fan, but like a good captain and team leader, he controlled his emotions and didn't let them get the better of him. Sy had tasted an NIT Championship his sophomore year and wanted to win another this year. He had to lead, and lead he did—more by his actions than verbally; he wasn't usually vocal. He thought about anti-Semitism and wondered why fans yelled ethnic slurs. Why was it was so prevalent now here, seemingly everywhere in America as well as in Europe. He was a religious Christian, went to church regularly, and treated all people with respect and dignity regardless of religion or race. Sy respected everyone and protected his teammates, and with a purposeful glare he shut the fan up directing his stern eyes in the fan's direction, flaring his nostrils. The fan silenced and left the arena a couple of minutes thereafter.

As the LIU players left the court, the band and the cheerleaders came onto the floor to practice. The band played and the cheerleaders sang the Michigan State Fight Song:

"On the banks of the Red Cedar
There's a school that's known to all
Its specialty is winning
And those Spartans play good ball
Spartan teams are never beaten
All through the game they'll fight
Fight for the only colors
Green and white
Go right through for MSU
Watch the points keep growing
Spartan teams are bound to win
They're fighting with a vim
Rah! Rah! Rah!
See their team is weakening
We're going to fight to win this game!
Fight! Fight! Rah, Team, Fight!
Victory for MSU!

Photo Below, LIU Basketball Team Flies into Lansing, Michigan, to take on Michigan State, February1941. The undefeated 14-0 University of Baltimore had already been invited to the NIT and LIU had not. LIU played DePaul and U of Baltimore after the Michigan State game all on the road with the NIT birth in the balance.

Long Island Team First to Fly Here

—State Journal Photo

First athletic team in history to make a trip here by airplane, the Long Island basketball team arrived late yesterday afternoon at the Capital City airport in a chartered ship. The picture shows the group on arrival. In the picture, first row, extreme left, is Coach Clair Bee, famous teacher of basketball. Beside him stands Pete Riley, an ardent Blackbird fan. Extreme right, first row, is Irving Marcus, graduate manager in charge of the party. The Blackbirds made the trip from La Guardia field to Lansing in slightly more than three hours, and then due to the fact that the motor on their bus froze while waiting their arrival, required nearly two hours to travel from the field to Michigan State college for practice.

Photo: (Michigan) State Journal

Jenison Field House

Photo: MSU Archives

On the campus of Michigan State University

Victor Mario Perez, in his LIU practice jersey, heard the cheer as he exited the court. He called out after the brief singing of the Michigan State fight song with his San Juan accent, "Hey guys, what means vim?" Everybody had a good laugh because no one could explain it to Victor. They didn't know themselves. Victor thought everyone was making fun of him even though they weren't, and it caused everyone to have a good laugh with the bemused Victor, who laughed along with his teammates when he realized that no one really knew what the word meant.

The team showered and headed back to the hotel. They had to prepare for the game the next day and lay out their pants, blazers, and ties that they would wear to the games. That night they also had to pack up the rest of their gear and clothing in their suitcase to get ready for the trip to Chicago. They were checking out of the hotel in the late morning and had to be ready to get on the team bus immediately afterward.

Wednesday was game day and you couldn't have asked for a nicer day. There was not a cloud in the sky, and the weather, while sunny, remained refreshingly chilly as the early morning temperature of 4 degrees Fahrenheit had warmed to a moderate 25 degrees Fahrenheit by the time the bus left the hotel in the late afternoon. The winds out of the west played with the banks of shoveled snow, dusting the sidewalk and streets outside the hotel with wisps of winter's powder.

The game was to start at 7:00 p.m, so the team was slated to play the game; shower; get their suits, jackets, and ties on; pack up their gear; and leave the arena to get on the bus to the airport for their charter flight to Chicago. From the hotel to the bus, Spider walked with Coach Picarello. "Hey, Spider, are you going to tape your ankles tonight?" "Let me answer that for you," said Coach Pic rhetorically, "Heck yeah, you are going to tape!" Spider grinned sheepishly. He didn't know what to say, so a sly grin did the job and he scooted onto the bus. Sy Lobello as usual was already sitting in the third seat to the left of the front of the bus, next to the window located two rows behind the coaches. The team sat in brown leather-cushioned bench seats, two players together on each side of the aisle. Shortly afterward, the rest of the team, coaches, and staff began to come onto the bus. Sy was the most affable player on the team. He was not as muscular as Bill King, but he was solid and strong and could run like an antelope and jump high enough to grab a rebound on both ends of the floor when it was needed. He was soft spoken and a peaceful and spiritual man. He was engaged to his Bryant High School sweetheart, Dorothy, and they had already decided to get married in Queens, New York, in March 1943. Simon had just turned 21 on December 16. The dark hair and moustache made the dapper Simon resemble a young Tyrone Power, the actor.

Spider sat next to Sy on the bus.

"Hey, Solly, how's it going? How are you enjoying the trip?"

Spider responded, "Everything is pretty neat. I'd like to get a bit more sleep. That plane ride tuckered me out, and after the game we have another plane trip and I don't like flying much." There they sat, a Christian and a Jew brought together from the schoolyards of Queens and the Bronx. They had the intense love of basketball as their common bond. While they came from different schoolyards, they learned the same crafty lessons about the game of basketball that prepared them for this important road trip. They talked about the game, the plays, the offense and defensive plans, and that night's opponent, the Michigan State Spartans.

Sy recalled a scene from the fall trip to San Juan. "Remember the Puerto Rico trip? That was the best time! So many crazy things happened on that trip, remember? What was the name of that girl you and Dolly took a liking to? That was funny!" Spider started to daydream, and his mind wandered off, not realizing that Sy had asked him a question. He didn't answer Sy at first, so Sy asked him again, "Solly, do you remember that girl on the boat coming back from San Juan, what was her name?"

"Sorry, Sy, I was thinking about the game. Sorry I didn't answer you. I never found out her real name. Can you believe that? Sorry, Sy. She said she was Carmen Miranda, but we all know that wasn't serious," Spider said.

"I remember you guys hanging out on the deck, and she jumped in your lap," Sy added.

"Yeah, Sy, that was a great trip. I think she liked Dolly too. I think she goes to college in New York City. I wonder whatever happened to her? She didn't appear too attractive that day, but when I saw her at night at the dance, she had makeup on and got all dressed up and she looked gorgeous." The two teammates reminisced about the Puerto Rico trip and the mysterious girl, a highlight of the boat trip back to Brooklyn from San Juan.

On the right side of the bus, several rows behind Lobello and Spider, Ossie Schectman, the All-Metropolitan selection from Tilden High School in Brooklyn, was sitting next to his buddy Sol "Butch" Schwartz. Ossie was wiry and 6 feet 1, and never stopped working on the court, an energy player and hard driving natural point guard. He joked with his pal Butch, the star of Seward Park High School in New York City. "Butchie," the sinewy brown-haired competitor began, "did you see where Marius Russo did really well with the Yankees this past year? I think he's won fourteen games, pitching for them. Too bad they didn't make the World Series!" Ossie was teasing his good pal.

Butch was a big Yankee fan, and Ossie loved the Brooklyn Dodgers. They liked to rib each other in a good-natured fashion about their favorite teams. "Oss, Marius was on that great 1936 LIU team. We could use some of them now. They won what thirty-three straight? 'Lefty' Russo, Kramer, Julie Bender, Art Hillhouse, and Leo Merson. Say, didn't you know Leo? His dad had a grocery store in the Brownsville Section of Brooklyn? Sad, the dad was killed rushing to return some change to a customer who had overpaid and had forgotten about paying too much. Leo's dad was killed by an errant cab while trying to do the right thing."

"Yeah, that was tragic," said Ossie, "but I think we'll be OK with this team. I think we are gonna surprise some folks and get back to the NIT. I don't wanna jinx it, but I feel that we are really starting to play well. But you are right. All those guys on that '36 team were incredible athletes. And don't forget the other players on that team—Ken Norton, Harry Grant, and Bill Schwartz. I think Grant became a pro bowler. But 'Lefty' Russo was the best athlete. Lefty was and still is an excellent basketball player! He'll probably have to stop playing in the alumni games now that he is a star with the Yanks."

"Yeah, this was his last year playing with the alumni. He told me so after the alumni game this year," said Butch. Spider overheard Ossie and Butch talking, and he marveled at the discussion, appreciating that great '36 team. Spider had read about that LIU squad, but he never dreamed that he would put on the same LIU Jersey as those legendary players. He looked back starting at CCNY night school, when LIU, NYU, and City College (CCNY) varsity coaches weren't interested in offering him a scholarship. How fortunate it was that Coach Pic saw him play in a couple of the CCNY night school games and offered him a full scholarship by LIU through Coach Pic. He had grown into a regular starter now as a varsity player.

"Sy," continued Spider, "do you remember that game we had down in San Juan at that outdoor stadium near the bay? We beat that Puerto Rico Olympic team by sixteen. We both scored a lot. You were really hitting them. But the thing that I remember the most is those green iguanas!"

"Yeah, Solly, that was crazy. They swarmed the court at sunset. There had to be about two-hundred of them. The refs couldn't start the game." The boys loved to talk about those crazy green iguanas. They had never seen anything like it. "It took forever to get 'em off the court!"

"That was nuts, and what about those parrots flying around? I've seen pigeons in the City, but nothing as wild as the dozens of parrots flying in the open like that!" Shortly, the reminiscing ended, and the boys were ready to play a game.

CHAPTER 14

Narcos at a Biker Rally

✳ ✳ ✳

THE MICHIGAN STATE FANS LOVED their Spartans. It was an agricultural school, and many of its basketball fans were local folks who came in from surrounding small towns and villages to the state campus to watch its Spartans' basketball games. The students attending the games were loud and boisterous. The state basketball team had become popular with the building of the new arena on campus, which had just opened. The new 12,500-seat Jenison Arena had everybody in town excited about attending events in the new facility.

When the LIU squad came onto the floor, the students stomped their feet rattling the wooden bleachers and shaking them. It seemed like the two referees knew everyone on the Michigan State coaching staff. "For heaven's sakes," Clair Bee thought, "those coaches and refs are calling each other by their first names like they're first cousins!"

The Michigan State fans booed louder and louder as the Blackbirds warmed up with their slick passing, showing their adept weaves and layups. Dick Holub did a couple of ball skills, spinning the ball on his index finger with his right hand, then the same with his left, impressing the fans as he did this for a couple of minutes to warm up. Then LIU did their layup drill where they didn't shoot the layup but just laid the ball off the glass on the right side of the basket, and each successive player tapped the ball against the backboard, until the whole team had done this two times.

The band played as loud as they could, and the arena fans cheered rabidly as the Green-and-White came out onto the newly polished hardwood floor with the MSU Spartans' "S" painted at Center Court. The LIU players were like narcos at a biker rally.[23] "Murder them, kill them, destroy them!" yelled the angry fanatics expecting another Spartans' victory.

The Jenison Field House on campus opened in 1940 and was named after Frederick Jenison, who willed his entire estate to the college. The US Public Works Administration funds along with funds from Mr. Jenison's estate were used to build a state-of-the art arena. The Art Deco three-story redbrick building sported a distinguished entry foyer with three large murals above each lobby door. There was one giant mural of a player from the three major sports—baseball, football, and basketball—above each door.

Eager for the game, the students crammed into the student section. They booed every single LIU player throughout the warm-ups and into the introductions and the start of the game. When the LIU boys went back into the locker room after their warm-up, Spider lost his dinner in the bathroom, and several of his teammates were likewise busy occupying the commodes in the locker room. Once they were relieved, they felt ready to take the floor and play a game.

Jenison Field House had four banks of stadium lights, which hung from the arena rafters and were so bright that several of the Long Island players felt a slight glare that distorted their vision and hindered their ability to shoot. Spider, in particular, was affected by the glare. His vision worsened still when a scintilla of residue of his applied leg liniment got in his eye after wiping the sweat off his brow during warm-ups. The LIU players barely noticed the new hardwood court made from the Midwest's finest finished wood and the fresh varnish on the floor that shone brilliant and still had a fresh new smell. Reporters and team personnel surrounded the court, and each team flanked opposite sides of the floor. Just prior to the start of the game, the officials discussed the rules with each other and the official scorer at the scorer's table.

The 1979 NCAA Championship banner, which Magic Johnson and the Spartans would win, would be raised to the rafters on this same court thirty-eight years later. But there were no banners hanging yet for Michigan State, and the cavernous arena reverberated with the exhortations of the home team's fans who cheered on and on, desperately wanting their beloved Spartans to crush their opponent.

The starting lineups were announced, and with each player's name echoing through the Fieldhouse, the lights were turned off and a spotlight alighted on the announced player who dribbled just onto the court; then he turned and passed the ball to the next starter who, in turn, was then announced and spotlighted. After the LIU starters were called out, the five Michigan State starting players entered the court likewise dribbling the ball and then passing it to their next starting teammate upon entering the court. An incredible roar went up when the Spartan players each came out. The fans chanted and clapped rhythmically as the band played the fight song followed by the public announcer calling each home player's name. The fans chanted, "Let's go, State! Let's go, State! Let's go, State!" As if it wasn't loud enough, the band started playing Benny Goodman's "Sing, Sing, Sing," and when the drummer played his solo part, the crowd went into a frenzy clapping and screaming.

The noise was deafening for the opening tip-off. Beenders jumping center for LIU lost the tip, and Michigan State got the basketball. Ossie, Butch Schwartz, Spider, Beenders, and Lobello fell back into their 1-3-1 wheel zone half-court defense. The Blackbirds started slower than

Coach Bee would have liked, and the men from Brooklyn fell behind quickly 11–2 midway through the first half, just what Coach Bee had hoped to avoid. The Spartans played slowly and deliberately offensively and stifled the Blackbird players on defense, and the Birds could not get many shots at the basket. Bee started to become concerned about the Spartans going into a stall now that they had a substantial lead, just like they had done in the Garden earlier in the year.

Back in New York, Genie Wallach and Lucio Rossini listened to the game on the radio, troubled by their pal Spider's team being down early in the game. They listened on the campus of St. John's University at a recreation hall. They didn't have a game to play but were intent on listening to Spider's game, rooting him on. Phil Rick and Dave Polansky were listening to the game back in the Bronx at Phil's parents' house, and Dave told Phil confidently, "Watch, Solly will get hot in the second half and LIU will win."

"I totally agree. We've seen him get hot so many times in the schoolyard; it's just a matter of time for him," replied the confident Philly Rick.

The shots that LIU was able to get off in the early going were but one-handed wild shots from poor angles. The coaches remained calm and did not panic. They rotated Dick Holub and Al Schneider into the game. The Brooklynites were off their game early on, and it almost seemed as if they were letting the raucous crowd impact their concentration. The Spartans were tenaciously guarding LIU's star, Ossie Schectman, rotating defenders to wear out the future NBA's NY Knickerbocker. Ossie just couldn't get going. At halftime, the Spartans led 17–11. David Eisenberg, a reporter from New York, was listening to the game on the radio back in New York City. He was rooting for LIU of course, but he was not optimistic about the Blackbirds' chances. There was no Hillhouse, Merson, Kramer, Torghoff, King, or Russo in the LIU lineup. "This was not a championship team," he thought. "Besides, King had now graduated, and the best player on the team, Dick Holub, wasn't playing enough. What could Clair Bee be thinking?" he thought.

He remembered what Bee had told him in January prior to the Duquesne loss in the Garden, "David, I don't expect a ranking position for this club among the national leaders in college basketball. This is going to be a tough game against Duquesne, and I don't expect to win half of our remaining games after this one. That's not good enough to make it back to the NIT like we did the past two years, and we will be lucky to end up with eighteen or nineteen wins and five or six losses. Seton Hall hasn't lost with Davies, Ohio U., and City College will likely have better records, and look at our away game schedule, going on the road for three games in four days at Michigan State, DePaul, and the University of Baltimore. After that we have to go to Philadelphia and play LaSalle at the Convention Center. I don't have a Julie Bender on this team, no Leo Merson, no Danny Kaplowitz, and definitely not a consensus All-American like Irv Torgoff from my 1939 NIT champs. We shall see what these boys have got in their hearts."

"Bee was convincing," thought Eisenberg. "But maybe that sly fox was sandbagging me. Maybe he is building another championship club, maybe Holub is a great player, but maybe Bee is trying to get the team chemistry aligned with other combinations of players." Bee had done it in the past, and who knows, he might have a few tricks left up his sleeve. There was no craftier coach.

Coach Bee was not happy in the locker room. "You boys dug a hole for yourselves. It's not going to be easy to do it, but I believe that you are all champions, and if you play our system of good basketball, execute the weave, pass and pick on offense, and press hard with our attacking zone defense all over the floor, we will come back and win. You must do it. We are not going to let them stall on us again. So let's go out and get on them early. Let's start out with the same players that started the game, and let's get on the press early and fierce. OK, boys, let's go out there and play hard!"

Sy Lobello walked out of the locker room, joining Spider as they came onto the court. Spider, like Ossie, had been held scoreless in the first half. His eyes had been bothering him because of the liniment, but he had soaked his face in a hot wet towel at halftime and successfully cleared the burning liniment out of his eyes. He could see clearly now.

LIU came out in the second half with a purpose, and as they jogged through layups to warm up, the sailor suit flap on the back of their warm-up jackets flopped up and down, as if waving mockingly to the Spartan crowd. The Spartan band played, the cheerleaders held their megaphones high and called out cheers, the crowd revved its collective engine, and the second half started in a frenzy. They started the half with a jump ball, and as they awaited the tap, Lobello grabbed Spider by the arm and inspired the young sophomore, "Solly, when you come out of the figure-8 weave, fake like you are going to rub by the post, go into the lane quickly but only halfway, then pop out to either the corner or the foul line extended at the wing. I'll set a pick at the end of the weave, and we'll hit you. We got to get going here!"

Lobello tapped Spider on the back as Spider said, "If I get it I'll make it." Lobello's reassurance had a calming effect on Spider. All he had to do now was shoot like he had done so many thousands of time at the schoolyard. He was in focus mode, and like Billy Chapel (Kevin Costner's character), in the movie *For the Love of the Game*, Spider "cleared the mechanism," and the crowd noise silenced in his mind. He was focused and "all in."

The three-man weave or figure 8 was a staple of the LIU offense. The LIU guards and forwards passed and went behind the man to whom the ball was passed; the pass recipient then passed the ball to the third player in the opposite direction and went behind him, and so on. This could be done with three or four players and a post-up man or center. What Sy Lobello audibled to Spider was a variation on the theme. The fourth man in the weave would break from the weave and burst out to the corner or the foul line extended at the wing, and the last player to pass in the weave would pass it to Spider, who was that fourth man moving to get open. The maneuver would be punctuated by Sy Lobello stopping to set a pick on Spider's man, leaving Spider with room to get open for a long-range set shot.

The Blackbirds lost the tap to start the second half, but the Spartans lost the ball when Ossie Schectman stole it back. A visceral booing rang out from the hostile home crowd each time LIU got the ball on offense and tried to score, relenting only when the Spartans retrieved possession of the ball. Beenders missed a running one-hander in the lane, and the Spartans got the ball, still leading 17–11. Emulating their winning strategy in the Garden, the team from the Midwest began to stall, holding the ball along with its lead. But Sy Lobello willed a steal from Michigan State's guard, Burk, giving LIU back the basketball. LIU went into its weave, and as Lobello set a screen for him, Spider popped out to the wing about 22 feet from the basket and nailed a high-arcing two-handed set shot to close the LIU deficit to 4 points. The crowd hushed for a moment as the ball went cleanly through the net for a swish. There were fourteen minutes left on the clock, and once again Michigan State began to stall, spreading out their offense and holding the ball. After a defensive breakdown, Michigan State's leading scorer, Frank Merkules, found an opening, and his driving layup put the Spartans back up by six. After Schectman made a foul shot, State got the ball back and tried to catch LIU sleeping. LIU's Beenders alertly beat his man to the spot and blocked a Spartan shot giving the Blackbirds possession. The Blackbirds turned it over again; however, they gave the ball back to the Spartans.

With the score 19–14, Michigan State called time-out. Were they going to go into the stall again? Coach Bee gathered his players in the time-out huddle and exhorted, "OK, we are going to go full court press in the 1-3-1 wheel zone. Let's go and get the ball; we don't want to lay back and have them run out the clock with another stall."

Coach Bee had just finished an intense brief talk when Ossie interjected. "Let's get it going, boys. Let's win this." The 1-3-1 wheel zone pressured the Spartans' guards who couldn't get the ball over half-court. They turned the possession over again. Ossie inbounded the ball and made a long pass out to Schwartz, who settled the ball down and started the offense. The ball went into Beenders, who spotted Spider moving off Lobello's screen as Spider popped out again, this time finding an opening in the corner. Spider got the pass, and as the defender, Gerard, tried to switch off Lobello, Sy gently brushed the Spartan, creating just enough interference so Gerard couldn't get out in time to contest the shot. Spider's 20-foot set shot went cleanly through the bright white netting once again. Now down by only 3 points, 19–16, the Blackbirds really started to hear it from the crowd. The Michigan State fans were yelling louder than they ever had, once again trying to throw the visitors off their game. The students began once again to stomp their feet on the wooden bleachers, which rattled and reverberated. The LIU players had never seen such a frenetic crowd nor heard anything louder.

After Phillips canned a 15-foot shot for Michigan State, Beenders connected on a hook shot from the post position to close the LIU deficit to 21–18. This time Coach Bee called time-out himself after the LIU basket. Seeing what was going on, he inspired his players, "OK, boys, this is what we are going to do. You have two options. Ossie and Butch, you can get the ball down into the post to Hank for a shot, or you guys or Hank can kick the ball out to Spider. OK. Got it?"

"OK, Coach," the boys responded in unison.

At this moment in the game, the boisterous Spartan crowd ironically motivated the away team. The cheers and jeers had an unintended effect; they had fired up LIU's players, and they pulled together as away teams sometimes do on the road against all odds.

It was the turning point in the game. The clock was ticking, LIU was away from home, and they weren't going to get any favors from the referees. It was not only a pivotal moment in the game but also a pivotal moment in LIU's entire season. The outside quick set shots or "pop shots" were working. Spider was hot, and he felt like he could score on any of the home team's defenders. The seniors were inspired by Spider's play. Nobody else on LIU was finding their mark from outside in this dazzling brightly lit new arena. The conditions and lighting were difficult, and LIU was struggling to convert its shots. It had seemed for a while, even to the coaches, that this would not be the Blackbird's night. Spider was not deterred. He could feel his teammates feeding off his shot-making, positively impacting the team's play. Another couple of swishes just might be enough to carry his team through.

The second half change in LIU's play was palpable, and the Spartans began to sense it. The home team was losing momentum. The Michigan boys responded out of the time-out and came out aggressively to try to retake the lead. They ran their offense and got the ball to Merkules, but Ossie was all over him, bodying up on him without fouling. The Spartan guard tried to get around Schectman but mustered a weak baby hook shot which missed. Lobello came up with a big rebound, and LIU went on offense. The Long Island team went into their weave again, staying disciplined. They got the ball out to Spider this time on the left wing. The defender Phillips was ready this time and anticipated the play, timing his move perfectly, lunging out on Spider. Spider reacted and moved back to 29 feet out.

Then instinctively he did something he had never done before. Seeing Phillips in hot pursuit and sensing that the he might block the shot at that moment, Spider faked hard like he was going to shoot, only to pull the ball back into his body as he watched Phillips fly by him. Then Spider composed himself and saw that he was all alone. He launched a high spiraling shot that Holub later said "came down from the heavens!" Spider's third swish in a row momentarily silenced the intense crowd, which breathed a collective "ugh" when the ball went in, and LIU trailed by a point, 21–20. "Way to go, Spider. Did I just see a bird fly by you?" Lobello yelled out, calling Solly by his nickname, as the captain led his team back down the court.

The Blackbirds went into their wheel zone full court press angling the Spartan guards toward the sidelines, using the out-of-bounds line, in effect, like another of its defenders. Spartan Coach Ben Van Alstyne wanted to insert guard Mel Peterson into the game to break the daunted Blackbird press, but Peterson had been out since early in the season with an injury and still was not ready to go.

Michigan State tried to penetrate on offense to get to the hoop, but this time Lobello tied up Joe Gerard trying his luck in the lane. LIU won the jump ball to regain possession with seven minutes and thirty-nine seconds to go. The Spartan fans were relentless and tried to will a victory for their boys, chanting, "Let's go, State, Let's go, State," over and over! LIU again worked the weave. This time from 10 feet beyond the foul line off a Lobello pick, Spider nailed his fourth straight missile, and after his little hop toward the net follow-through, Spider clapped his hands in celebration as the LIU players sprinted back down the court, taking the lead for the first time in the game, 22–21.

The Spartans called time-out and set up a play for Merkules to get the ball and score off a pick from Hindman, the center. Coach Bee urged his players on. "This time we are going to play the 1-3-1 zone in our defensive zone just like the full court press but in the half-court, and let's force them out of the middle where they are the most dangerous. We are going to stop them, and when we get the ball back we are going to give them a taste of their own medicine. When we get possession, we'll start the weave, but this time spread out the floor and stall on them! Let's go, men!"

"Let's go, fellas," urged Captain Lobello.

Merkules got the ball and dribbled to his left, hoping to catch Butch Schwartz, his defender, off guard on a pick play with Hindman. But Schwartz was too quick; he slid over the Hindman screen with Ossie's help, talking him through the screen and supporting him. Mekules again could not connect on the shot, and LIU got the ball back with seven minutes exactly to go in the game. LIU now spread their offense out on the floor after getting the ball over the half-court line. The Beemen stalled, dribbling and passing at the deep perimeter, like Dean Smith's North Carolina "four corners," which the great coach would deploy some thirty years later. The Spartan players did not come out of their zone defense to contest the stall. The Spartan fans grew restless and began to boo and boo and boo. They started chanting unspeakable slurs at the Blackbirds. The LIU cagers held the ball for over four minutes, and with less than three minutes to go in the game, the booing was so loud that neither coach could hear. Players and coaches could simply not communicate. The angry Spartan fans started throwing things. Coach Bee was the first to notice that the fans were throwing nickels and pennies at the LIU players. The coins landed on the court, and one hit Coach Bee in the head and angered him. Then, Coach Bee motioned to the referee and called his final time-out. The crowd continued to boo and would not stop throwing coins onto the court. Coach Bee instructed his players carefully, "Go back onto the floor now during the time-out and pick up as many of the coins as you can and give them to Marcus and Isaacs (the managers)." The boys went onto the court during the time-out and quickly gathered up most of the coins. The fans saw this and went crazy yelling! The crowd could not believe what the New Yorkers were doing. "City Slickers, stiffs, panhandlers, losers," the fans yelled.

The game finally resumed after a bit of a delay as one of the Michigan State coaches tried to calm the crowd down. The students, for their part, started to rattle the stands, stomping in unison on the wooden bleachers creating an even louder sound than before. The rafters were visibly shaking, the noise louder than a plane engine. The police at the game started to close in around the LIU team as the booing and war-like threats became louder and more vicious.

When the game resumed there was just over two minutes remaining. The fans booed louder and louder; the students kept stomping their feet, rattling the bleachers. The home fans were hateful, and their angry savage comments, threats, and projectiles foisted upon the LIU players could not be controlled by the small police group in attendance. The crowd was out of control, and one of the police officers would later say that he feared for the lives of the visiting players.

Finally, with just over a minute to go, Butch Schwartz made a running layup to give the Blackbirds a three-point cushion, 24–21. The booing and hurling of garbage onto the floor was now so far out of control that the police were calling back to the station for backup police officers to come to the arena immediately. The Spartan faithful hardly noticed the Bob Phillips basket with thirty seconds to go to make the score LIU 24–Spartans 23. LIU held the ball for the last twenty-five seconds of the game as time ran out with the Spartans unable to regain possession of the ball.

The fans were in a frenzy like no other. They were throwing everything they could get their hands on when the final buzzer sounded. First coins, then toilet paper, popcorn, and finally soda cups, some partially full. The projectiles were attacking the LIU players, who were trapped and blocked by an angry mob of fans. LIU could not exit their side of the floor to gain entrance to their locker room.

The local police desperately pleaded with Coach Bee and his staff, "Have your team bus ready outside for an immediate departure. Have your staff get up all of your equipment and clothing out of the locker and head for the bus immediately, or we cannot guarantee your safety. This crowd is out of control and crazy. We've called in for backup but this is a small town and our reinforcements won't get here in time, and even if they did it would not be enough support to hold off this crowd. We have never seen anything like this."

Thinking quickly with his rapier-sharp mind, Clair Bee protected his players like family. Poised and gracefully eloquent under the pressure of the moment, Bee instructed his players, "Everyone put on your warm-up suits and head for the bus, we will get up all the clothes, gear, and equipment off of the bench and in the locker room. Now, and I mean right now, let's get out of here!"

The boys from Brooklyn obeyed their smart coach, and they were glad to exit the arena and to see their bus ready to go, this time without a frozen motor. The players felt lucky that all of their belongings were successfully gathered by the team managers. They rushed to make it onto the bus. The bus was no safe harbor however, and the boys were not out of the woods yet. Now the crazed fans pelted the bus with rocks that they launched at the bus windows as if they were trying the baseball toss game to win a stuffed animal at the county fair. Several of the fans began to rock the bus, but as the bus started to move back and forth, one of the Lansing police sergeants vaulted onto the scene, temporarily stopping the onslaught of the Spartan fanatics. He fired a flare into the air, and the sound stunned the crowd just enough for the LIU players, coaches, and staff to hop on the charter bus to make its getaway to the airport. When their chartered American Airways plane to Chicago took off, the boys felt like they had made the greatest escape of their lives. The mob just barely missed the LIU group at the airport, and the great escape was successful. The game against DePaul in Chicago would be easy, by comparison.

The boys felt like they had been through a war, and they had. The team's narrow escape had punctuated the victory, and like the escape of narcos at a biker rally, LIU had fled the perils of their unpopular victory in Lansing. Spider looked out the window as the plane lifted off and saw the angry mob that had followed the bus to the airport. Once those rabid fans realized that the LIU team had escaped and had lifted out of town, the group quickly dispersed and Spider could no longer see them as the plane ascended into the heavens. After fifteen minutes or so

Spider glanced back, and there were no longer any signs that this crazy game with the wild hostile Spartan fans had actually happened. It was over, seemingly vanished like a distant memory. He knew it had all happened, he was there, but he put it all behind him as the lights of Lansing faded into the night clouds.

The boys didn't get out of their sailor warm-up suits until they reached the Downtowner Hotel in Chicago three hours later. The team went to bed quickly, and they all slept very well. They had cleared perhaps the most difficult hurdle in their climb to get back in the national championship picture. Spider was the big hero, and his sharpshooting had accounted for eight second-half points. The next day, Thursday, Coach Bee had just finished eating breakfast in the hotel lobby in Chicago. The esteemed coach was approached by the press. Responding to questions about the exciting win against the Spartans the night before, Bee instructed the media, "Well, every one of the players deserves credit for our victory last night, and hopefully the winning will continue. The three newcomers really have been a pleasant surprise to the lineup. These fellas, Holub, Beenders, and Cohen, should get a little extra credit for doing the unexpected. Solly's just a sophomore; we knew he was a fine shot, but he wasn't expected to be ready for regular work. Nobody hoped that Beenders and Holub would share Bill King's work and do the job. But last night Solly and his long-range pop shooting was the story of our second-half comeback victory against Michigan State in a very hostile environment."

One of the pool writers asked Bee, "So, Coach, how good is this kid?"

Bee turned slowly and with a wry smile replied, "Solly, he's a deadeye, and he showed it tonight! We needed a spark, and he gave it to us."

Spider had lingered long enough in the lobby to overhear Coach Bee singing his praises, and his confidence soared. He marveled at how far he had come. No one had wanted him after graduating Clinton High School, and here he was with all these great players on this great team with perhaps a chance at the national championship! This great coach was giving him the highest compliment he had ever gotten. He thought of his dad and wished his dad could have heard what the coach said. After he had graduated Clinton High School, all he wanted to do was play college ball and continue his journey. The coaches at NYU, CCNY, Seton Hall, and St. John's had told him he was not good enough. They had tried to define him and his game. He didn't permit himself to accept this setback, because he knew without knowing that he was good enough, and he instinctively refused to let anyone limit him, including some of the best college coaches in America.

In years to come, Beenders and Holub would have better careers than Spider. But as the alchemy of people, places, and time can be magic, Spider's 1941 season elevated him above both of these future superstars in that one great season. The chemistry with Sy Lobello and the confidence and belief that Clair Bee had in Spider's ability catered to Spider's outside shooting skills and maximized his chances and those of LIU. The Michigan State game was Spider's best at LIU. When he left the hotel lobby, Ossie Schectman approached him and said, "Boychek, that was a heckuva a game. You keep this up, and we're just liable to have a very special season." Ossie was LIU's best player, and he would be rewarded for a career of hard-nose play with acclaim that would go down in history in the game of basketball. Ossie would move on and play in the BAA/NBA and was credited with scoring the first basket in the newly formed league (NBA) in Toronto for the New York Knickerbockers in 1947.[24]

L. I. U. VICTOR, 24-23, AT MICHIGAN STATE

Rallies From Deficits of 2-11 and 11-17 to Down Spartans in Basketball Contest

Special to The New York Times.

EAST LANSING, Mich., Feb. 19—
Long Island University defeated
Michigan State College, 24—23, in a
slow basketball game tonight, after
coming from far behind.

Michigan State set the pace and
was in front by 11—2 midway
through the first half. The Spartans played slowly and deliberately,
allowing Long Island few shots. To
add to their trouble, the Blackbirds were far off form in their
field-goal shooting early in the
game.

Dad's Favorite Game vs Michigan State Away. He was the star of the game. Clair Bee stalled and the angry crowd mandated a hurried police escort from the Arena...

Behind by 11—17 at half time,
Long Island finally went into the
lead at 22—21 and then put on a
dead stall. For six minutes the
Blackbirds walked about passing
the ball while Michigan State refused to come out of its defensive
position. Each team made a basket
later in the game.

Saul Cohen was the Blackbirds'
hero. His four field goals in the
second half saved the day for the
visitors, who left soon after the
game for Chicago.

The result evened the count for
the season between the teams, the
Spartans having beaten the Long
Islanders in a New York game.

The line-up:

L. I. U. (24)	G.	F.	P.	MICH. STATE (23)	G.	F.	P.
Lobello, lf	1	1	3	Mekules, lf	1	0	2
Cohen	4	0	8	Gerard, rf	5	0	10
Schneider, rf	2	0	4	Hindman, c	1	2	4
Beenders, c	2	1		Burk, lg	0	3	3
Holub	0	0	0	Phillips, rg	2	0	4
Sch'chtm'n, lg	0	1	1				
Schwartz, rg	2	0	4	Total	9	5	23
Total	10	4	24				

Referee—Eddie Powers, Western Michigan.
Umpire—Jack Travnicek, Armour Tech.

CHAPTER 15

Getting Ready for the NIT

✳ ✳ ✳

THE HARD WORK AND TEAMWORK paid off for the LIU club. Their blend of talent and energy helped them go undefeated for the remainder of their games. After victories at DePaul, at the University of Baltimore, against Canisius, and at LaSalle, LIU defeated Toledo to end the season 22–2. The Beemen were selected to play in the NIT. The University of Baltimore and Toledo University were left out of the field and did not make the tournament as many of the writers had predicted. In fact, the LIU regular season ended with an LIU victory over Toledo in Madison Square Garden, knocking the Rockets out of NIT consideration.

The NIT field had the best eight teams in the country as decided upon by Ned Irish and a group of renowned coaches and writers. The teams included undefeated Seton Hall led by All-American Bob Davies, and the great Ohio University team and their All-American Frankie Baumholtz. The University of Virginia, Long Island University, Westminster College, City College of New York (CCNY), the University of Rhode Island, and Duquesne rounded out the tournament selections.

The LIU success on the road was a pleasant turn of events for Coach Bee, who had been hopeful of a string of wins to close out the season. The team had lost its star, Dolly King, and somehow prevailed in his absence. In the face of its naysayers, the Beemen bonded and went on a run of victories in largely adversarial venues. Finally they came together as one.

"They instinctively began to draw closer together. They took to huddling ... before and after workouts, talking about what, precisely, they could do to make each ... better ... than before... They began to grow serious in a way they had never been before. Each of them knew that a defining moment in his life was nearly at hand; none wanted to waste it. And none wanted to waste it for the others."[25]

The LIU players, to a man, started their quest for a championship after its last regular season game. Having finished their midterm examinations, the team began its NIT practices.

Sy Lobello had a lot on his mind. He had an offer to play for the independent pro basketball team, the Long Island Gruman Flyers. The pay wasn't much, $45 per game, but he loved basketball and it was inevitable that he continue his playing career. Many boys were already enlisting in the army for World War II. The United States had not yet entered the war, but it seemed likely that it would sooner than later. All of these preoccupations could wait, as this was Sy's last year at LIU—a big moment—and he wanted to make his mark with this team and for Coach Bee, whom he greatly admired.

Sy, always optimistic, always positive, was fiercely competitive yet still the nicest guy in the room. At the start of the season, he saw the inexperience of his young sophomore teammates and wanted to help them succeed. Just as Irving Torghoff had helped him when he was a sophomore, he wanted to help his young teammates. That was the type of leadership that LIU basketball was all about. He continued the great tradition of the school in mentoring the younger players. Sy saw talent in Spider, and he was glad when Spider came through for the team on the last road trip, especially at Michigan State. Spider, with average size and slender physique, was not forecast to help the team, but he was a good kid and Sy gravitated to working with him and it was paying off. Spider, with Sy's help, now fit in on the team like a puzzle piece. Spider was looking forward to the NIT. He had never played in the NIT before but knew the names of the LIU stars on the 1936 and 1939 LIU undefeated teams. He revered the tradition of the school and its great teams. He had met Leo Merson and Julie Bender from the 1936 team and Irving Torgoff and Art Hillhouse from the 1939 team. The 1936 team was legend. Not only did they have an undefeated record, but Spider felt that they did the right thing in boycotting the Berlin Olympics. He had been told that Julie Bender, the star of that team, had wanted to play in the Olympics like all great athletes, but he had been greatly influenced to boycott the games by his grandfather, who was a religious Jew. No one in the Jewish community in Brooklyn wanted to support anything of economic benefit to Germany, and the Olympics would be a shot in the arm for the German economy. There were protests in the Jewish neighborhoods against the German oppression of Jews in Europe. Hitler's treatment of the Jews was horrible and perverse. Anti-Semitism there was spreading like a drought-fed California wildfire.

Prior to his first NIT game, Spider relaxed at home. His mother called out to him, "Solly, make sure that you get Murray a ticket to the tournament game. He wants to go."

"OK, Mom, I'll get him one," said Spider, just 2 years older than his younger brother, Murray.

Spider's mom, Jennie, always encouraged him to take care of his younger brother. There were pool halls with prevalent gambling in the neighborhood. A mother's vigilance sought to make sure her sons avoid any involvement with the "wrong kind of people." Spider loved his little brother who had dark hair, thick handsome eyebrows, and an intelligent demeanor. Spider always did the most to help him in every way. He taught Murray how to shoot the basketball and made sure that Murray also played in the schoolyard games.

"Hey, Solly," said Murray, "the paper says to expect record crowds at the Garden for the NIT this year. I thought last year's crowds were huge, but it says they are going to sell out every game this year!" "Sol," continued, Murray, "Honey Russell has got a great team with Bob Davies at Seton Hall. Have they lost a game this year?"

"Nope," said Spider putting a bit of a game face on. He was very superstitious about his rituals and conversations, especially leading up to a game. He didn't want to think about everybody's All-American, Bob Davies. Spider continued, "You're right, Murray, they haven't lost a game, and Davies may be the best player in America. But I like our chances against anyone the way we are playing now. We know each other, we're working well now, and you know we got the best coach. I don't think they can stop us, and for that matter, I don't think anyone can!" "Coach Bee is always a step ahead of the competition," continued Spider. "This isn't his first time in the NIT, and he knows how to win it. You know he won forty-three straight games at LIU until Luisetti beat them in the Garden, and then they won their next sixteen in a row. The school's got a heck of a tradition, Murray. We lost a couple this year, but I think we may be as good as those '36 and '39 undefeated teams. We played a really tough road schedule. The refs on the road don't give you anything, so those wins were well earned."

The boys shared a room at their family apartment on Grand Avenue; they grew tired as they talked, and soon they both fell soundly asleep.

The next morning the team had a day to relax. Schools were not in session for spring break. Spider went down and got the *Daily News* early in the morning; it was filled with feature articles and photos about international events. The Germans were attacking in Africa with the Afrika Corps. The Desert Fox, General Rommel, was scoring decisive victories there against Allied forces. The German encroachments and conquest of the various countries in Europe and the stories in the newspaper concerned him. Who could stop Hitler?

His parents were fearful that Europe's persecution of the Jews would follow them to America. They could never forget the persecution they had escaped in Europe. Spider sat in the second-floor apartment living room, alone. Grand Avenue had the usual cacophony of the sounds of street vendors, people chatting loudly, buses, and trolleys. An ambulance screeched by. As he read, he savored a cup of hot tea, with milk and sugar. When he was done reading he noshed on pieces of rye bread, butter, and a hard-boiled egg sprinkled with salt and pepper. His mother offered him some borscht to drink, but he declined. He wanted to have some sardines and mustard but resisted the temptation before the game.

He didn't know what to do with himself. It seemed as if time stood still, and he reflected on the moment, promising himself that he would always remember this mundane nosh and his thoughts before this, his first NIT. He had all the time in the world. He sat down, finished his snack, and returned to his newspaper. He zeroed in on a photograph that moved him. It was a newspaper photo of the children in the Syndlow Ghetto in Nazi-occupied Poland. The photo showed little Jewish boys forced to wear white arm bands stigmatizing them and marking them as Jews, effectively branding them like cattle. In the background of the photo, the caption explained that the little girls shown in the photo were "running like chickens," terrified of the foreign photographer attempting to capture their images. Spider sensed the fear hidden by a boy's smile in the forefront of the photo. Next to the photo there was another photo entitled "House Divided." A Polish city streetcar was depicted in the photo like those that Spider took in the Bronx. The difference in Poland was that the streetcar was divided into two sections. One side of the bus had a sign that was labeled "Jews," and the other side was marked, "Aryans." In another newspaper photo, it showed a concrete wall, which confined over a half a million Polish Jews in the city of Warsaw. The Nazis had closed off two-hundred streets and streetcar lines, which confined these Polish Jews to live with no contact beyond the walls of the ghetto. Spider tried not to think about these images indicative of alarming events, but he couldn't help feel the pain and apprehension of the restricted Jews in Poland, not far from where his father and mother had been born in nearby Russia. He was thankful to be in America.

The German advance on Europe was relentless. They now occupied Czechoslovakia, Poland, Denmark, Norway, France, Holland, Belgium, and Luxembourg, and they had their sights set on further conquests. British prime minister, Neville Chamberlain, tried to appease Hitler, but the Nazis continued their onslaught, and despite mixed signals to Chamberlain, German fighter planes and bombers started to air raid Great Britain itself. American supply ships bound for England were being regularly attacked and destroyed by German U-Boats in the Atlantic Ocean. The United States entry into the war was inevitable, and the world seemed to be turned upside down.

America was still reeling from the devastating impact of both the Dust Bowl and the Depression, which started in the plains and spread across the whole of the United States. Despite the many public works programs of President Franklyn D. Roosevelt, economic progress was slow. People were worried. In Newton, Massachusetts, like many cities in the northeast, vigilant night patrol monitors enforced a "no lights at night and curtains closed" policy, subject to fines. German U-boats were spotted off the coast of Cape Cod, and some of the worrisome Massachusetts residents were getting ready for a perceived German takeover. They were already studying German in adult learning classes.

"The world is in deep trouble," Spider thought as he read about the chaos that touched him and came alive from the pages of the newspaper. There were workers striking at the Bethlehem Steel plant, and the plant sent in the police inciting clashes between ownership and the workers.

The Russians had occupied Lithuania, which had been part of Russia itself when Spider's mother was born there. Latvia and Estonia were also engulfed by Russian troops. Hitler's bombing of London and blockade of Britain created havoc for America's biggest European ally. It seemed that Great Britain would be the next German conquest and occupation.

Many in the country favored staying out of the war, and were called "isolationists." These isolationists didn't perceive the German threat to the United States and wanted to ignore what was going on an ocean away.

Spider was lost off the basketball court. He was perplexed as to what he could do to earn a living after graduating LIU. Would he go into the army? Maybe to the police force, which had accepted him before? Nothing seemed to be clear to him except for his basketball at LIU. There was safety and security in that. The sport was his sanctuary. He wanted to make his mark in the world, and he was driven by his father's words, "I voudn't give you a nickl for my son's futcha!" While he had been raised by religious Jewish parents and his uncle was a rabbi, he was not equally as observant, and he was not as focused on religion as much as he once was as a boy. Sports were his interest and most particularly basketball.

It seemed like an eternity since he had regularly played ball at the Creston Schoolyard, but each time he picked up a basketball, he was transfixed back to its grounds. He clenched his teeth, his brown eyes clear with electric concentration, the wild thick black hair untamed, legs and arms coiled, fingertips at the ready. His checklist of movements ingrained, he never expected to miss. His arm and leg movements were mechanically grooved into his brain and body after the many hours of repetition. He always finished his shot with a little follow-through hop toward the basket.

"It has been a fantastic season," thought Spider. He wasn't a Holtzman, Davies, Baumholtz, or Luisetti. He had, however, made the most of his big opportunity. He wasn't fast like Ossie, King, Lobello, Holub, or Schwartz, but he could play good ball, and with the right teammates and in the right system, he could provide the long-range shooting spark that could help a very good team.

He had showcased his talents in the AAU tournament with the varsity at Saratoga Springs. He showed toughness in the Manhattan Beach night summer basketball. Coach Bee had an office there, and that was where he could see and scrutinize his players. The Manhattan Beach court was the perfect showcase for his talent. It had been constructed on a new 20,000-foot roller-skating area with special portable backboards on a smaller 84-by-48-foot playing surface. In the competitive summer games, the venue provided Spider a spotlight that gave him a leg up with his coaches. He was able to connect on enough set shots to curry favor, and at summer's end, he was within striking distance getting playing time. It was a dream come through.

Spider recalled how hard the whole team and coaching staff had worked to get to this point. The LIU team had stars, which attracted loyal fans, even in the summer. Dolly King, Ossie Schectman, and Sy Lobello were established big-time players, and the fans and the press followed their trials in summer ball. Coach Bee ran the Manhattan Beach parks sports programs, and many of the players took jobs there during the day and played ball at night. Players worked with Coach Bee as counselors for his Manhattan Beach basketball camps as well.

The summer league games were rugged. During a summer game, the Manhattan Beach Athletic Club, the MBAC team, consisting of mainly LIU players, defeated the Washington Heights Americans 40–32 before almost 6,000 fans. The game was hard fought, and it took the referees ten minutes to clear the court after a free-for-all fist fight started between the two teams. Al Schneider drove to the hoop and got undercut by one of the Americans' cagers, and the hard foul provoked a ruckus. When

MBAC played the Jewish Community House of Bensonhurst, 14,500 fans attended and cheered passionately. When MBAC took on the Flatbush Boys Club, over 15,000 spectators came, and the LIU players held a one-hour post-game autograph session.

As Director of Recreation at Manhattan Beach, then the world's largest privately owned playground, Bee gave Spider a lifeguard job for $4 a day. He needed the money and was happy to be with his future teammates who worked alongside him. There were big crowds who followed LIU basketball, so Bee brought in other talented teams to generate revenue for the parks by charging admission. The success warranted installation of night lights and a speaker system to announce the games and give the fans up-to-date statistics of players and the team and future game schedule information as the game progressed.

The highlight of the LIU preseason was the trip to Puerto Rico. The trip had opened things, and Spider felt part of the varsity team and looked forward to a good season. At the start of the season, however, Spider had been unsure of his place on the team. There were many players returning and excellent newcomers that were the top high school players in the country. He would be pressed to make the starting lineup with returning stars Ossie Schectman, Butch Schwartz, and Sy Lobello, a trio that had been on LIU's 1939 championship team. Dolly King and the other returners, such as Irving Zeitlin, Al Schneider, Lou Simon, Max Sharf, and Alex Walterson, would all start the season ahead of Spider in the team plans. As the fall practices ramped up, Spider felt ill at ease. Things were not going his way; perhaps he would only be a benchwarmer this year when the season began? He had been a star player at DeWitt Clinton High School, but everyone on the LIU roster had been a star in their respective high school.

In spite of all of his concerns, he had somehow found his way, and here he was in the starting lineup for the biggest game of his life. He thought about how much stronger he had become over the summer and the good work that he had done with Dave Polansky. Dave's playground work-outs strengthened his body, making it wiry and stronger. Dave had also improved his stamina, training him to run with proper form—sprinting and long-distance running around the Mullaly playground track. He was still slender, but he had added the needed strength and weight to maneuver on the court against some of the game's giants and strongmen. He was now powerful enough to rebound and play tough defense to complement his good set shot. His confidence soared thanks to his pal Dave. Spider was now a tougher player, harder for opponents to play against.

Going into the 1940–1941 season, veterans like Ossie and Butch were confident. They were regulars in the starting lineup. Ossie was a fiery and inspirational player. Schectman was strong like King and Lobello, with quick feet and lightning hands that could create steals at critical points of a game. He could score and was the team's best defender and the team's voice, always talking it up on the floor. Butch Schwartz was the best scorer on the team, a good shot who could put the ball on the floor, get to the net, and finish. Lobello was the captain who led by actions on the court; he was competitive and fierce. If there was a critical play to be made, Sy made it and did so, consistently it seemed. Spider remembered how hard he had fought for the final berth on the starting team, and he relished this moment. It was now the quiet before the storm of Madison Square Garden's biggest college basketball event. Spider had come a long way from the schoolyard and had risen above athletes that he never imagined he could surpass to make the starting 5. He had read the newspaper articles that said he was not expected to be ready to contribute as a sophomore. His hard work had paid off, and Coach Bee loved his shooting accuracy and range and the fact that he had now developed a complete game at both ends of the floor.

While Bee felt that this LIU team was not as gifted as his two prior championship teams, he was quietly confident that if his current team worked hard, it just might be gritty enough to win it all again this year. Spider and his mates believed in themselves. It was going to be an exciting week of basketball at the world's most famous arena, Madison Square Garden. They had overcome all obstacles and had won their last 8 games. As he sat alone in the apartment, there was suddenly a surprising quiet on Grand Avenue. He thought clearly in great anticipation of the upcoming big event, "I'm ready for a big tournament, and I think all the guys are. This is the best moment in my life!"

Nazis in Madison Square Garden

Photo: by AP
Nazi salute HEIL HITLER, 1939

CHAPTER 16

The NIT

✳ ✳ ✳

HE DIDN'T WANT TO STAY in the apartment all day nor hang around the neighborhood. So Spider found his way into Manhattan the day before the NIT. He got off the subway's D Line, walked up the stairs, and headed south, then west along 50th street. The brisk wind chilled the 37-degree air. The snow had largely melted but stubbornly remained in piles on the side of the roads. Several police on horseback clicked along and passed him as he walked. His nervous energy walked Manhattan's avenues bustling with street vendors, squealing trolley wheels, subway trains, and peevish taxicabs.

Soon Spider found himself on the west side of 8th Avenue at the corner of 50th Street. It was as if a magnet had drawn him to "The Garden." The regular season had given his team 7 games at Madison Square Garden, but the arena seemed more majestic now, more animated, and more relevant. There it stood, the world's most famous arena, with flowing Broadway marquee, gargantuan bold letters spelling out the name that headlined the white backlit sign on one of its sides. The upcoming event card displayed the events in large black letters. With dusk slowly beginning, Spider noticed that the lights of the arena marquee seemed off. He noticed some lights were, in fact, out on the marquee. The side marquee usually featured the lighted letters, "MADISON SQ. GARDEN." Tonight, it was different. The "ON" was out in the word MADISON, and the letter "S" was out in the abbreviation "SQ." It showed MADIS Q.

GARDEN. Was this a good omen? The sign had three letters that were not illuminated. Spider wanted this to symbolize that LIU would knock the lights out of three opponents. That meant that they not only would make the finals but defeat their opponent in the championship (3rd) game. "It was indeed a good omen," thought Spider. He was superstitious. Now this sign! Surely it was destiny and LIU was meant to win! It was an illogical deduction, or was it?

Spider looked on the bright side of things. He had matured this season and was beginning to overcome his insecurities and feel confident. His ruminating gave way to a stunning encounter. There, just across the street walking alone, was Victor Mario Perez. "What is he doing here?" Spider thought, as he called out to his teammate and friend, "Victor, how ya doing?" The two players approached each other, with Spider crossing the street to joint Victor. They greeted each other with glee and chatted a bit. They decided to have a late lunch/early dinner and decided to split a cab and head up to the Horn and Hardart, the Automat restaurant, up at W 57th Street and 6th Avenue. As they departed, they looked back at the Garden marquee.

The letters below the arena sign on the front side of the three-sided Marquee said:

NIT
Westminster v/s LIU
Ohio U. v/s DUQUESNE
VIRGINIA v/s CCNY
SETON HALL v/s R.I. STATE

Unlike the error on the side marquee sign display, the main front side of the Garden marquee was impeccable. It had the largest letters, more than twice as big as the 2 side marquees. "MADISON SQ. GARDEN" shone brightly with all letters flawless, all of its bulbs clear and bright.

They got out of the cab, and Victor and Spider entered the modern restaurant with its Plexiglas-protected compartments, each housing a variety of delicious freshly made main dishes and sides. They each had the same dinner of Salisbury steak and mashed potatoes, a buttered club roll, and a club soda. They didn't have dessert, and as they ate they talked about what a great season it had been. They had accomplished what everyone said they could not. LIU and Coach Bee had a chance at another NIT. They stood alone as the only team to participate in every NIT since inception. Victor was fascinating to Spider, and Spider was so different from him that Victor enjoyed exchanging perspectives with Spider. Victor had not played as much as he had hoped, but he was still thrilled to be on such a talented team. Both boys were team first all the way, and their hearts were fully engaged in the team winning.

The boys finished their meal at Horn and Hardart, and they parted ways. Victor headed back in a cab to the Hotel Earl, and Spider took the subway back to the Bronx and quickly dozed off, resting his head against his sweater and coat that he had taken off inside the subway car, using them as a makeshift pillow and partial covering.

He fell into a deep peaceful sleep. He dreamt of the Rice game, where he had gotten his first big chance in competition. The game was played on a cold and rainy Monday night during the winter break, and over 17,000 fans were eager to watch elite college basketball at Madison Square Garden. Spider knew he was going to get his chance off the bench, and was ready. Coach Pic had given him a nice pep talk before the game. "Spider, when you put on that uniform, you represent Long Island University, the greatest program in the country. You are in the plans tonight, so get ready to play the game of your life!" Spider hit the floor with his teammates, and the near-capacity crowd cheered the hometown LIU cagers with a thunderous roar. Rice Institute had been the champions of the Southwest Conference the year before and was leading the conference again this year with an undefeated record going into its game with LIU. LIU was a

2-point underdog, and many of the sportswriters were skeptical about the season. The consensus of the beat writers was that LIU would not have enough manpower to be a great team.

LIU started out fast, but the Rice Owls soon recovered to tie the score 28–28, going on a 10–0 run. The smoke-filled shirt-and-tie Garden crowd hushed when Rice took a brief lead with only 2 minutes to go in the half. Simon Lobello dropped an impressive set shot from 20 feet out on the left wing with 5 seconds to go in the half to give LIU a 2-point lead at the midway point.

Rice went ahead by 2 points, 3 minutes into the second period, and Coach Bee called time-out. Coach Pic motioned Spider into the game. He wasted no time as he got a perfect pass from Schectman, which he, in turn, bounce-passed to Lobello who scored on a driving layup to tie the score. After Rice scored to take the lead again, Spider had a moment. Like his stealth second chance in the tryout line at DeWitt Clinton, Spider made his own luck. Rice's guard Chester Palmer brought the ball up the court and accelerated his dribble, crossing over to speed past Spider. Anticipating Palmer's move Spider clamped down on the ball when Palmer put the ball on the floor on a crossover dribble. The ball bounced low, staying not far above the Garden's planked floor.

Remembering Dave Polansky's advice in defending Lefty at the night center, Spider used his quick hands to trap the ball on the hardwood. It was a good steal, and somehow, the ball stuck on a plank, trapped by Spider's right hand. Palmer continued to dribble the ghost of the ball on the other side of the mid-court stripe. With Palmer past him by 10 feet, Spider gained full control of the ball, bending over to snag it just inside half-court. Spider picked up the ball and took 2 quick dribbles, and then Palmer turned around and took four quick strides to catch up to Spider. Spider, sensing Palmer's recovery, quickly let the ball fly from 35 feet out, following through falling forward from his momentum and follow-through. Spider propelled the ball from a crouched position on the Garden court. Thinking he was going to fall, but gaining full possession of the basketball, Spider heaved the ball toward the goal. It was an absurd high-arcing spinner that seemed to whistle aerodynamically through the rising cloud of smoke that hung over the arena. Spider lost his balance after he released the ball, and as he hit the floor he happily watched the ball whoosh through the netting while on his stomach. The large crowd was incredulous and for a moment hesitated. Then, there was an explosion of sound, like a massive ocean wave crashing into giant rocks.

"Whoah, yeah, yeah, yeah! L-I-U, L-I-U, L-I-U!" yelled the Garden fans. Coach Bee shouted out, "Way to go, Solly!" "Way to go," encouraged Coach Pic! As Spider ran down the court, Lobello patted him on the shoulder, and said, "Attaboy, kid!"

He had taken advantage of his chance to shine, and the coaches appreciated his effort. Several minutes later with the score tied, Lobello threw a baseball bounce pass through 3 defenders to Ossie Schectman driving to the hoop to give the Beemen the lead. The Blackbirds won the game 61–57 to boost their record to 7–0 to start the season. Spider would stay in the plans after that Rice Institute game. He was promoted to the starting 5. He began to rely more and more on Captain Lobello, who was always encouraging and instructing him: "Play him close, he can shoot," or "He can't go left," or "Box out, he crashes the boards hard," or "Switch on the screen, I got him, Solly!" Playing with Sy boosted his level of play and made him attentive to the little details of the game, which was the difference between success and failure.

Suddenly, there was the sound of the screeching of wheels, and Spider opened his eyes. He looked around, then quickly went back to sleep once again as the train moved on after its brief station stop. He thought about Sy Lobello, the determined spirit who valued winning and good sportsmanship. Sy was one of the team's leaders and a hero. Eventually,

Bee would pay homage to Sy and dedicate his book, *Championship Ball*,[26] in Sy's memory, saying, "Sy gave his life and soul to his team and his country!"

Spider's thoughts moved on to the NIT. He thought of the NIT competition, the undefeated Seton Hall and Bob Davies, and the dynamic Frank Baumholtz with the formidable Ohio University Bobcats. Davies and Baumholtz were both incredible athletes. Both were extraordinary players who could run, jump, shoot, and dribble. Most of all, they both were tenacious competitors.

LIU was not without its own skilled athletes. They had an extraordinary player in Ossie Schectman. Ossie could stop anyone when he wanted to. Seton Hall, however, had a great team, and would be tough to beat, coming into the NIT with a chance to break the LIU major college 43-consecutive-game winning streak. "Wouldn't it be something if we met Davies in the tournament with their streak on the line?" Spider thought.

The NIT was the premier college basketball tournament of its time. There was no NCAA March Madness. In fact, Rhodes Scholar, Princeton All-American, and New York Knicks standout, Bill Bradley, supports the supremacy of the era's NIT in his book, *A Sense of Where You Are: Bill Bradley at Princeton*. In his book Bradley writes, "In the 1940s, when the NCAA Tournament was less than 10 years old, the National Invitational Tournament, a Saturnalia held in New York at Madison Square Garden by the Metropolitan Intercollegiate Basketball Association, was the most glamorous of the postseason tournaments and generally had the better teams. The winner of the National Invitation Tournament was regarded as more of a national champion than the actual titular, national champion, or winner of the NCAA Tournament."

Spider's thoughts froze when a long loud screech of the subway train wheels convinced him that he had arrived at the stop near Grand

Avenue just in time to get off the train. He arrived home tired and went right to bed. He slept peacefully before his first NIT game against Westminster. The *Brooklyn Eagle* and the *Daily News* were saying that the undefeated Seton Hall Pirates and All-American Bob Davies were the sure bet to win the NIT. CCNY was not to be overlooked either as they had Bill "Red" Holtzman, the future coach of the NBA Champion New York Knickerbockers, later elected to the NBA Hall of Fame.

The papers picked Seton Hall to win the NIT reasoning that Seton Hall was primed to win in the same way that the 1939 LIU undefeated club had won the 1939 NIT. The fact that the team was undefeated implied that Seton Hall would likewise win the NIT.

The next morning, Spider woke up and was perturbed, and he didn't know why. Perhaps it was his game face, or way to prepare mentally for the big game and the NIT. He went right to the newsstand to read the newspapers. He usually enjoyed reading the *Daily News*. He could get a paper at the newsstand for 2 cents. When they had a good write-up on his games, his sister Mary would cut the article or box score out and put it in the scrapbook she and her sister Rose had created for him.

Today he was further irked because the *Daily News* headline asserted, "NIT begins, Seton Hall favored." Spider could not envision anything but a tournament win for his team. Yet there is always some level of uncertainty in a novel new experience, and as this was his first NIT, he didn't know what it would take for his team to win. Spider was, nevertheless, somehow bothered by the newspaper article, and he couldn't wait to get to the Garden and play the game. His mom, Jennie, made his favorite "good luck" pregame meal. She prepared hot chicken soup with pieces of chicken, carrots, and some boiled potatoes. He drank some hot tea with milk and sugar as well. He was ready to play.

"I'm going to play the big game in the big tournament at Madison Square Garden. How ironic and appropriate," he thought. Just 2 years prior, February 20, 1939, he had passed by the Garden hoping to see a game. There were no basketball games, however. Flicky Fields worked in the Garden ticket office, and Spider thought Mel could get him access to the game. But there was no basketball game, and Mel wasn't working. Instead, Spider looked up at the marquee.

The bright lights were unmistakable in their message: "German American Bund Tonight." "Wow," he thought. "This is incredible. That's the Nazi party." The place looked mobbed. There were no seats available as the sign outside the ticket office said "SOLD OUT." It looked like the Nazis had taken over the Garden and New York City for that matter. He would find out the next day that 22,000 Nazis had celebrated and marched in the Garden. He had read the newspapers' stories about Kristallnacht, the anti-Jewish purges in Germany, and the zealous Nuremburg "Zeek Heil" rallies. Jews in Europe were being persecuted everywhere. On that day in 1939 it had looked like the Nazis were invading New York. Yes, there were Nazi sympathizers and isolationists in the United States, but surely they were the exception. The persecution of the European Jewry, it seemed, was far away and out of his neighborhood. Here now, however, the Nazis were in his backyard. He recalled that Garden scene and trying to make sense of it all. It was time now to stop thinking about anything but tonight's game. He shut off his mind to everything else, and he grabbed the subway to the Garden for the Westminster College game.

When he entered the locker room at the Garden, Spider and the entire LIU team could feel it. They were coming together. It was powerful. Like some uplifting force. The practices, the summer training, the fall trip to Puerto Rico had brought the boys together. They had a rhythm, a glue that bound them. They were playing in sync, like a fine rowing team.

"There is a thing that sometimes happens in rowing that is hard to achieve and hard to define. Many crews, even winning crews, never really find it. Others find it but can't sustain it. It's called 'swing'; it only happens when all 8 oarsmen are rowing in such perfect unison that no single action by any one is out of sync with those of all the others. It's not just that the oars enter and leave the water at precisely the same instant. Sixteen arms must begin to pull, sixteen knees must begin to fold and unfold, eight bodies must begin to slide forward and backward, eight backs must bend and straighten all at once. Each minute action, each subtle turning of wrists must be mirrored exactly by each oarsman, from one end of the boat to the other. Only then will the boat continue to run, unchecked, fluidly and gracefully between pulls of the oars. Only then will it feel as if the boat is a part of each of them, moving as if on its own. Only then does pain entirely give way to exultation. Rowing then becomes a kind of perfect language. Poetry—that's what a good swing feels like."[25]

As the LIU team laced up their sneakers, all of its players were uplifted, having made their way into the NIT when most had doubted them. It brought the boys together and they had developed a strong team bond.

Lobello came up to Spider in the locker room. "Hey, Solly, they are going to be all over Ossie and me all night. You and Butchie need to keep moving, and we'll set some screens for you out of the weave, like we've been doing. That should open things up, and we can get some give-and-gos to the basket. When we run the offense, I'll set a weak side screen for you as well when I can, and all you have to do is follow my lead. If they come up on you, look for Hank or Holub in the post. They should be wide open. Get warmed up. You're going to have a big game tonight!" Sy had been there; he knew, as he had won a championship before. He was a generous soul, and he passed his experience on to the underclassman.

The first play of the game, Ossie, the point guard, dribbled the ball up taking it over the half-court line. He passed to Butch Schwartz, and then Ossie cut down the lane; Beenders came up and set a screen for Lobello, who got the ball and motioned to Spider to take his step back two-handed set shot. The two-handed pop shot went cleanly through the elongated net just 45 seconds into the game, giving the Brooklyn boys the lead they would never relinquish as Butchie's 15 points, Beenders 12 points, and Spider's 8 points led the way to an LIU 48–36 victory. The loss was only the second in 24 games for the Westminster Titans, propelling LIU into the semifinals. "Thanks, Sy," Spider wanted to say in the locker room after the game, but both Sy and Ossie had not scored and Spider kept quiet, appreciative of the kindness and warmth shown him by the captain, but respectful of the fact that they were not particularly talkative knowing that there was still a lot of work to do to get to where they wanted to go. They did not speak much, but you didn't have to with Sy; he communicated on the court with his glow, his generosity, his pervasive smile, and occasionally his words. Ossie and Sy had not scored, but their presence was felt. The team was just getting revved up.

The next game was the semifinals versus undefeated Bob Davies and the Seton Hall Pirates. It had happened! The Pirates had now won 43 games in a row and had tied LIU's NCAA winning streak mark. The other semifinal game was simply Frank versus Bill; Baumholtz vs. Holtzman, Ohio University versus CCNY.

The 3 best players in the tournament did not play for LIU. Often team chemistry, however, is more powerful than a collection of individual talents. Davies, Baumholtz, and Holtzman were "superstars." They were the difference makers and three of the best players of their time. Coach Nat Holman of CCNY called Bob Davies an even better player than the Stanford great Hank Luisetti, the LIU 43-game winning streak killer of 1938.

The big Garden crowds were setting records for tournament organizer Ned Irish, and the 1941 edition of the NIT would show a 40 percent increase in attendance, selling out virtually every game. The 70,000 tournament fans for the event would be an NIT attendance record. College basketball had become big business. The crowds were intense, and the college hoop fanatics loved their basketball. Davies was a speedster, and his "Hallsters" had crushed Rhode Island State 70–54 in the first round of the NIT. Seton Hall, however, would be no match for LIU in the semifinals, and the press noticed it, writing that "the boys from South Orange, New Jersey, were a bit nervous and intimidated by the scene and by the experienced LIU cagers."[27] Seton Hall had been perfect in their first 20 games of the season, had that great winning streak going, and were a highly confident group. There had been talk that the Pirates would skip the tournament altogether because they didn't need to play it on the basis of their perfect record which could have made them deemed National Intercollegiate Champs.

Coach Honey Russell of Seton Hall would not think of skipping the prestigious tournament, however, and he was abundantly confident in his star Bob Davies, whose great speed and fantastic shooting made him a standout against any competition. In these semifinals, however, the favored Pirates were defeated by LIU, and the losers shot only 7 for 57 from the field. LIU won the game by a decisive margin of 49–26. Butch Schwartz and Ossie Schectman both guarded Davies and held him to a single field goal and only 4 points, after he had scored 19 against Rhode Island State in the first round of the tournament. Any game can rest on a decisive play, which alters the course of the game and its outcome. With 5 minutes to go in the first half of this semifinal game, Ossie was on Davies, guarding him tight and knowing that Lobello, Beenders, and Spider would help out if he got beat.

That was the greatness of Coach Bee's 1-3-1 wheel zone. It was a zone that could fool a defense by appearing to be man-to-man defense at times. It had additional variations as Coach Bee would call out numbers alternating the wheel zone, then changing to straight man-to-man defense and then back to zone again. The great deception was that the opponents could not readily distinguish between the two LIU defenses, and the confusion would create steals, turnovers, and momentum for LIU. Its defense became a key to its offense. Employing the wheel zone, it always seemed like two guys on LIU were guarding one opponent at all times. Then the critical moment happened. Davies tried to beat Schectman to the hoop, exploding off the dribble drive. He dribbled the ball behind his back to avoid Ossie and beat Ossie by half a step. But as he tried to drive past Schectman, the tenacious Ossie leaned his legs into Davies and without fouling him knocked Davies down and stole the ball. No one on Seton Hall had ever seen anyone do that to Davies. It was a shocker and game changer. After that play it seemed like LIU got the edge on the Pirates, and after that the Pirates went down 23–15 at the half. In the end, LIU finished off Seton Hall, winning by 23 points. The one play by Ossie on Davies seemed to give the Blackbirds the momentum they needed to turn the tables on the Hallsters. The result left college hoop fans exuberant about the finals, which would match LIU against the Ohio University Bobcats and Frank Baumholtz, who had triumphed over the great Bill "Red" Holtzman and CCNY, 45–43, in the other semifinal that night.

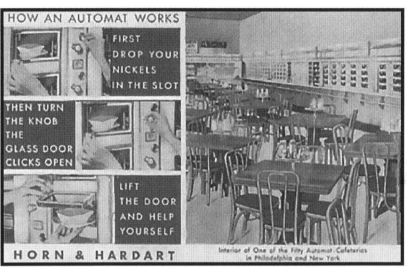

HOW AN AUTOMAT WORKS

FIRST DROP YOUR NICKELS IN THE SLOT

THEN TURN THE KNOB THE GLASS DOOR CLICKS OPEN

LIFT THE DOOR AND HELP YOURSELF

HORN & HARDART

Interior of One of the Fifty Automat-Cafeterias in Philadelphia and New York

HORN AND HARDART AUTOMAT
—SAMPLE MENU—

Heart of Lettuce Salad with Russian Dressing......25 cents
Macaroni and Cheese "The Best In The City"....25 cents
Baked Beans..25 cents
Ham and Cheese Sandwich on Hard Roll........25 cents
Chopped Sirloin Steak.....................................50 cents
Salisbury Steak... 50 cents
Beef or Chicken Pot Pie................................35 cents
Meatloaf..50 cents
Club Roll, Biscuit or Corn Bread....................10 cents
Meringue or Custard Pie................................15 cents
Soft Drink, Tea or Coffee..............................10 cents

AUTOMAT

Saul and Victor Perez had a NIT Champion Pre Game meal here at HORN AND HARDART'S AUTOMAT.

March 24, 1941 , NIT Championship Game Program

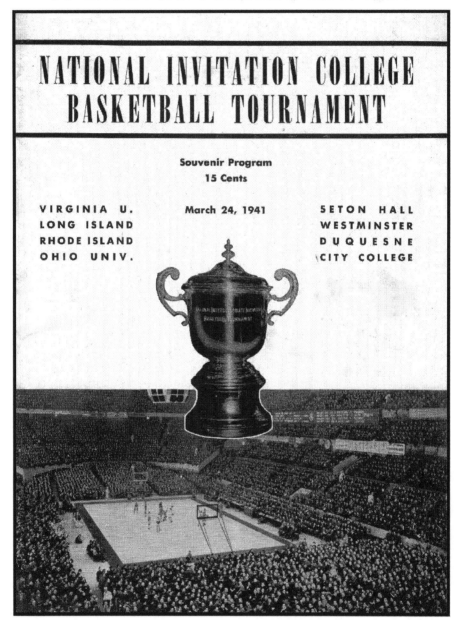

March 24, 1941 , NIT Championship Scorecard

March 24, 1941, NIT Championship Game

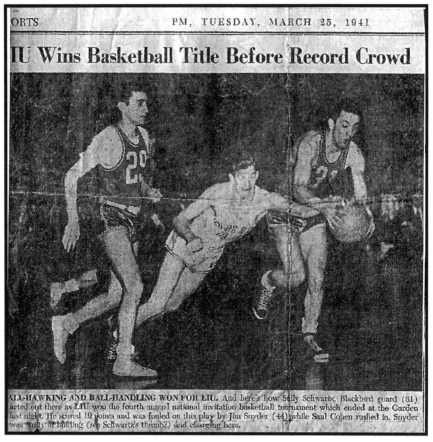

ORTS   PM, TUESDAY, MARCH 25, 1941

IU Wins Basketball Title Before Record Crowd

ALL-HAWKING AND BALL-HANDLING WON FOR LIU. And here's how Sully Schwartz, Blackbird guard (31) acted out there as LIU won the fourth annual national invitation basketball tournament which ended at the Garden last night. He scored 19 points and was fouled on this play by Jim Snyder (44) while Saul Cohen rushed in. Snyder was guilty of holding (see Schwartz's thumb?) and charging here.

Photo: Article appeared in the Brooklyn Eagle

Spider and Schwartz for LIU

March 24, 1941, NIT Championship Game

Photo: Article appeared in the *Brooklyn Eagle*
Ossie Schectman #24, Saul Cohen #29 for LIU vs Carl Ott #25 Ohio University

LIU 1940-1941 NATIONAL INVITATION TOURNAMENT CHAMPIONS

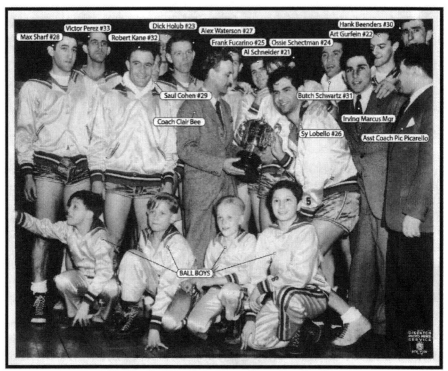

Photo: by Dispatch Photo News Service NY

Left to Right: Max Sharf #28, Victor Perez #33, Robert Kane #32,
Saul Cohen #29, Dick Holub #23, Alex Waterson #27,
Coach Clair Bee, Frank Fucarino #25, Al Schneider #21,
Ossie Schectman #24, Sy Lobello #26, Butch Schwartz #31,
Manager Irving Marcus, Art Gurfein #22,
Assistant Coach Pic Picarello, Hank Beenders #30.

CHAPTER 17

The Finals

✳ ✳ ✳

THE GARDEN WAS JAMMED WITH another sellout crowd of 18,500 for the Monday night finals matchup between LIU and Ohio University. Spider took the subway into Manhattan from the Bronx, and as he walked into the Garden there was Philly waiting for him to wish him good luck in this the most important game of his life. It was 2 hours before game time, and there was his old pal from the schoolyard. Phil approached Spider and offered words of reassurance. "Solly, you guys are going to win. There is no question about it. We are all here to root you on. Lucio, Dave, Lenny, Lester, Flicky, Genie, and Wally are all coming. I heard that Flicky is bringing Dolph too. So the whole schoolyard is behind you. I just saw Milty Gries, Lester Hirschfield, Red Schwartz, and Siggy Shore too. Everyone's here to root you guys on. Good luck, we'll be hollering for you!" It made Spider feel good that his mates were behind him and that they were behind him and LIU and coming to the game. The schoolyard was there, and he felt great. "Bye, Philly, I'll see you guys soon. Thanks for coming." And with that Spider entered the world's most famous arena, cleared the Garden security, and found his way to the LIU locker room.

Most of the big LIU alumni were in the locker room by the time Spider arrived for the championship game. Irving Torghoff, Dolly King, Joe Shelly, Art Hillhouse, Leo Merson, and Julie Bender joined the team in the locker room. They were so pumped up they looked like they were ready to play the game, bubbling with enthusiasm, rooting on the current edition of their alma mater. The champion LIU pedigree was everywhere as Shelly; Hillhouse, the 6-foot-7 second team All-American; and Torghoff, the 6-foot-2 first team All-American had played with Lobello, Schectman, and Schwartz on the 1939 NIT Championship team. Coach Bee introduced each alumnus to the team, emphasizing that Torghoff, Hillhouse, and King were now playing professional basketball. The locker room was animated, and the team seemed inspired and ready to play hard against the boys from Ohio.

Merson and Bender were clapping their hands, urging the team on. Dolly King was now playing with the New York Renaissance "Rens" professional basketball team. Marius "Lefty" Russo could not make it as he was at spring training camp for the New York Yankees in St. Petersburg, Florida. He did send a telegram to Coach Bee wishing the team good luck. Coach Bee read the telegram aloud to the boys in the locker room before the game: "Dear Coach Bee, tell the boys that while I cannot make the game, I'll be listening to the game on radio and will be there with them in spirit. I know you are winners. Good luck, and carry on to victory, … yours truly, Lefty Russo."

Using a wool string spool with different pegs attached to his basketball court display board, Bee illustrated the plays and aligned the players using the wool and pegs on the board to show his defensive alignment, the positioning of the players, and his strategies. He outlined the man-to-man matchups and defensive game plan that would feature an attacking 1-3-1 zone defense. The offensive plan would activate open shots off their tight three-man-weave ball movement and continuity of passing. "Let's look to give-and-go and attack the basket against them," Coach Bee fired up, speaking to the boys, and pounding the metal locker room door. "Men, if they back off, I want to take those pop shots from deep!"

His team was ready, and the LIU players sprinted out onto the Garden floor charging past the courtside table displaying the NIT

Championship Trophy and the gold-plated miniature basketballs awarded to the Finals' Championship players individually. The championship mementos were individually wrapped in plastic sleeves, awaiting the post-game award ceremony. Both teams would receive the mini-basketball mementos, and the winning team would also get Seiko watches, which were packed in little black boxes with the inscription, "NIT Champs, March 24, 1941," written on the inside face of the watch. Coach Picarello was not thinking about the trophies or mementos; that could wait. He was concerned about Ohio University's Frankie Baumholtz, and he had good reason to be apprehensive. Baumholtz was a threat to score every time his team went on offense and he touched the basketball.

With their 10-game-win streak and all of the momentum in the world, the coaches would have thought the Blackbirds ready to come out and steamroll the Bobcats. When they came onto the floor just prior to the start, however, LIU looked lethargic, lacking energy. LIU started Beenders, Schwartz, Schectman, Lobello, and Spider. Standing around the jump ball circle, prior to the opening tip-off, the Bobcats' Harry McSherry looked at Schectman, pointed his finger at the LIU star, and barked out, "I'm warning you, Schectman." As McSherry said this he looked at Baumholtz and Schectman, and then looking back at Ossie he said, "No rough stuff, or else you'll be sorry." Ossie knew that Harry McSherry was the leader and enforcer of the Ohio University team. Gamesmanship was on display, and both McSherry and Schectman knew that "to defeat an adversary that was your equal, maybe even your superior, it wasn't necessarily enough just to give it your all from start to finish. You had to master your opponent mentally. When a critical moment .... is upon you, you had to know something that he did not-that down in your core you still had something in reserve, something that you had not yet shown, something that once revealed would make him doubt himself, make him falter just when it counted the most..."[25]

Both Ossie and his Ohio University counterpart McSherry were trying to see what was in each other's hearts. At first it looked like McSherry was not going to give an inch and neither would Ossie, who always made his presence known. The battle would be fierce.

"Wait until next year, we'll have a great team then!" Coach Bee told the writers earlier in the season prior to the LIU vs. Butler game. Bee was once again lamenting the loss of his greatest athlete, Dolly King, who was playing his last game of the season that evening. It seemed like LIU's chances for a good season were lost. The sportswriter George E. Colemen of the *Brooklyn Daily Eagle* wrote: "So right now, the Beemen have a team that is a 100-1 shot to make the NIT at the Garden in March."[28] LIU's fortunes had changed, however; they had made their way, and they were now playing in the NIT finals. They had met their goal to play in the very last game of the season. Their ultimate goal would be met if they won tonight's finals game.

LIU, despite the coach's pregame speech, did not play well at the start. As much as both LIU coaches tried to motivate the team, clapping and urging them on, the players did not respond.

It seemed eerily similar to the disappointing Duquesne game where the Beemen started off slowly and let their opponent hang around too long. LIU lost that game at the buzzer. The coaches were trying to figure out which LIU team had shown up for this championship game. Was it the good LIU squad, focused and engaged squad, or was it the other LIU team that played sloppy basketball? The coaches knew how impressionable youngsters 18–22 years old could be. The coaching staff, nevertheless, hoped that the team would settle down and execute. At the start of the game it looked like LIU was outclassed and were a mismatch for the more athletic, undaunted Ohio University Bobcat club. "Perhaps," one observer thought, "New York basketball was overrated. Maybe Ohio University was just too good."

The Bobcats jumped out to a 14–3 first-half lead, 10 minutes into the game. Butchie Schwartz, a great scorer, started out on Baumholtz, who connected on 5 shots for 10 points early in the game. The Beemen started out like Sunday morning in rural Montana, moving without energy, without purpose. It was their worst opening 10 minutes of the season. Their comeback season would be for naught unless they could reverse the momentum of Ohio University, who was off to a torrid start. LIU was getting blown off the court in the most important game of the season, the championship game.

Bee called time-out. "Ossie, you take "#54 (Baumholtz); Butch, switch and take #57 (Ott)."

"OK, Coach," the two seniors responded. Butchie was tough as nails, but he was not able to match up to the speed and quickness of Baumholtz. Ossie was a different story, and he was ready to pounce like a tiger. Number 49, McSherry, once again confronted Ossie, glaring at him as the teams came out of their huddles and returned to the court. Harry McSherry was the strongman for the Bobcats. He protected the high-scoring duo of Baumholtz and Ott and was always at the ready. Nostrils flaring again, he eyed Ossie. He meant for Ossie to take it easy on Baumholtz. If he thought that he could make Ossie dial it down a notch, he could forget it. That was not Ossie; he didn't back down and was an expert defender, fast, quick, and sporting strong, elastic legs. Coaches say that defense wins championships, and Ossie was the best defender in the tournament.

Ossie ignored McSherry's banter, and the Ohio player turned away to focus on his game assignment. Ossie went to work on Baumholtz, talking to him repeatedly during the game, guarding him tightly and chirping the Ohio University star, yelling out, "No, Frank, don't shoot, it's too far, you can't make it!"[29]

Schectman, more vocal than usual, was intent on getting Baumholtz off of his game, forcing him to give up the basketball prior to launching his stellar outside shot and neutralizing his penetration to the basket by fighting off the tough screens that McSherry set for Baumholtz. Ossie communicated with his teammates, and if there was a switch off of Baumholtz, Ossie was quick to get back on Frankie, with Ossie's teammates going out of their way to let Ossie work through screens to stay on Baumholtz. After a while, Ossie gained enough of a mental edge to disrupt the Ohio University star's rhythm. McSherry and Baumholtz tried the pick-and-roll play, but Ossie was too tough and hung right there so that Baumholtz's effectiveness was greatly reduced. The sportswriters had already penciled Baumholtz in for the NIT Most Valuable Player Award prior to the start of the game, based on leading his team to 2 victories in the first 2 games of the tournament.

Baumholtz was on the verge of setting a tournament scoring record as well. But in order to win the tournament Baumholtz would have to regain his form in the second half in spite of Schectman's tenacious defense. For LIU's part, holding down the Ohio U. ace would not be easy. Most of the press corps felt it impossible to contain the swift Ohio University star. The Beemen did not rattle, though, and continued nibbling at the Ohio University lead. Three times in the last 4 minutes of the first half, LIU came within a basket of the Bobcats. The Bobcats responded each time with a bucket of their own. The first half ended with the Ohioans leading the men from Brooklyn 25–21. Carl Ott and Baumholtz had the Beemen where they wanted, or so they thought.

Ossie started the second half by guarding Baumholtz once again on defense. The Blackbirds started to press the Bobcats all over the court employing their 1-3-1 wheel zone defense. In the first half the Bobcats had smothered the Blackbirds' outside shot attempts, and none of the LIU marksmen were able to connect. Now in the second half, the Blackbird shooters found their mark. Quickly at the start of the half, Lobello hit Spider on the wing, and Spider connected. It was

LIU's first set shot from long range. Then Lobello passed to Schwartz on a give-and-go, penetrating the Bobcat defense for another hoop. The Long Island University boys had deadlocked the score at 25–25.

Coach Bill Trautwein of Ohio University called time-out, perplexed at his team's inability to execute their proficient offense to start the second half on the Garden floor. Schectman and McSherry bumped each other as the teams came together to begin the time-out. The two glared at each other, but no one made a move. There would be no fighting, not on the big stage of the NIT finals. Had this been a schoolyard game, perhaps there would have been some fisticuffs. It was, however, not the time for such juvenile confrontations, and both chest-beaters went about their business trying to execute their assignments on the court. Ohio University desperately tried to get their potent offense activated, and the Beemen used their defense to ignite their offense. Dr. James Naismith, the inventor of the game of basketball, applauded both teams from courtside as they emerged from the time-out. Dr. Naismith had tossed the ceremonial first jump ball to start this championship. Naismith afterward noted that he was inspired by the effervescent play of both teams. The teams each played hard, and neither team wanted to back down. They were both champions and neither wanted to lose.

With the score tied 31 all, the Garden crowd's buzz simmered in anticipation. It was a pivotal point in the game. Eleven minutes remained in the contest. The moment proved propitious for LIU as the boys from Brooklyn found their rhythm. Everything came together for the team at just the perfect time. Every player knew what to expect from the coaches and most importantly from each other. They knew each other's moves and how to work as a unit completely synchronized, like it was second nature. Clair Bee's vision and training had the team playing at its best. The LIU squad was working in unison. This was the moment during the game that every player on the LIU team realized that they were going to win and that no one could beat them. They may not have had the most talent, but they were so perfectly in harmony with each other and the systems they played that the whole was far greater than the sum of the parts.

Smoke filled the arena, and the fans rose to their feet each time the ball swished through the hoop. There was a lively, loud Ohio contingent of fans who cheered boldly at each Ohio basket or free throw. The smoke wafted through Spider's brain, and he couldn't think; he began to almost gasp for air. The tension of the moment made him start to hyperventilate. He almost forgot that he had been fouled and was walking involuntarily to the foul line to shoot a single free throw with the scored tied in the biggest game of his life. Behind the basket about 15 rows up he could hear a loud broken voice. He saw his brothers Murray and Benny, but it wasn't either of their voices that was making the sound he had heard. No, it was a white-haired man. It was Abraham, his father, calling out in his broken English. The same father who thought that basketball was a waste of time. There he was shouting, "Zookem, Solly, comen, Solly!" The words of encouragement were well intended but made Spider even more tense. As the stout red-haired referee, Pat Kennedy, bounced the ball several times waiting for Spider to compose himself, Spider heard another voice and then felt a slap on the back. The score was tied, and the record Madison Square Garden crowd was sizzling with excitement. Would the slender sophomore break the tie or would he be the goat, many in the crowd wondered.

At Creston Junior High School, the schoolyard was empty, but somehow in the distance, the radio broadcast of the game echoed out of the open window of a nearby apartment. The announcer said, "And now Sol Cohen is going to the free throw line with a chance to put Long Island University in the lead." The bouquet of cigarette and cigar smoke was a dense cloud, and the roaring and cheering of the spectators was deafening. Remembering his father's words, "I vudn't give you a nickel for my son's future....!" he was at the precipice of the abyss. Would his nerves permit his body to function? The sound of someone speaking to him at a moment like this was incredible. He was almost sure now that his arms would not even lift the ball let alone put it through the net. He lifted his face and turned only to see the jocular smiling face and heard the reassuring voice of Sy Lobello, "Hey, Solly, I bet ya a nickel that ya miss this shot!"

Spider was so taken aback and surprised by the captain that he laughed. "Oh yeah, Sy, we'll see about that!" The disarming remark put Spider more at ease. In his mind, he released his apprehension. Unshackled, he cleared his brain of all the noise and was transported back to Creston Schoolyard; he forgot that he was in the Garden and relaxed. It just felt like he was shooting a simple free throw in the empty schoolyard. Spider made the free throw and ran back down the court. Through the corner of his eye, Spider saw his dad. He had never seen Spider play before. Now after he'd made the free throw his dad was actually jumping up and down with joy and shaking Benny and Murray in the excitement. The old man must have bought a ticket for himself! Spider had made himself (and his dad) proud. The Long Island University boys had taken a 1-point lead. Spider rushed back down the floor and into the zone defense and realized at that moment why his dad had taken him to see Benny Leonard fight.

It had planted a seed of toughness in him that bore fruit at this unforeseen moment. He quickly said to himself, "Thank you, Dad, and thank you, Sy Lobello, for your sangfroid and for showing me the way." Spider would never forget that magical moment and would cherish that memory of both Sy and his father. Way up in the balcony, the boys from the schoolyard were yelling out, "Way to go, Solly, let's go!" The whole crew from Creston was up in the same section rooting on their schoolyard mate and praying for an LIU victory.

After the LIU group took the lead, it was all LIU after that, and Spider would combine with Sy Lobello, Hank Beenders, and Ossie to play heads-up ball and a tough pressing zone defense the rest of the game. Ossie, the real star, and Butch Schwartz, a co-star, helped defeat the Bobcats 56–42. Ossie had 12 points, Butch 19, and Sy 11 points. Baumholtz got 19 points on limited second-half scoring, often passing up shots he otherwise would have taken but for Ossie's chatter and aggressive defense. Baumholtz was named the tournament MVP, and Ossie finished second in the voting. Ossie had gotten the last word and had taken care of business to vanquish a tough opponent, showing his heart and reaching deep down to his core to beat a strong and dynamic player.

After the game, the locker room celebrated with the boys all taking turns kissing the NIT Championship Trophy, embracing their individual gold-plated mini-basketball mementos, and showing off to each other those elegant watches received from Ned Irish, which displayed the NIT Championship inscription and date.

The LIU players hooped and hollered in the locker room. "Don't you guys think Butchie deserved the MVP?" Ossie was going around saying. But nobody worried about the individual awards; they were the champs. The Blackbirds came back out onto the court to pose for a victory photo for the newspapers. Team captain, Sy Lobello, couldn't stop smiling. He grinned from ear to ear as he shook Coach Bee's hand, shaking it up and down repeatedly. His smile was infectious. The shy Spider posed on the left of the photographer, his profile intently eyeing the trophy and the happy scene. Ossie and Butch stood next to Sy and the coach, congratulations circulating all around. Ironically, Spider would lose his gold-plated championship memento later that night in the celebration, but he was still a champion, and no one could take that away from him. The victory was the 3rd National Intercollegiate Championship in 5 years for LIU, and the team had now participated in every NIT tournament since its inception. They were a powerhouse team and a dynasty in college basketball. One of the former LIU players then playing professionally,

Art Hillhouse, told a reporter, "That was the smartest half of basketball played at the Garden this season."[29] He was referring to LIU's play in the second half. LIU was the 1941 NIT champ. They were a great combination of youth, leadership, and experience and had overcome all obstacles against overwhelming odds and the toughest road schedule in their history to win the national championship[30] and rank up there with the best LIU teams of all time.

CHAPTER 18

After the National Invitation Tournament

✳ ✳ ✳

THE SCHOOLYARD WAS QUIET ON March 25, 1941. Creston Junior High School was off on spring recess and the forlorn baskets welcomed an old friend, as he walked through the schoolyard, pensive the day after his team had won the championship. He instinctively came back to share his victory with the schoolyard and imbibe all of the great memories there. It had all started there. He had accomplished his goal to play college ball and win a championship. It had been a great season. He was much better when he had goals.

Now that he been to the mountaintop, he wondered what was next. How could he possibly top this dream season? He had exceeded his expectations and those of his coaches and the media. The only ones who had believed in him all along were his pals from this schoolyard. He saw them all in his mind as he walked once around the perimeter of the yard. He knew every part of the schoolyard and remembered the games that were played there, and his friends. They had all grown up now, and there were new kids who played in the yards now. The newcomers carried the torch and continued the tradition. But Spider remembered his generation of schoolyard games and his buddies, and he remembered fondly the pickup ball at the schoolyard. It had all started there.

The next week, the 1941 LIU varsity basketball team arrived in Brooklyn one last time as a group. The university set up tables on the Brooklyn Pharmacy floor. The managers had organized silver and white balloons in the shape of a giant horseshoe and had placed these in front of each basket on the full court of the Pharmacy floor, effectively making book-ends on either side of the group of tables that congregated around mid-court and seated the team, its staff, the coaches, and the important school administrators and deans. Dean Metcalfe accompanied Coach Bee and the staff when they entered the proceedings last, greeted by a rousing series of applause and the cry of "Hip, hip, hoorah!" The small luncheon was served, and the boys were treated to a steak dinner with mashed potatoes and a medley of vegetables. Chocolate cake with choc-olate filling was served to the boys as dessert, and a good time was had by all. When the championship celebration ended, everyone congratu-lated each other on the outstanding season. Dolly King attended and was awarded a championship memento and happily embraced the NIT Championship Trophy. He felt good seeing his old teammates; after all he had been a big part of the team.

At the victory luncheon, Coach Bee was already preparing for the next season and told the team about the late-spring and summer tourna-ments they would play. Basketball was a year-round sport for Coach Bee. They would begin their quest for another championship almost immediately. Bee's vision was like that of Billy Bob Thornton's character at Permian High School, in the movie *Friday Night Lights*. In that final movie scene, Coach Gaines contemplates the loss of his senior athletes. He then moves on looking forward to next year, taking off the name tags representing the graduating seniors on his depth chart, replacing them with new name tags of the underclassman scheduled to take over the next season and start on the varsity.

Next year, the 1941–1942 season, Clair Bee hoped to lead his team to repeat as NIT Champions, something that no other team had ever done before. It would be another difficult schedule with a trip to New Orleans for the Sugar Bowl, to play the University of Tennessee, and back to Madison Square Garden to take on the nationally ranked University of Southern California Trojans.

There would be spring, summer, and fall basketball and possibly another trip to Puerto Rico or Cuba. The incoming freshman class looked promising with the addition of many of the Madison High School City championship team, and Beenders, Holub, Fucarino, and Spider would be back.

Subsequent teams, however, did not live up to their potential and did not have the same chemistry as the 1941 NIT Championship team. Later that year, on December 7, 1941, the disruption of war ensued after the Japanese bombed Pearl Harbor, destroying much of the United States' naval fleet leading to the country's entry into World War II. In fact, LIU did not field a team following the spring of 1943 until after the war.

Sadly, the Long Island University basketball team was shaken by a point-shaving gambling scandal, in the early '50s, along with CCNY, Kentucky, and several other colleges in New York area. The gamblers had infiltrated college basketball, and it would be the end of the LIU dynasty.

But in that 1941 Championship season, they had come together, and for his part, Spider had been commended for a very good season, at times being a great player. He had contributed well on the tough road trips, in the big Garden games, and in the NIT Tournament.

Spider's senior year showed promise, but the season was cut short by the United States' war effort and entry of the players into the armed forces in World War II.

Following his graduation, Sy Lobello's great smile, generosity, and leadership were missed. He had been the great mentor. Spider would still have some big scoring games and would regain his shooting touch, but it was not the same without Sy. The flashes of excellence that Spider achieved subsequently were fleeting reminders of the past. After the 1942 Southern Cal game, after Spider scored 19 points, Bee praised Spider, saying, "Solly, he's the best…" It was difficult, however, as the subsequent teams at LIU did not have the same chemistry or cohesiveness.

Spider graduated LIU in 1943; he went on to serve his country prior to returning to the game of basketball after the war. He played 4 years of professional basketball. His performance in the American Basketball League (the ABL) was stellar with the Brooklyn and New York Gothams, once breaking an arena scoring record with 28 points for the Gothams. The ABL games were spirited affairs played for the most part in old hockey rinks adapted for basketball. In the case of a rival league team, the New York Visitations, home games on their court could feature thrown beer bottles onto the floor by hometown fans, if displeased at the results of the game.

Ironically, Spider reunited with Barney Sedran, who had mentored him at the Creston Schoolyard. Sedran was the coach of the 1945 Gothams, and Spider would be his star player. What a coincidence that the same man that had singled him out in the schoolyard and mentored him as a preteenager would end up as his coach in professional basketball!

He would meet a teammate with the Gothams named Frito Frey, and they worked well together playing an effective two-man game using the pick-and-roll play that became a staple of the Gotham's offense. Spider became one of the ABL's top scorers his first 2 seasons.

After 4 pro seasons, Spider chose his profession. He was going to law school at NYU and simultaneously play pro ball with frequent road games in the ABL. The Gothams played their first year's home games at the St. Nicholas Arena in Manhattan, an old hockey rink and boxing facility that seated 6,600 fans and was located at 66th Street and Columbus Avenue in Manhattan. In his second year with the Gothams, they played their home games at the Broadway Arena in the Bushwick Section of Brooklyn. The home games were manageable, but the road games made it difficult for him to study for and attend law school classes. Often he would return from a long road trip by car or train, traveling all night without sleep. In those cases he simply stopped off in the library or an off campus coffeehouse with his luggage and gear, and lay back in a chair to get a couple of hours' sleep prior to class. Sometimes, he just got coffee and went to class, going without sleep until he could garner a quick afternoon nap before Gothams' practice.

It was difficult as well to earn a living in pro basketball at the time (they paid $40–$50 per game); ultimately, he stopped playing. He did not sign a contract when asked by Red Auerbach for his Washington Capitals, a BAA/NBA team. Other talented college basketball players in the mid-to-late '40s and into the '50s did not see playing basketball as gainful employment. One had to earn a living, especially if one wanted to get married and raise a family. Don Goldstein, one of the University of Louisville's all-time greats,[31] and Bob Kurland of Oklahoma A&M (whose team defeated NYU and Dolph Schayes in the 1945 NCAA Finals)[32] were two extraordinary college players who went into non-basketball professions. Both great players opted out of pro basketball, despite being drafted in the NBA.

Spider was fortunate. His deployment for the war was delayed. His mother had written to the draft board and asked for a delay in his deployment so that he could help with the care of his father, who was dying of cancer. Ultimately service duty called, and he was deployed in late 1944. While he experienced enemy fire, the delay likely helped him survive the war.

The 1940–1941 season and NIT tournament win would be Spider's fondest sports memory. The evening after the championship game, Spider read the *Daily News* and the other New York papers. The sports sections simply said, "LIU NIT Champs!" He was a champion. "What a difference a year made," he thought. Only last year, he had been an insecure freshman, worried about making the LIU varsity and enduring the unending slings and arrows of his father's didactic and harsh criticisms. His father had disturbed him then, but now there was a silver lining, and he took satisfaction in what he had accomplished. His tough Russian father had shown his paternal pride as well, purchasing a ticket for the NIT finals and being there to share the championship victory and celebration in Madison Square Garden. Spider remembered the moment that he held the championship trophy, posing with it for the *Daily News'* photo. He had eyeballed his father who had descended to the Garden floor, craning to see his son, and for the first time that he could remember, his father had smiled. While Abraham never told him, Spider knew that his dad respected what he had achieved. He now appreciated his son's worth, and the father had approved of what the son had accomplished.

CHAPTER 19

PFC Simon Lobello

THE MOIST SNOW HAD INTERMITTENT encounters with mounds of mud formed from the pounding on the snow and ice by the Sherman tanks and armored vehicles, which were unceremoniously pursued at various intervals by German Panzer tanks, strategic support vehicles, and battle equipment. It was a bone-chilling 1944 winter that would continue its frigid attitude for months to come. The snow-covered grounds capitulated amid the constant grind of machinery in the border areas of Germany, Belgium, France, and Luxembourg. Snowstorms caused frostbite and trench foot for the American, British, and German troops encamped in proximity to one another. Warren Spahn, the great Milwaukee Braves Hall of Fame pitcher, was at the battlefront and said, "I am from Buffalo, and I'm used to the cold, but I have never felt anything as cold as the cold of the Battle of the Bulge in the Ardennes!"[33] Private First Class Simon Lobello of the 8th Infantry Division, 13th Regiment, was entrenched in a snowbank on a hill. His groin no longer hurt in the aftermath of his inguinal hernia surgery that he had undergone in Ireland in May, just 7 months earlier. He had injured his groin playing professional basketball for Grumman Aircraft Company just prior to entering the service but had played with the pain and lived with it for over a year. Post-surgery, Sy felt much better and was released in time to rejoin his unit in July. His unit, Company E, was a proud part of the 13th Regiment. They were transported from their European training ground in Ireland by boat and headed for combat duty.

Lobello's division landed at Omaha Beach, Normandy, in July 1944. After the launch, they moved from the beach onward, taking town after town all the way to the western front of Germany. German troops were now on the run, and Hitler ordered his troops to aggregate in the Ardennes forest to launch what he hoped would be a successful blitzkrieg attack like they had executed successfully from the same location earlier in the war, successfully conquering Belgium and France. The first German invasions had begun when Germany attacked Poland on September 1, 1939. The United States did not join the war until Hitler declared war on the United States, which promptly responded by entering the war on the Allied side on December 11, 1941, just 4 days after the Japanese attack on Pearl Harbor.

Sy Lobello was part of the transport and support group attached to the First Army with the 8th Infantry Division. This had been a particularly grueling winter; all of the soldiers were underfed, cold, and in need of medical assistance. They were now being limited to 10 rounds a day as ammunition began to run short. The conditions were awful. Sy dreamt about going back home to Queens. He missed Dorothy, and her weekly letters kept him going in the cold and dire conditions. He tried to write her every week but could not always be as diligent as his new wife in this regard. Company E was not always in a position to have the time to write. It seemed that they had been marching and waiting and remaining vigilant forever, and he couldn't remember the last good night's sleep he had enjoyed. Having a shower would have been nice, but he had gone weeks without one. The mail was slow, and due to his company's movements it took Dorothy's letters too long to get to him. They had just gotten married before he began active army duty in March 1943. PFC Lobello started basic training two months later.

The sound of bullets and shrapnel deflecting off trees, tanks, and bodies reverberated around Company E's entrenched position. The soldiers in the company were sick from wallowing in the mud, repairing vehicles that had been damaged from enemy fire and warding off the forays of enemy soldiers. German troops, however, had been weakened further as well, and their supply lines had been broken due to the prolonged attack and siege of Germany by the Allied forces. Every day more Allied troops poured into the battle. Sy and his company mates felt Germany would be defeated soon, but the fighting was fierce and the elements like no other he had ever experienced. He visualized a positive outcome, always ebullient with optimism. It was his nature to see good and to overcome and to win. He was undefeated in this way. He imagined the taste of Dorothy's cooking and felt certain that he would be back in time for some of her savory home-cooked meals before summer. He regretted the fact that he would miss Christmas with her this year. He also missed playing basketball, and he learned that there were a couple of new professional basketball leagues starting up. In one of her letters, Dorothy told him that he had received some letters from pro teams and that he'd been invited to tryouts when he returned home.

Suddenly, he heard a sound. "Rat-tat-tat-tat–tat, rat-tat-tat!" There were two Panzer tanks in the vicinity, audaciously moving in his direction. He could hear the wheels and the metal grinding and squealing, echoing through the dense forest like a giant monster bent on destroying anything in its path.

"OK, everybody move out," said the sergeant. It was the beginning of a last-ditch effort by the German Army to counterattack, divide, and surround the British and American lines to break them apart. Their mission was to get to the Port of Antwerp to buy some more time until they could negotiate a settlement with the Allies. Hitler's plan to surround the United States and British forces might even enable the Germans to gain a victory in the Ardennes, and then perhaps the Allies would surrender. Against all odds, Hitler hoped for a victory at the Battle of the Bulge so he could send his troops back to Russia and finish off the Russians as well.

The American sergeant cried out again, "Move out!" Sy's unit was moving out to reconnoiter the German positions, moving around the right flank of the two approaching Panzers, successfully avoiding their path.

PFC Lobello was a good soldier. He had been trained to use a rifle and a pistol in Ireland, and he could shoot both with accuracy. He could run as fast as anyone in his division, and his muscular 6-foot-4 body could scale small obstacles in the dense forest, navigate hills, traverse small gullies, and secure the correct positions in combat.

Sy was at the ready, alert, in light of the gunfire he heard in the distance. He had almost become accustomed to it over these past weeks in this battle, which would become known as the Battle of the Bulge. As it happens in protracted battles and skirmishes, suddenly, there was a lull in the action. Sy's mind began to wander. He thought about his LIU team winning that last NIT, a little over a year and half prior. He smiled redolently as he contemplated how he had shaken Coach Bee's hand, kissed the NIT Championship Trophy, and, as the team captain, accepted the large NIT Champions Trophy, which now shone brightly in the university trophy case at the Brooklyn Pharmacy gym. He remembered how his languishing smile did not waiver until they had to tell him that they were closing up the Garden for the evening. After they had beaten Ohio University, he had not wanted to leave the scene of the great victory. He had lingered with his teammates shaking Coach Bee's hand and those of his teammates to congratulate all as the LIU players posed for the newsreels and the newspapers. The LIU family, friends, and fans had mobbed the players on the Garden floor. Coach Bee was elated and smiled deeply. It was the happiest Sy had ever seen his coach.

They had done their best, and it had paid off. He had given Dorothy his NIT Championship commemorative gold-plated miniature basketball and watch, and she had put them in her jewelry drawer. He remembered fondly those magic words on the memento: "NIT Champion, March 24, 1941." His thoughts gave way to sleep, and while he did not expect to doze off, he started to. After about 5 minutes or so, he forced his eyes to stay open, in a daze, wanting to sleep but not permitting himself to succumb to his fatigue.

Sy reflected on the wonderful coach and man that had taught him so much. Coach Bee's philosophy and his motivations and teaching had a profound impact on his life. He wistfully recalled how he had loved signing autographs at school when they came back from spring break to campus after the victory. It had made him feel like a celebrity, and he guessed that he, in fact, was well known and appreciated by the student body, the faculty, his teammates, and their coaches.

The 8th Infantry Division stopped and hunkered down on the north flank of the front line and with binoculars eyeballed the German attack force. The central flank would bulge, as would the southern flank, but the 8th Infantry Division stood its ground, as the Germans launched their blitzkrieg attack. The attack was made under protection of the heavy cloud cover and the passing snowstorms, which neutralized the Allies' superior air power. The Germans attacked the Allied forces under this cloud cover moving out in secret early in the morning at 5:30 a.m., concealed in the cover of the dark morning, catching the weak point in the Allied lines unprepared. The Germans pushed back the Allies, ultimately encircling the Allies at Bastogne in Belgium. General Patton would eventually come to the rescue, pushing the Germans all the way back to Berlin.

Sy's 8th Division advanced, holding its ground near the Roer River in Germany. They fought through heavily mined woods and dug in concrete and log bunkers. They occupied a 6-mile stretch east of Bergstein, Germany, holding off the German counterattack on December 16. The 8th Infantry Division further held the position until well after New Year's. Early in February, the division moved north to take over the Roer Riverfront opposite the German towns of Duren and Niederau. On February 23, 1945, the 8th crossed the Roer at the south flank of the 1st and 9th US Armies in a combined offensive under the direction of the British General Montgomery and his 21st Army. On February 25th, the 8th Division cleared the southern half of the city of Duren and drove to the Rhine River in Germany in a 10-day span, taking 50 German towns, critical enemy equipment, and over 10,000 prisoners!

Somehow shrapnel mortally wounded Sy Lobello, fighting the good fight on German soil. His official date of death was reported to be March 3, 1945.[34] He would ultimately be awarded the Bronze Star and a Purple Heart for his heroic efforts in combat. Lobello's Company E fought valiantly, and 90 of its soldiers perished out of the approximately 150 soldiers in the company, with most cited for medals and commendations including the captain of Company E, Richard C. Warren, who was awarded the "Croix de Guerre," along with a Silver Star. PFC Lobello was given a Combat Infantryman Badge, a Marksmanship Badge, a World War II Victory Medal, an American Campaign Medal, an Army Presidential Unit Citation, and an Army Good Conduct Medal to go with his Bronze Star and Purple Heart.[35] PFC Lobello had been killed less than 1 year after he had entered active service.

He was only 25 years old, but his spirit pervaded that of his LIU teammates, coaches, classmates, and teachers who never forgot his great energy, generosity, guidance, leadership, sense of humor, and proud positive spirit. Simon surely would have joined the newly formed NBA Professional Basketball League had he made it back from the war. The LIU coaching staff, faculty, and alumni, including many of his teammates, had a fundraiser for him back in Brooklyn when the news of his death circulated. He was a hero to LIU and to his country.

Spider was in Europe at the war's end, August 15, 1945. He had heard about Sy's death from shrapnel wounds in late March. He was overcome with grief, mourning the loss of his teammate and mentor. Sy's memory would remain with him; he would share stories of Sy and that championship season with his surviving teammates, Ossie Schectman and Butch Schwartz. They would be fixtures at the South Florida Basketball Association Luncheon every year, and they would always speak of Sy Lobello with great admiration. Spider returned to the United States and his home in the Bronx after the war. He would never forget Simon Lobello and appreciated the sacrifice that his great teammate had made for his country.

Simon Lobello, 1940

Photo: ancestry.com

Simon Lobello
Commemorative Memorial
Henri-Chapelle American Cemetary Hombourg, Belgium

IN MEMORY OF

★★★★★

SIMON LOBELLO

RANK

PRIVATE FIRST CLASS, U.S. ARMY

UNIT

13TH INFANTRY REGIMENT, 8TH INFANTRY DIVISION

DATE OF DEATH

MARCH 3, 1945

COMMEMORATED IN PERPETUITY AT

HENRI-CHAPELLE AMERICAN CEMETERY

HOMBOURG, BELGIUM

"Time will not dim the glory of their deeds."

— GENERAL JOHN J. PERSHING

Dave Polansky　　　　　　　Lou Rossini

Gene Wallach　　　　　　　Saul Cohen

Photos from: Barry Cohen's Family Album

LIU Basketball Players and Coach Get Ready to Go to War in the Army

Photo from: Barry Cohen's Family Album

Kneeling Left to Right: Marius "Lefty" Russo, Max Sharf, Saul "Spider" Cohen, Phil Rabinowitz, Lou Simon

Standing Left to Right are: Coach "Pic" Picarello, Sol "Butch" Schwartz, Irv Torghoff, Ossie Schechtman, Mike Sewictch, Pop Gates, Irv Rothenberg, Julie Bender, Art Hillhouse, Howie Radar, Dolly King, Freddy Lewis, Lennie Radar, Leo Merson, and Coach Bee

Saul Cohen in the Army, circa 1944

Photo from: Barry Cohen's Family Album
Saul, bottom row, second from right.

Europe, parts unknown
winter of 1945.

V-J Day War is over! August
15, 1945. Newspaper says
simply "Japan Quits",
Saul Cohen and army pal in
Germany on same date.

Photo from: Barry Cohen's Family Album

CHAPTER 20

Scandal

* * *

JACKIE GOLDSMITH WAS 5 FEET, 8 inches tall, but he was the Steph Curry of his day. He could fire a two-handed set shot accurately from up to 35 feet away from the basket. There were no 3-point lines to reward his marksmanship, but everyone who saw him confirmed his phenomenal skill from long range.

Clair Bee called Jackie Goldsmith "the greatest two-handed set shooter in the history of New York City college basketball."[36]

Goldsmith would become a great college player after World War II at LIU. Jackie averaged 17 points per game at LIU, was name second team All-America, and set LIU game and season scoring records. He was a first team All-Metropolitan selection. Goldsmith went on to play pro basketball. He was his own worst enemy, however, and got involved with Eddie Gard (LIU) and Jack Molinas (Columbia). He became a part of the worst college basketball scandal of the time. The scandal caused several major schools to go on probation and other programs to lose their status as major college basketball programs. The scandal upset the college basketball world.

While both Gard and Molinas were excellent ballplayers, they got involved with gamblers who organized point-shaving on college bas-ketball games, usually in Madison Square Garden. Jackie's poor associations ultimately led to time in prison. He was arrested in April 1951 and sentenced to 2½ years in prison. The money in pro basketball was different than it is now. Players got $40–$50 per game in the ABL, and the same emoluments or slightly higher in other pro leagues. The rival pro leagues did not pay its players enough to support a viable livelihood. The Basketball Association of America (BAA) and the National Basketball League (NBL) merged to become the National Basketball League (NBA); however, professional basketball players had to have a second job to support themselves and their families.

Jackie Goldsmith, Sherman White, and Eddie Gard—the best college player of his time and LIU teammate—arranged point-shaving on games to help gamblers, most notably Salvatore Sollazzo. Sollazzo bet and won on college games involving CCNY, Manhattan, LIU, Kentucky, and several other colleges. All teams along with the individuals involved were punished. The teams were all sanctioned, and CCNY was banned from ever playing in Madison Square Garden.

Mrs. Sollazzo leaves court in a Cab.

Photo: APWirephoto

Some ballplayers knew nothing outside of the game of basketball. They were not inclined to any gainful profession. They fell easy prey to gamblers. The gamblers frequented the college games more so than the pro games in that era as the college game was better attended.

Jack Molinas was a 6-foot-6 skilled player who rivaled any NBA player in the 1950s. The son of parents who owned a bar in Coney Island, Molinas graduated Stuyvesant High School in New York City to star at Columbia University. He became the greatest basketball player in that school's history. He was picked third overall in the 1953 NBA draft by the Fort Wayne Pistons and selected to the 1954 NBA All-Star game, averaging 12 points per game that year and setting the team individual game scoring record. He was, however, suspended before the NBA All-Star game and did not play in it as planned, soon leaving the game of basketball. Molinas went to law school after his pro career ended and became an attorney. He became involved in a point-shaving scandal in 1961 involving 50 players from 27 colleges, including future Hall of Famers Connie Hawkins and Roger Brown. In 1963, Molinas was convicted of the crimes committed in the scandal and served 5 years in prison.

Molinas was murdered at his home in Los Angeles at the age of 43 in 1975 by gunmen. He was awaiting trial at the time for the crime of the interstate shipment of pornography. He had contacts to organized crime organizations. Molinas never sustained a prolonged professional basketball career, having taken a wrong turn along his path in life. Ironically, Molinas was a product of the Creston Junior High School Schoolyard. When Spider watched the kids leave the schoolyard and steal from the fruit stands on the avenue just outside the schoolyard, he was tempted, but he had learned to take the correct path and was determined not to fall into the snare of the petty thieves and gamblers, and other temptations of the streets. Jackie Goldsmith, Eddie Gard, and Jack Molinas from the streets of New York City and its schoolyards took a wrong turn in the road, and they suffered the consequences.

Saul Cohen Was One of the High Scorers for the ABL Gothams

Gothams and Vissies Repeat Double Victory

For the second successive week Brooklyn's two entries in professional basketball emerged victorious after second half uphill battles at the Broadway Arena last night. The Gothams, league leader in the Northern Division of the American Basketball League, conquered Troy, 60—55, and Visitations downed Bayonne, 52—38, in a New York and New Jersey League clash.

The Gothams in scoring their 18th triumph against five setbacks marred the local debut of Dave Banks, former Celtic star, as coach of the Troy Celtics. The Brooklynites took the lead in the last quarter after trailing throughout the game. It was the ninth win in 11 starts on the Broadway Arena court for the Gothams.

Saul Cohen led the Gothams' scoring attack with 28 points, a new high for the season on the Broadway Arena court. Johnny Ezersky aided the Brooklyn cagers cause with 15 tallies. Ash Besnick, former New Utrecht High ace, led the Troy quintet with 16 points.

Visitation registered seven straight points in the last three minutes while holding Bayonne scoreless to record its seventh win against three defeats. Bill Peters was the top scorer for the victors with 15 points.

Next week's pro twin bill at the Broadway pits the Gothams against Wilmington and Visitation against the leading Orange Triangles.

The lineups:

Gothams	G.	F.	P.	Troy	G.	F.	P.
Cohen	11	6	28	Dubilier	4	5	13
Prey	3	5	11	Flanagan	0	0	0
Kopitko	0	0	0	Resnick	5	6	16
Delson	1	0	2	N. Frankel	1	0	2
Rabin	1	1	3	M. Frankel	0	2	2
Walsh	0	0	0	Laub	0	1	1
Ezersky	5	5	15	Kasner	7	0	14
Banks	0	1	1	Judenfr'nd	3	3	9
Totals	22	18	60	Totals	20	15	55

Referee—Begovich.

Visitation	G.	F.	P.	Bayonne	G.	F.	P.
Rosenman	0	2	2	McCabe	2	1	5
Peters	5	5	15	Melofchick	7	2	16
Courtney	2	1	5	Studwell	1	0	2
Mariaschin	4	0	8	Wright	3	0	6
O'Hare	2	2	6	Gabbanelli	3	2	8
Kennedy	2	2	6	Paulick	0	1	1
Mulholland	0	0	0				
Totals	15	12	42	Totals	16	6	38

Referee—Mahon.

Gothams Draw Praise In Rout of Sphas, 68-47

"They looked better than any team we've met this year" was the way Coach Harry Litwack of the Philadelphia Sphas termed the sparkling showing of the Brooklyn Gothams at the Broadway Arena last night.

The Gothams, sparked by Capt. Saul Cohen, swamped the Quaker outfit, 68 to 47, handing the invaders their worst local setback in ten years. It was Brooklyn's sixth American League victory in eight games and cemented their hold on first place in the Northern Division.

Although the Sphas held a 13-to-10 lead in the first half, the Gothams kept plugging away until Cohen's baskets put them ahead. At the intermission mark it was 37 to 19. Cohen scored 22 points, 17 of them

in the first half, to skyrocket himself among the loop's leading scorers.

Dave Soden, Brooklyn's favorite sports fan, tossed out the first ball. Sid Gordon of the Giants and President John O'Brien of the league was also spectators.

The Gothams encounter the Wilmington Blue Bombers in their next league game a the Arena next Sunday night.

The lineup:

GOTHAMS	G.	F.	P.	SPHAS	G.	F.	P.
Cohen	6	10	22	Opper	5	2	12
Rabin	2	1	7	Snyder	3	0	6
Frey	2	4	8	Schwartz	3	0	6
Kovner	0	0	0	Brown	0	0	0
Kopitko	3	2	8	Davis	1	2	4
Ezersky	3	1	8	Weiner	3	1	7
Delson	0	0	0	Lautman	1	2	4
Banks	2	0	4	Klotz	1	3	5
Walsh	6	2	14	Freeman	1	1	3
Totals	23	22	68	Totals	18	11	47

Referee—Sollerman.

The Philadelphia Sphas Team was noted for excellent ball movement.

The fact that the Gothams soundly defeated them was impressive.

It is a marvel to me that Dad played Pro Ball and did well, and went to Law School at NYU at the same time!

Gotham '5' Tops Crescents, 68-57

The Gothams made their first home start as Brooklyn representatives in the American Basketball League a successful one when they defeated the Paterson Crescents, 68-57, at the Broadway Arena last night.

Sol Cohen, with 19 points, led the attack for the Gothams, who were tied at the half, 34-all, after trailing, 20-10, at the end of the first quarter.

GOTHAMS	G.	F.	Pts.	PATERSON	G.	F.	Pts.
Walsh	1	1	3	Goebel	5	3	13
Rabin	5	3	13	Krygier	1	0	2
Frey	3	4	10	Nochims'n	2	1	5
Kovner	1	0	2	Auerb'h	0	1	1
Kopitko	1	2	4	Dorn	8	8	12
Mintz	0	0	0	Lesser	3	3	9
Delson	2	0	4	Juenger	5	1	11
Cohen	6	7	19	Boardm'n	2	0	4
Ezersky	6	1	13				
Totals	25	18	68	Totals	26	17	57

Saul Breaking Base Scoring Mark vs Robbins Field at Hunter Field

L. I. U. TOPS FT. DIX, 69-23

Cohen and Holub Get 15 Points Each in Basketball Victory

The Long Island University basketball team romped to a 69-23 victory over Fort Dix at the Brooklyn College of Pharmacy gym last night. The victors led, 37—12, at the half.

The Blackbirds jumped into an early lead on baskets by Saul Cohen and Fred Lewis and quickly increased their advantage. Cohen and Dick Holub shared scoring honors with 15 points each. Dave Conway led the soldiers with eight.

The line-up:

L. I. U. (69)	G.	F.	P.	FORT DIX (23)	G.	F.	P.
Beenders, lf	2	0	4	Katz, lf	1	1	3
Sapan	2	0	4	Lor, rf	1	1	3
Lewis, rf	2	1	5	Cantelmo	0	0	0
Waxman	2	0	4	Waller, c	3	0	6
Fronczak	0	0	0	Goldstein, lg	1	0	2
Holub, c	5	5	15	Dino	0	0	0
Gurfein	2	0	4	Condit	0	0	0
H. Rader, lg	0	0	0	Gavin, rg	0	1	1
L. Rader	3	1	7	Eggers	0	0	0
Berman	0	0	0	Conway	4	0	8
Cohen, rg	7	1	15				
Schneider	3	2	8	Total	10	3	23
Fucarino	1	1	3				
Total	29	11	69				

Officials—Russell Belsswanger and Lou Eisenstein, E. I. A. Time of halves—20 minutes.

BOMBERS SCORE 65-55 TRIUMPH

Cohen Sets Base Mark As Robins Field Loses

Paced by former All-American Saul Cohen the Bombers upset the Robins Field team, which is rated among the top ten service outfits in the nation, by a 65-55 margin last night.

Cohen copped high scoring honors and at the same time set a Hunter Field record by sinking eleven field goals and six foul shots. Center Marvin Neal, former All-Conference star in California, took second place with seventeen points.

The lead see-sawed back and forth but the Bombers led 26-23 at the half. The Robins Field men sank thirteen out of fourteen foul shots.

Box score:

Air Base.	FG.	F.	TP.
Saul Cohen, f.	11	6	28
Woodward, f.	2	3	7
Keeney, f.	0	0	0
Reynolds, f.	2	1	5
Neal, c.	8	1	17
Smith, g.	3	0	6
Katz, g.	0	0	0
Hooker, g.	1	0	2
Thomas, g.	0	0	0
Totals	27	11	65

Robins Field.	FG.	F.	TP.
Gentry, f.	5	3	13
Patterson, f.	1	0	2
Gannon, f.	2	2	6
Drish, c.	6	4	16
Anderson, g.	3	2	8
Combs, g.	4	2	10
Totals	21	13	55

Scores at half, 26-23.

ABL NEW YORK GOTHAMS

Photo from: Barry Cohen's Family Album

Brooklyn Gothams Team Photo Bottom Row Right Lester Mintz,
two players to the left of Lester is Saul "Spider" Cohen, holding basketball.

Victor Mario Perez (#33)
LIU and myself in
San Juan, Puerto Rico1995.
He was a charmer and could
still drink 3 martinis.
He was 80 years old
at the time.

Saul Cohen, Ossie Schechtman,
and Butch Schwartz at the
1998 Basketball Fraternity.

Old LIU Teammates
Saul Cohen and
Ossie Schechtman at the 1999
Basketball Fraternity
Luncheon.

Photos from: Barry Cohen's Family Album

CHAPTER 21
Epilogue

✻ ✻ ✻

THE BASKETBALL PLAYERS OF TODAY are far superior to those who played during the period from 1933 to 1949. Each generation gets bigger, faster, stronger, and more skilled. There has also been radical improvement in athletic training in all sports. It is virtually impossible to compare athletes of different generations. How would Bob Cousy have done against Magic Johnson, or Larry Bird or Michael Jordan, Lebron James, Kobe Bryant, or Kevin Durant? Is it even fair to compare athletes of different generations? In hockey, what would Gump Worsley or Jacques Plante as goalies do with the powerful shot of Shea Weber or Zdeno Chara? Besides the increasing strength and power of today's athletes, the current-day equipment enhances performance. The athletes have better sneakers and lighter and more powerful sticks, clubs, or rackets to showcase their talent with more efficient tools.

The training techniques in basketball as in all sports have been impacted by technology; improvements in monitoring diet; studies of sleep, vitamin supplements, and psychology, and that is why it is almost impossible to compare athletes of one generation to another. In his brilliant treatise on baseball, *The New Historical Baseball Abstract*, Bill James uses numbers and metrics to compare generations of the greatest baseball players of all time. This type of intergenerational comparison is more challenging in basketball as the players today are far superior and reasonable metrics have not been developed as a common denominator for any such cross-generational comparisons.

Wilt Chamberlain, Jim Brown, Bobby Orr, Wayne Gretzky, Bob Gibson, and Sandy Koufax are exceptions. These extraordinary athletes were ahead of their time and had transcended the eras of their playing careers. Their abilities were so advanced they could likely compete favorably with today's athletes. These players were game changers both in their era and thereafter, their impact enduring in their respective sports. Tom Brady and Lebron James will likewise follow these great athletes as great players in their respective sports who would be able to compete against future athletes, many years into the future.

Internationalization has vastly improved the game of basketball, which at its inception was almost exclusively an American game. The NBA game did not have many athletes born of European, Asian, Australian, Canadian, South American, African, or Caribbean parents. The 1992 dream team changed that, effectively exporting the game of basketball, rivaling the impact of the Beatles on pop culture in America. The result was a wider range of athletes playing the sport of basketball, the Euro step, and more exposure of the game to the masses, especially internationally on all continents. More athletes worldwide began to play the sport and the athletes became more skilled and the competition in the pros got even better.

The dream team was not the first attempt to export the game. In fact, Clair Bee started teaching and marketing the game of basketball on an international level in the late '30s and early 40s, traveling to Puerto Rico and Cuba with his LIU teams to play in exhibition games and to provide clinics on the game. But the United States still dominated the sport, especially in the Olympic Games. Until that unsavory and perverse 1972 finals loss to the USSR, the United States had never lost in the Olympics. Doug Collins' courage taking it to the hoop and getting fouled flagrantly and making both free throws against Russia in that Olympic Game deserved a gold medal, and most importantly, the US Olympic team deserved the gold medal.

In the 1930s and 1940s, many African Americans were excluded from playing college and pro basketball. Those who got to play were often treated unfairly, limiting their success and not given the opportunity to freely excel.

Dolly King was an example of an African American athlete who overcame these limitations. Referees ignored the flagrant blows and contact that Dolly took in the pivot. Racially motivated, the blows were designed to impact Dolly's temperament, but he kept his cool, playing and focusing to help his team win, which they usually did.

King was a dominant player in both basketball and football. Like Jackie Robinson, he was a trailblazer, paving the way for future African American NBA players. The NBA's tribute to King in a Hall of Fame tribute by Blake Griffin, a modern-day NBA All-Star[37] shows what a great player Dolly King was. There were many other African American ballplayers of that era who never got the chance to show what they could do.

Schoolyard basketball is played for the love of the game. The schoolyards in New York in the 1930s and 1940s were cauldrons for players to develop their basketball skills. There was no TV, no sponsorships, and no sneaker money for pro ballplayers, and the sport was not a viable option as a sole profession. In spite of the lack of the lure of future emoluments, players loved to play the game. They studied it and enjoyed a special camaraderie. These schoolyards produced high school, college, and pro basketball players. The kids lived to play the game and shared ideas and strategies with each other. When they got a good coach, they revered him. A coach was a powerful, dedicated teacher, and the young boys soaked up the teachings and the experience of the era's disciplined, dedicated, and savvy coaches.

The schoolyards were great to learn game skills. They gave kids the chance to nurture those skills and meld them with other schoolyard friends. Having a coach to guide them was the dream of every young basketball player. The whole was always greater than the sum of the parts, and when everyone bought in, coaches were appreciated and great results followed.

The NBA was founded in 1949, when its predecessor leagues—the BAA and the NBL—merged in June 1946, and the NBA was formed in August 1949.

Prior to that there were several professional basketball leagues. The first attempt at a professional basketball league in the United States from 1925 to 1931 was the American Basketball League (ABL). The president of the National Football League (NFL) at the time, Joseph Carr, organized the ABL with 9 of the best teams independent professional teams from the East and Midwest. George Halas of the Chicago Bears owned the ABL Chicago Bruins; Max Rosenblum, who also owned the NFL Cleveland Bulldogs and was a department store magnate, owned the ABL Cleveland Rosenblums; and future Washington Redskins owner George Preston Marshall owned the ABL's Washington Palace Five team.

Saul "Spider" Cohen played on the New York and Brooklyn Gothams from 1945 to 1948. He was invited to play for the BAA's Washington Capitals team by Coach Red Auerbach in 1948. The BAA was the first pro league to try and enable the players to train full time. Players had training camps, and they were in excellent shape. As a result they were a step ahead of the ABL, whose players had other jobs and a split focus, according to Sonny Hertzberg, who played in both leagues.[38] The BAA was a serious league that was a full-time job without full-time pay except for a few of the superstars. Spider left the game after the 1948 season, graduating NYU Law School. He never went to the Washington Capitals camp. Many of the players that he played with at LIU played in the BAA and then in the NBA, such as Ossie Schectman, Dick Holub, Irving Rothenberg, Freddie Lewis, Hank Beenders, and Butch Schwartz.

Spider became a lawyer in the hope of a more remunerative profession. Little did he know that they would one day pay players a bit more than $50 per game!

The Creston Crew are all gone now. Yet somehow in some multiverse, some parallel universe, the boys are playing. All of the kids who ever played at Creston are on the courts, and there are 5 sets of players waiting to play the winners on every court. They stop for a moment and reflect. The sun hits their collective faces; a slight breeze requires the boys to remember the very moment as everlasting. They stop to kibitz, and a friendly argument ensues about baseball. "Who is better? The Brooklyn Dodgers, the New York Giants, or the New York Yankees? Is Cool Papa Bell a better player than Bill Dickey?" The boys understand each other and accept each other, and they both tolerate and respect their differences. They simply agree to disagree. In all matters, respect is one of the important factors in how people get along with each other. If you respect someone and they respect you, even polemic differences in philosophy, politics, or determining who the better baseball team is, can be tolerated and even appreciated. Most importantly, the schoolyard kids listen to each other and are genuinely concerned for each other. They are brethren of an informal yet cogent fraternity.

The boys are bouncing balls, chewing bubble gum, teasing each other, and needling one another to death or life. I know they are there, imperceptible yet paradoxically palpable. Spider gets in the game. He sees the pick-and-roll, and Lucio cuts to the basket just in time to get a pass from Spider. Genie and Philly Rick applaud, and Dave Polansky dribbles up court. Wally Sencer makes a layup, and Artie Reichner, Lester Mintz, Lenny Lesser, and Flicky call for the ball as Spider inbounds. They get the ball downcourt, and they pass and cut away, going backdoor for another bucket. They laugh with happiness at a nice play, winking at their friends, teammates, and opponents in the schoolyard. Another play and a quick bounce pass for a bucket off a layup, and Benny lays it up and in on Ralph Kaplowitz. Benny smiles and points back to his brother, acknowledging his fine pass. It feels good, and the boys in the schoolyard are having fun. The game ends, everyone wins. Who's got next? "Wanna play?"

Of his parents and his 5 siblings, Spider was the last to go. Of the LIU 1941 NIT Championship team, he was the last to go. Of his Creston Schoolyard crew, he was the last to go. He could not thrive as he once had without his pals from the schoolyard. They were waiting for him in the heavens. Genie Wallach would surely ask him to play some ball again, and Wally Sencer would be laughing and hosting a party in Spider's honor. Sometimes exactly 26 miles north of Key West late at night, when no one else is watching, at the exact point where the Atlantic Ocean meets the Gulf of Mexico, you can see the lonesome stars shining on the shadows of the phantoms of boys playing in the schoolyard.

SAUL "SPIDER COHEN AND SON BARRY COHEN

Saul "Spider" Cohen, age 20, LIU 1941   The Author, Barry Cohen, age 20, UVM 1972

Photo from: Barry Cohen's Family Album

AUTHOR'S NOTE

The accounts and events described in this work are primarily based on stories told to me by my father throughout his life for as long as I can remember. The events, scores, articles, and many of the photos have been culled from the *Brooklyn Eagle*, *New York Times*, and *New York Daily News* from "newspapers.com" and the references listed below in support of the various events depicted. The interactions of many of the characters have been surmised and estimated based on my father's stories and based on documented events where the characters were likely to have interacted.

NOTES AND BIBLIOGRAPHY

[1]. Dick McGuire would play 3 on 3 ball at Cantiague Park on Long Island, New York, circa 1966–1967. He made the game so much fun. It was old-time schoolyard ball with cutting and passing and his positive exhortations. He never shot the ball; he just passed and set picks and told you what to do and was always so positive and helpful. "I got you," he would say as he set a mean pick for you. Or he would raise his eyebrows, signaling you to cut to the basket as he delivered you a gift-wrapped perfect bounce pass, crisp and on the mark, hitting you in stride perfectly. He just made everyone on the court feel good about playing. It was a different game. You didn't feel the game; it just floated by on a cloud, and you were transported. When you played with him on your team you remembered it. It was magic, a wonderful game.

[2]. "The City Game, Basketball from the Garden to the Playgrounds," by Pete Axthelm, University of Nebraska Press, Bison Books (1999). Introduction to the Bison Books Edition, by Rick Telander.

[3]. "The Heart of the Order," by Thomas Boswell, Penguin Books (1989).

[4]. Friedrich Nietzsche "The Will to Power," "A. Morality as the work of Immortality.

[5]. Ancestry.com, "Abraham Knobel" aka Abraham Cohen, Ship Manifest. (In Yiddish, Knobel means garlic").

[6]. Famous Basketball commentator Dick Vitale refers to 'PTPers' as prime time players or blue chip players.

[7]. http://wilburcoach0.tripod.com/psalchamps.html

[8]. Wikipedia "Ralph Kaplowitz."

[9]. Moses Malone's actual quote was "I be a Greyhound in the 4th Quarter." His most famous quote was "Fo Fo and Fo," which was his response to a reporter's question as to his thoughts on how the 76ers would do in the 1983 NBA playoffs. This was his way of asserting that the 76ers would win each playoff round in a 4-game

sweep. He was basically correct as the 76ers won each round in 4 games, 5 games, and finally in 4 games in a Finals sweep.

[10]. Wikipedia, "Catskill Resorts."

[11]. Wikipedia, "Dolph Schayes."

[12]. Stories told by Dolph Schayes at the South Florida Basketball Luncheon, circa 2008.

[13]. Premo-Porretta Power Poll (The results of this poll were recently published in the ESPN College Basketball Encyclopedia) (see below):

The Premo-Porretta Power Poll is a retroactive end-of-year ranking for American college basketball teams competing in the 1895–96 through the 1947–48 seasons.

The Premo-Porretta Polls are intended to serve collectively as a source of information regarding the relative standings of college basketball teams within given seasons during the early decades of the sport. No systematic end-of-season national tournament existed in college basketball until the founding of the National Invitation Tournament in 1938 and the NCAA Men's Division I Basketball Championship Tournament in 1939, the latter of which determines the NCAA Champion for a given season. Furthermore, no regular, recognized national polling took place for college basketball prior to the establishment of the Associated Press Poll and the Coaches Poll in the 1948–49 and 1950–51 seasons, respectively.

Patrick Premo, a professor emeritus of accounting at St. Bonaventure University, and Phil Porretta, a former computer programmer, have each spent more than 40 years—first separately, and later collaboratively—researching the early history of college basketball. Their archival work has often uncovered game results that had not previously been reported in books and basketball program media guides, such as the results of competition against AAU, semi-professional, club, and YMCA teams. Whereas Bill Schroeder of the Helms Athletic Foundation only retroactively named his choice of the top team nationally for each season, Premo and Porretta have used the data they have compiled to compare teams against one another and assign rankings to multiple teams for each season—15 teams for the 1895–96 season, 20 teams for each season from the 1896–97 through the 1908–09 seasons, and 25 teams for each season from the 1909–10 through the 1947–48 seasons.

Premo and Porretta first published results of their early collaboration in 1995. Most recently, in 2009, their full rankings were included with the core information for each season prior to 1949 in the ESPN College Basketball Encyclopedia.

[14]. Wikipedia Citation under "History of the NIT."

[15]. Wikipedia, "Clair Bee."

[16]. "ESPN College Basketball Encyclopedia: The Complete History of the Men's Game," by ESPN, ESPN Books, New York, NY (2009), p. 526, ISBN 978-0-345-51392-2.

[17]. "A team that chose principles over gold medals," By Michael Weinreb, Special to Page 2 (Archive) Updated: April 20, 2009, 12:33 PM ET.

[18]. Holocaust Encyclopedia, Anti-Jewish Legislation in Prewar Germany, https://encyclopedia.ushmm.org/content/en/article/anti-jewish-legislation-in-prewar-germany

[19]. *Brooklyn Eagle* newspaper article, Clair Bee quote on Julie Bender.

[20]. Ancestry.com Passenger List 1940.

[21]. New York Daily News, January 29, 1941.

[22]. The footnote below is from the following website verbatim. "Blackfives.org/www.blackfivesfoundation.com"

The Black Fives Era In Perspective: Just after the game of basketball was invented in 1891, teams were called "fives" in reference to their five starting players. Basketball, like American society, was racially segregated. Teams made up entirely of African American players were often known as "colored quints," "Negro cagers," or "black fives." The sport remained divided from 1904—when basketball was first introduced to African Americans on a wide-scale organized basis—until the racial integration of the National Basketball League in the 1940s and the National Basketball Association in 1950. The period in between became known as the Black Fives Era, when dozens of all-Black teams emerged, flourished, and excelled. African Americans were making moves in basketball generations before the N.B.A. was born. At first, those teams—sponsored by churches, athletic and social clubs, "Colored" YMCAs, businesses, and newspapers – had few places to play, since gymnasiums and athletic clubs were whites-only. But when the phonograph emerged in the early 1900s, Black music—ragtime, jazz, and blues—became so popular that a dance craze swept America. Almost overnight, sheet music and player pianos in the parlor gave way to dance halls and ballrooms. Positive and culturally affirming opportunities in the entertainment industry replaced the insulting, degrading minstrelsy of the past. For observant and enterprising African American sports promoters, these spaces became ready-made basketball venues on off nights, featuring music by top Black musicians and dancing afterward until well past midnight. In urban industrial centers like New York, Washington, Pittsburgh, and Chicago, Black people were in motion. New migrants from the South, as well as new immigrants from all parts of the Caribbean, Africa, Central, and South America, were looking for ways to meet each other and assimilate. As a result, Black Fives Era basketball games went beyond the sport itself and became meaningful social events. Though commonplace today, the marriage of basketball and music was an African American innovation that grew out of necessity, opportunism, timing, and broad cultural awareness by community leaders. This is why so many early game advertisements included the headline, "Basket Ball and Dance." There never existed a Black professional basketball league akin to baseball's Negro Leagues. However, independent African American teams played within a well-organized nationwide barnstorming circuit. They commanded national attention in the Negro press and headlines in local papers while battling for the annual right to be called "Colored Basketball World's Champions." The Black Fives Era spanned what were perhaps America's darkest yet most colorful years, a rich period that included the First Black Migration, the emergence of the phonograph and radio, the growth of entertainment culture, the explosion of jazz, ragtime, and the blues, vice reform, lynchings and race riots, the ballroom dancing craze, Prohibition, the Roaring '20s, the Harlem Renaissance, the Great Depression, two World Wars, and the Golden Age of Sports. Out of many, one African American team, the New York Renaissance (aka Harlem "Rens") stood apart as arguably the most successful basketball team of the century, irrespective of race or ethnicity. From 1923 to 1948, the Rens won 2,588 of 3,117 games – a staggering winning percentage of 83% sustained over a 25-year period! The Rens ushered in the Harlem Renaissance period, smashed the color barrier in pro basketball, and helped pave the way for the Civil Rights Movement. The teams and players of the Black Fives Era created something from nothing, with no road map, no instructions, and no recipes, despite many fears, doubts, and obstacles—and for little more than the love of the game. With definite plans, collective purpose, and relentless pursuit, they kept climbing to higher levels of success on increasingly bigger stages, in front of ever-growing audiences. All the while they fostered hope, aspiration, pride, unity, pragmatism, and self-esteem among African Americans during a time— the most pivotal period in Black history of the last century—when those attributes were prerequisites for sheer survival. The men and women of the Black Fives Era were true basketball pioneers whose desire simply to play their best and innovate the game opened doors for generations of African American players. In doing so they left a worldwide legacy that inspires not only ballers, but also all of us to this day. Now you can find out more!

[23]. Expression first coined by comedian Dennis Miller.

[24]. The Documentary Film *The First Basket,* released 2008, Laemmle/ Zeller Films.

[25]. "The Boys in the Boat," by Daniel James Brown, Penguin Books (2014).

[26]. Clair Bee, Broadman, and Holman Publisher Nashville Tennessee Copyright 1998.

[27]. *Brooklyn Eagle, March 23, 1941*

[28]. *Brooklyn Eagle, January 30, 1941, George E. Coleman, writer.*

[29]. *Brooklyn Eagle, March 25, 1941.*

[30]. In the book by Terry Frei, *March 1939 Before the Madness, the Story of the First NCAA Tournament Champions,** the author impugns conventional wisdom. The book seeks to evaluate which tournament in the year 1939 was more apt to determine the National Collegiate Basketball Champions, the NIT or the fledgling NCAA Tournament. Despite the Premo Porretta Power Poll, Mr. Frei argues that the 1939 "Tall Firs" Oregon NCAA Tournament Champions were a better club than the 1939 NIT Champions from Long Island University. This perspective in my view is speculative and hypothetical. While an interesting argument, it neglects the realities of the specific players on each of the comparative teams in the relevant year of comparison. It uses as a reference point subsequent and prior years where the players on both teams were completely different. The Premo Porretta Poll chose LIU as its 1939 national champion based on wins and losses of all NCAA teams for that year against common opponents and the opponents of those teams as well. This power poll is therefore, in my view, more relevant and accurate. The Premo Porretta Power Poll retroactively named LIU the National Champion in 1939 and 1941 in part based on data and comparative scores of opponents as well as a result of the tournament outcomes and relative strength of the respective tournaments and their fields at the time. In the case of the comparison in 1939, the common opponent of LIU and

Oregon clearly show LIU as the better team. They both played Bradley Tech with LIU defeating Bradley 36–32 in the semifinals of the NIT. Oregon lost to Bradley 52–39 during the regular season, and both LIU and Oregon beat the other common opponent, Canisius, by 12 points. The NIT was the better, more prestigious tournament as well, and that was paramount. In 1941 LIU won the NIT and finished the season 25–2. The University of Wisconsin won the NCAA Tournament with a record of 20–3. They shared a common opponent, Butler, which they both beat. Wisconsin won 59–55 at home and LIU beat Butler in the Garden 46–35. LIU beat Toledo 49–43, and while Wisconsin didn't play Toledo, the Badgers beat Dartmouth 51–50 which lost to Toledo 54–48. Finally, Wisconsin lost at home to an 11–9 University of Minnesota Team 44–27. By contrast LIU lost only 2 games, one on a half-court shot by Moe Becker of Duquesne at the buzzer in its 36–34 loss, and then against Michigan State 31–26. However, LIU later beat Michigan State on the Spartans' home court in front of very hostile crowd, 25–24. Michigan State was not then in the Big Ten and did not play Wisconsin. Clearly, the NIT was the premier tournament of its time. The Premo Porretta Power Poll conclusively deemed the 1941 LIU team the National Collegiate Champions. Bill Bradley asserts this priority and preference, in his book *A Sense of Where You Are: Bill Bradley Basketball at Princeton*. In the book Bradley writes, "In the 1940s, when the NCAA Tournament was less than 10 years old, the National Invitational Tournament, a Saturnalia held in New York at Madison Square Garden by the Metropolitan Intercollegiate Basketball Association, was the most glamorous of the post-season tournaments and generally had the better teams. The winner of the National Invitation Tournament was regarded as more of a national champion than the actual titular, national champion, or winner of the NCAA Tournament."

Hindsight can be 20–20, and it is easy to get sentimental about one's favorite team so as to lose one's perspective. In this case in regard to the NIT's significance, Mr. Frei's assertions in his book are misguided in that at that time the NIT Tournament was the significantly better tournament and the benchmark for collegiate basketball supremacy.

[31]. *Basketball Is My Life, A Basketball Addict's Autobiography,* by Martin Groveman (2017), Library of Congress, Number 2017918427. At page 42, Chapter 3 Groveman says, "Don was selected in the second round (of the NBA Draft), by the Pistons...Don thought long and hard and made a decision not to play professional basketball. Instead he opted for a career in dentistry...the stability of an esteemed profession and settled home life as opposed to a tenuous basketball future helped to solidify Don's decision. He followed his plan and for 5 decades has been a respected and skilled dentist." As Regards Bob Kurland, the *New York Times* article dated September 30, 2013, by Richard Goldstein, made a similar comment about the 6-foot-11 stalwart Kurland, "Viewing the business world as promising a secure future, Kurland shunned the pros and joined the Phillips Petroleum Company of Bartlesville, Oklahoma, as an executive." (Kurland had been drafted in the NBA, 7th overall).

[32]. Wikipedia, "Bob Kurland."

[33]. Warren Spahn quote "Battle of the Bulge," by history.com editor, and "The Love of Baseball, Essays by Lifelong Fans," edited by Chris Arvidson and Diana Nelson Jones, McFarland and Company, Inc. Publishers, Jefferson, North Carolina.

[34]. "HonorStates.org" Re: Simon Lobello PFC.

[35]. www.fieldsofhonor-database.com/index   reference   Simon Lobello.

[36]. *Brooklyn Eagle* newspaper article Clair Bee quote on Jackie Goldsmith.

[37]. NBA Hall of Fame video tribute by Blake Griffin, NBA All-Star, All Rights Reserved NBA and Basketball Hall of Fame.

[38]. Wikipedia, "Sonny Hertzberg."

OTHER REFERENCES AND SOURCES

1. Frostino, Nino (2004). Right on the Numbers. Trafford Publishing. ISBN 1-4120-3305-5. Retrieved February 6, 2011.
2. Jewish Sports Legends: The International Jewish Hall of Fame. Brassey's. 2000. ISBN 9781574882841. Retrieved February 6, 2011.
3. Wertsman, Vladimir F. (July 22, 2010). Salute to the Romanian Jews in America and Canada, 1850–2010. ISBN 9781453512807. Retrieved February 6, 2011.
4. Schayes, Adolph ("Dolph").
5. Othello Harris, George Kirsch, Claire Nolte (April 2000). Encyclopedia of Ethnicity and Sports in the United States. Westport, Connecticut: Greenwood Publishing Group. p. 401. ISBN 0-313-29911-0.
6. "The Depth of Ethnicity: Jewish Identity and Ideology in Interwar New York City" (PDF). Retrieved February 6, 2011.
7. Goldman, David J. (January 2006). Jewish Sports Stars: Athletic Heroes Past and Present. ISBN 9781580131834. Retrieved February 6, 2011.
8. Goldstein, Richard (December 10, 2015). "Dolph Schayes, a Bridge to Modern Basketball, Is Dead at 87". The New York Times.
9. Pluto, Terry (October 2000). Tall Tales: The Glory Years of the NBA. ISBN 0803287666. Retrieved February 6, 2011.
10. "Dolph Schayes NBA & ABA Statistics". Basketball-Reference.com. Retrieved February 6, 2011.
11. "NBA.com Schayes Summary". Retrieved August 26, 2007.
12. "NBL Rookie of the Year Award Winners". Basketball-Reference. com. Retrieved February 6, 2011.
13. Stewart, Mark (August 2007). The Philadelphia 76ers. ISBN 9781599531250. Retrieved February 6, 2011.
14. Purdy, Dennis (February 23, 2010). Kiss 'Em Goodbye: An ESPN Treasury of Failed, Forgotten, and Departed Teams. ISBN 9780345520470. Retrieved February 6, 2011.

15. *Who's Better, Who's Best in Basketball?: Mr. Stats Sets the Record Straight on the Top 50 NBA Players of All Time.* McGraw Hill. 2003. ISBN 9780071417884. Retrieved February 6, 2011.

16. Brown, Donald H. (October 2, 2007). A Basketball Handbook. ISBN 9781467805728. Retrieved February 6, 2011.

17. Gentile, Derek (2003). Smooth Moves: Juking, Jamming, Hooking & Slamming: Basketball's Plays, Players, Action &Style. ISBN 9781579122843. Retrieved February 6, 2011.

18. Wechsler, Bob (2008). Day by Dday in Jewish Sports History. ISBN 9781602800137. Retrieved February 6, 2011.

19. "Basketball-Reference.com: Dolph Schayes". Retrieved August 26, 2007.

20. Danilov, Victor J. (1997). *Hall of Fame Museums: A Reference Guide.* ISBN 9780313300004. Retrieved February 6, 2011.

21. Encyclopedia of Ethnicity and Sports in the United States. Greenwood Publishing Group. 2000. p. 402. Retrieved February 6, 2011. Dolph Schayes.

22. Carlson, Chris. "Dolph Schayes Will Have His Number Retired by Philadelphia 76ers". Syracuse. Syracuse Media Group. Retrieved March 12, 2016.

23. "Syracuse Crunch to Retire Jersey of Hall of Famer and 12-Time NBA All-Star Dolph Schayes March 26". Syracuse Crunch. February 23, 2016. Retrieved March 3, 2016.

24. Siegman, Joseph M. (May 19, 1928). The International Jewish Sports Hall of Fame. ISBN 9781561710287. Retrieved February 6, 2011.

25. Ellis Island to Ebbets Field: Sport and the American Jewish Experience. Oxford University Press. 1992. p. 316. Retrieved February 6, 2011. Dolph Schayes.

26. Klein, Steve. "NBA Hall-of-Famer Says Games in Israel Forged His Jewish Identity". Haaretz. Retrieved February 6, 2011.

27. "The Greatest – by Marc Tracy". Tablet Magazine. December 1, 2010. Retrieved February 6, 2011.

28. Araton, Harvey (September 19, 2001). "Sports of the Times – Giving in Wasn't the Answer". The New York Times. Retrieved February 6, 2011.

29. Goldin, Howard (May 18, 2015). "NBA Hall of Famer Adolph Schayes Inducted into the Bronx Walk of Fame". New York Sports Day. Retrieved June 10, 2015.

30. "Former Syracuse Nationals Star Dolph Schayes Dies at Age 87". Syracuse.com.

31. "Davies, 'Bob' (Robert E.)". HickokSports.com. Archived from the original on February 23, 2002. Retrieved March 17, 2007.

32. "Ossie Schectman, N.B.A.'s First Scorer, Dies at 94". The New York Times. Retrieved July 31, 2013.

33. Goldstein, Richard (July 30, 2013). "Ossie Schectman, N.B.A.'s First Scorer, Dies at 94". The New York Times.

34. "LIU Brooklyn to Honor Knick Who Scored the First Basket in NBA History". liu.edu. Retrieved July 31, 2013.

35. "Schectman, Ossie". Jews in Sports. Retrieved February 26, 2014.

36. "Do You Know Who Scored THE FIRST BASKET in the NBA?". Thefirstbasket.com. November 1, 1946. Archived from the original on June 25, 2003. Retrieved February 25, 2014.

37. "The Story". The First Basket. November 1, 1946. Archived from the original on March 7, 2009. Retrieved October 19, 2010.

38. "1946-47 BAA Player Stats: Per Game | Basketball-Reference.com". Basketball-Reference.com. Retrieved March 28, 2017.

39. Ossie Schectman at the National Jewish Sports Hall of Fame.

40. Corio, Ray (June 21, 2003). "Dave Polansky, 83, Who Guided City College Team After Scandal, Dies". The New York Times.

41. Goldstein, Richard (October 24, 2005). "Lou Rossini, N.Y. Basketball Coach, Dies at 84". The New York Times. Retrieved April 12, 2017.

42. "Press Maravich". bcshof.org.

43. "Press Maravich's Record vs. Kentucky". bigbluehistory.net.

44. Politika (January 4, 2018). "Velikan NBA srpskog porekla" (in Serbian). Retrieved June 27, 2020.

45. "LSU Fighting Tigers Coaches". sports-reference.com. Retrieved July 29, 2018.

46. One More Time: The Best of Mike Royko. University of Chicago. 1999, p. 29–31.

47. http://www.baseball-almanac.com/legendary/baseball_and_basketball_players.shtml

48. Richman, Joe (June 5, 1997). "The Starting Five". All Things Considered. National Public Radio. Retrieved July 11, 2007.

49. "Ralph Kaplowitz Stats". Basketball Reference. Retrieved June 26, 2017.

50. Maoz, Jason (June 27, 2007). "Court Jews: Pro Basketball's Forgotten History". The Jewish Press. Retrieved July 11, 2007.

51. Former FDU Men's Basketball Coach Dick Holub Passes Away. Northeast Conference. August 6, 2009. Retrieved December 18, 2012.

52. Former LIU Star Holub Dies at 87. ESPN. August 7, 2009. Retrieved August 10, 2009.

53. "Former Philadelphia Warriors Player Hank Beenders Dies at 87". Burlington County Times, October 27, 2003.

54. Hank Beenders. Basketball-Reference.com. Retrieved September 22, 2007.

55. "Beenders Played in NBA Forerunner". ESPN Classic, October 27, 2003. Retrieved July 15, 2007.

56. Ron Thomas. They Cleared the Lane Archived August 10, 2007, at the Wayback Machine. HoopsHype. Retrieved August 16, 2007.

57. Out of the Shadows Archived August 7, 2007, at the Wayback Machine. Retrieved August 16, 2007.

58. BBallSports Statistical Database. Retrieved August 16, 2007.

59. Known Deceased Basketball Individuals. APBR.org. Retrieved August 16, 2007.

60. "LIU Streaks". Archived from the original on December 22, 2004. Retrieved January 6, 2005.

61. "Archived Copy". Archived from the original on July 26, 2009. Retrieved July 22, 2009.

62. Luchter, P. S. (May 21, 2010). "Long Island University All-Time Football Records". List of Amazing Sports Lists. Retrieved February 4, 2020.

63. Basketball Hall of Fame Bio.

64. ESPN, ed. (2009). ESPN College Basketball Encyclopedia: The Complete History of the Men's Game. New York: ESPN Books. p. 544. ISBN 978-0-345-51392-2.

65. "Goldsmith, Garden Darling, Refutes Idea Star of Today Must Be One with Altitude". News-Herald, Franklin, PA. January 4, 1946. p. 8. Retrieved February 16, 2015 – via Newspapers.com.

66. "Police Probing into History of Jackie Goldsmith". The Sheboygan Press. April 25, 1951. p. 25. Retrieved February 16, 2015 – via Newspapers.com.

67. Goldstein, Joe (November 19, 2003). "Explosion: 1951 Scandals Threaten College Hoops". ESPN.com. Retrieved February 16, 2015.

68. "Molinas, Jack". JewsinSports.org. Retrieved March 12, 2008.

69. Konigsberg, Eric (2002-03-03). "Double Dribbling". The New York Times. Retrieved November 2, 2007.

70. "Molinas Presses $3,000,000 Case; Ex-Court Ace Sues N.B.A. for Banning Him After He Bet on Own Team". The New York Times. January 3, 1961.

71. "Molinas Loses Antitrust Suit". New York Times. January 12, 1961.

72. "Molinas's Past Sifted For Clues". The New York Times. August 6, 1975.

73. Goldstein, Joe (November 19, 2003). "Explosion II: The Molinas Period". ESPN.com. Retrieved November 10, 2012.

74. "ESPN Classic - Explosion II: The Molinas period". www.espn.com. Retrieved May 21, 2019.

75. Kudler, Adrian Glick (August 16, 2011). "House Where Point Shaver/ Pornographer Jack Molinas Was Killed". Curbed LA. Retrieved May 21, 2019.

1. Cohen Family Photo, Passover, 1940, The Cohens, left to right Saul, Abraham (Father), Israel, Jennie (Mother), Mary, Rose, Bennie, and Murray, Page 30.
2. Abraham and Jenny Cohen, 1940, Page 31.
3. Newspaper article showing life in the Warsaw Ghetto, Poland 1939, Page 32.
4. Creston Schoolyard crew at dinner, all grown up. Hirschfield, Wallack, Sencer, Lesser, Mintz, etc, Page 33.
5. Arthur Reichner, Spider Lester Mintz, Milty Gries horsing around in the Catskills at the Nevele, Page 149.
6. Mrs. Spider, the elegant, Bernice Rosenthal Cohen, the author's mother, Page 149.
7. Schoolyard pals forever at the Nevele at dinner, Dolph Schayes, Spider, Milty Gries, Flicky Fields, and others, Page 150.
8. Spider, Michael Wallack (Genie's son), with NY Knick, Carl Braun at the Jericho Country Club, 1959, Page 151.
9. DeWitt Clinton High School varsity basketball team, New York City, Champions 1937, Page 159.
10. Lucio Rossini photo, Page 168.
11. Dolph Schayes at the Nevele Country Club, Page 183.
12. Dolph Schayes, image of signed photo, Top 50 All Times players and Hall of Fame Induction, Page 184.
13. The Nevele Country Counselor Team, Nevele Country Club Basketball Team with the schoolyard gang left to right NBA Hall of Famer Dolph Schayes, unknown player, Lester Mintz, Flicky Fields, Saul Cohen, Milty Gries, and Arthur Reichner, Page 185.
14. LIU vs. Oregon, Saul Cohen, Madison Square Garden Page 195.
15. LIU NIT 1942 vs West Virginia Saul Cohen photo, Page 196.
16. Photo Duquesne vs. LIU at Madison Square Garden February 8, 1941, the last game LIU would lose before reeling off 11 straight to win

the National Intercollegiate Men's Basketball Championship, Ossie Schectman #24, Saul Cohen #29, Hank Beenders #30 for LIU, Paul Widowitz #12 and #5 Moe Becker for Duquesne. Becker hit a half-court shot at the buzzer for the 36–34 Duquesne victory, Page 197.

17. LIU vs. Rice, Madison Square Garden, 1940, Spider against Selmen of Rice, Page 198.

18. Spider vs. Rice and Chester Palmer in Madison Square Garden, Speed Ray photography, Page 199.

19. Saul Cohen 41 LIU vs Gene Rock #9 Southern California 1942, LIU Lost 48–40, Saul had 19 points, Coach Bee called him "simply the best" in the *Brooklyn Eagle* paper, Page 200.

20. Saul Cohen, #41 Long Island University, holding the ball with the seams for the photo, Page 201.

21. Photo of the famous 1935–1936 LIU Undefeated National Championship Team with left to right players Schwartz, Norton, Merson, Hillhouse, Russo, Kramer (C), and Bender, that boycotted the 1936 Olympics; also Photos of the St. John's, CCNY, NYU, Fordham, and St. Francis Basketball Teams, Page 212.

22. LIU 1941 team photo, prior to Dolly King graduation mid-season, Page 213.

23. LIU Fundamentals of Good Basketball, Clair Bee, Page 214.

24. Photo Saul Cohen and Moe Becker LIU vs. Duquesne, Page 215.

25. LIU vs. Oregon Saul Cohen #29, Sy Lobello #26 for LIU and McNeely of Oregon at Madison Square Garden, December 14, 1940, Page 216.

26. Coach Clair Bee Coaching Record, Page 217.

27. All-Time Best Men's College Basketball Winning Percentage, Page 218.

28. Coach Clair Bee, Page 221.

29. SS *Borinquen* carried passengers to and from Puerto Rico, Page 222.

30. Saul "Spider" Cohen, Hank Beenders, Dolly King, Sy Lobello, and Frank Fucarino, on SS *Borinquen* between New York City and San Juan Puerto Rico, Page 223.

46. Creston Schoolyard pals top left clockwise, Dave Polansky, Lou Rossini, Saul Cohen, Gene Wallack, Page 396.
47. Long Island University Players, Coaches, and Alumni Basketball Army Enlistment Photo (Top left to right : Sol "Butch Schwartz," Coach "Pic" Picarello, Irving Torghoff, Ossie Schechtman, Mike Sewtich, Pop Gates, Irving Rothenberg, Julie Bender, Art Hillhouse, Howie Rader, Dolly King, Freddie Lewis, Dick Holub, Lennie Rader, Leo Merson, Coach Clair Bee. Bottom row, left to right: Marius "Lefty" Russo, Max Sharf, Saul "Spider" Cohen, Phil Rabinowitz, and Lou Simon, Page 397.
48. Spider in the army in Europe, circa 1944 Page 398.
49. Spider marching in snow, Europe parts unknown, circa 1945, Page 399.
50. Spider and army buddy celebrate VJ Day in Europe ending the war, Page 399.
51. Scandal over, Mrs. Sollazzo gets in a cab after husband convicted for point-shaving basketball scandal, Page 402.
52. Saul Cohen, ABL Gothams high scorer box score, Page 405.
53. ABL Gothams draw praise from Philadelphia Sphas, box score with Spider top scorer, Page 406.
54. ABL Gothams top Crescents, Spider high point man, Page 406.
55. LIU and Hunter's Field Box Scores, Saul Cohen top scorer, Page 407.
56. ABL Gothams Team photo, Brooklyn Gothams Professional Basketball (ABL) Team (1946), Saul Cohen, holding basketball to the right, and bottom extreme right schoolyard pal Lester Mintz, who almost strangled Luccio Rossini on a schoolyard bet, Page 408.
57. Photos Top: Victor Mario Perez and the author Barry Cohen, 1998 San Juan Puerto Rico; Middle: Saul Cohen and Ossie Schectman; Bottom: Saul Cohen, Ossie Schectman, and Butch Schwartz, South Florida Basketball Luncheon, Polo Club, Boca Raton, Florida, Page 409.
58. Saul Spider Cohen, 1941, and Barry Cohen, the author, 1972, dribbling for their respective school basketball; photos at LIU and University of Vermont, respectively, Page 419.

NOTABLE PERSONS MENTIONED AND THEIR RECORDS AND STATISTICS

1. Dolph Schayes
2. Bob Davies
3. Butch Schwartz
4. Ossie Schechtman
5. Dave Polansky
6. Lou Rossini
7. Petar Maravich
8. Frankie Baumholtz
9. Ralph Kaplowitz
10. Simon Lobello
11. Saul Cohen
12. Dick Holub
13. Hank Beenders
14. Dolly King
15. Clair Bee
16. Jackie Goldsmith
17. Jack Molinas

DOLPH SCHAYES

Adolph Schayes (May 19, 1928–December 10, 2015) was an American professional basketball player and coach in the National Basketball Association (NBA). A top scorer and rebounder, he was a 12-time NBA All-Star and a 12-time All-NBA selection. Schayes won an NBA championship with the Syracuse Nationals in 1955. He was named one of the 50 Greatest Players in NBA History and inducted into the Naismith Memorial Basketball Hall of Fame.

Schayes played his entire career with the Nationals and their successor, the Philadelphia 76ers, from 1948 to 1964. In his 16-year career, he led his team into the playoffs 15 times. After the Nationals moved to Philadelphia, Schayes became player-coach of the newly minted 76ers. He retired after the 1963–64 season and stayed on as coach for two more seasons, earning NBA Coach of the Year honors in 1966. He briefly coached with the Buffalo Braves.

He attended Creston Junior High School 79 and DeWitt Clinton High School in the Bronx, New York, where he played for the basketball team and led it to a borough championship. He played his college basketball at New York University (NYU) in 1944–48. In 1945, as a 16-year-old freshman, Schayes helped NYU reach the NCAA final. Schayes earned an aeronautical engineering degree, was an All-American in basketball, and won the Haggerty Award in his final year.

Source: Dolph Schayes—https://en.wikipedia.org

DOLPH SCHAYES (continued)

Regular season

Year	Team	GP	MPG	FG%	FT%	RPG	APG	PPG
1949–50	Syracuse	64	–	.385	.774	–	4.0	16.8
1950–51	Syracuse	66	–	.357	.752	16.4*	3.8	17.0
1951–52	Syracuse	63	31.8	.355	.807	12.3	2.9	13.8
1952–53	Syracuse	71	37.6	.374	.827	13.0	3.2	17.8
1953–54	Syracuse	72	36.9	.380	.827	12.1	3.0	17.1
1954–55†	Syracuse	72	35.1	.383	.833	12.3	3.0	18.5
1955–56	Syracuse	72	35.0	.387	.858	12.4	2.8	20.4
1956–57	Syracuse	72	39.6*	.379	.904	14.0	3.2	22.5
1957–58	Syracuse	72	40.5*	.398	.904*	14.2	3.1	24.9
1958–59	Syracuse	72	36.7	.387	.864	13.4	2.5	21.3
1959–60	Syracuse	75	36.5	.401	.893*	12.8	3.4	22.5
1960–61	Syracuse	79	38.1	.372	.868	12.2	3.7	23.6
1961–62	Syracuse	56	26.4	.357	.897*	7.8	2.1	14.7
1962–63	Syracuse	66	21.8	.388	.879	5.7	2.7	9.5
1963–64	Philadelphia	24	14.6	.308	.807	4.6	2.0	5.6
Career		996	34.4	.380	.849	12.1	3.1	18.5
All-Star		11	22.5	.440	.840	9.5	1.5	12.5

Playoffs

Year	Team	GP	MPG	FG%	FT%	RPG	APG	PPG
1950	Syracuse	11	–	.385	.733	–	2.5	17.1
1951	Syracuse	7	–	.448	.766	14.6	2.9	20.4
1952	Syracuse	7	35.4	.451	.769	12.9	2.1	20.3
1953	Syracuse	2	29.0	.250	.769	8.5	0.5	9.0
1954	Syracuse	13	28.8	.457	.741	10.5	1.8	16.0
1955†	Syracuse	11	33.0	.359	.840	12.8	3.6	19.0
1956	Syracuse	8	38.8	.366	.880	13.9	3.4	22.1
1957	Syracuse	5	43.0	.305	.891	18.0	2.8	21.4
1958	Syracuse	3	43.7	.391	.833	15.0	3.1	26.7
1959	Syracuse	9	39.0	.400	.916	13.0	4.6	28.2
1960	Syracuse	3	42.0	.455	.933	16.0	2.7	29.3
1961	Syracuse	8	38.5	.336	.900	11.4	2.6	20.6
1962	Syracuse	5	19.0	.364	.692	7.0	1.0	11.4
1963	Syracuse	5	21.6	.455	.917	5.6	1.4	10.2
Career		97	34.0	.390	.825	12.2	2.6	19.5

BOB DAVIES

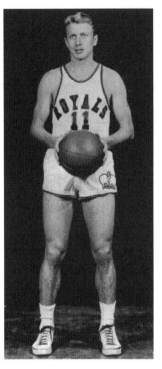

Robert Edris Davies (January 15, 1920–April 22, 1990) was an American professional basketball player. Alongside Bobby Wanzer he formed one of the best backcourt duos in the National Basketball Association's early years. Davies and Wanzer led the Rochester Royals to the 1951 NBA championship. Davies was also a former basketball coach at the Seton Hall University and was inducted to the Naismith Memorial Basketball Hall of Fame on April 11, 1970.

Davies entered Seton Hall in 1938 on a <u>baseball</u> scholarship, but Russell persuaded him to concentrate on basketball after seeing him practice once. Never a high scorer—his best college average was 11.8 points a game—Davies was a consummate passer and play-maker.

Known as the "Harrisburg Houdini," Davies led Seton Hall to 43 consecutive victories from 1939 into 1941. His spectacular skills helped attract the largest crowd in basketball history at the time, 18,403 people, to <u>Madison Square Garden</u> in March 1941, when Seton Hall beat <u>Rhode Island</u> in a quarter-final game of the <u>National Invitation Tournament</u>.

An All-American guard in 1941 and 1942, Davies joined the <u>U S Navy</u> during World War II and led the Great Lakes Naval Training Station team to a 34–3 record before going overseas.

Source: Bob Davies—https://en.wikipedia.org

BOB DAVIES (continued)

Regular season

Year	Team	GP	MPG	FG%	FT%	RPG	APG	PPG
1948–49	Rochester	60	–	.364	.776	–	5.4*	15.1
1949–50	Rochester	64	–	.357	.752	–	4.6	14.0
1950–51†	Rochester	63	–	.372	.795	3.1	4.6	15.2
1951–52	Rochester	65	36.8	.383	.776	2.9	6.0	16.2
1952–53	Rochester	66	33.6	.385	.753	3.0	4.2	15.6
1953–54	Rochester	72	29.7	.371	.718	2.7	4.5	12.3
1954–55	Rochester	72	26.0	.415	.751	2.8	4.9	12.1
Career		462	31.3	.378	.759	2.9	4.9	14.3
All-Star		4	18.8	.475	.714	3.3	4.3	12.0

Playoffs

Year	Team	GP	MPG	FG%	FT%	RPG	APG	PPG
1949	Rochester	4	–	.373	.769	–	3.3	12.0
1950	Rochester	2	–	.235	.875	–	4.5	7.5
1951†	Rochester	14	–	.338	.800	3.1	5.4	15.9
1952	Rochester	6	38.8	.402	.818	2.2	4.7	19.8
1953	Rochester	3	30.3	.207	.700	1.3	4.7	8.7
1954	Rochester	6	28.7	.327	.739	2.0	2.3	8.5
1955	Rochester	3	25.0	.333	.750	2.0	3.0	8.3
Career		38	31.7	.341	.788	2.4	4.3	13.3

BUTCH SCHWARTZ

After playing basketball at LIU, Schwartz went on to the New York Jewels before landing with the SPHAs. He played with the SPHAs for six seasons, missing a year and a half to serve in the US Navy during World War II.

Source: Butch Schwartz—http:// peachbasketsociety.blogspot. com/

BUTCH SCHWARTZ (continued)

Year	Team	GA	FGM	FTM	FTA	PCT.	AST	PTS	AVG
1937-38	Long Island (Frosh)								
1938-39	Long Island	20						91	4.6
1939-40	Long Island	22						208	9.5
1940-41	Long Island	24						207	8.6
1941-42	NY/PA	10	15	5				35	3.5
1941-42	Saratoga NYSL	14	45	23				113	8.1
1941-42	Long island								
1942-43	Philadelphia	12	37	16				90	7.5
1942-43	Long Island	21						179	8.5
1943-44	Philadelphia	20	54	27				135	6.8
1944-46	US Navy Military Service								
1945-46	Philadelphia	7	6	6				18	2.6
1946-47	Philadelphia	32	94	60				248	7.8
1947-48	Philadelphia	5	8	6	10	.600		22	4.4
1948-49	Paterson ABL	24	56	46	69	.667		158	6.6
1948-49	Danbury ECL								
1949-50	Trenton ABL	2	2	2	2	1.000	2	6	3.0
Major League Totals		49	112	54				278	5.7

			POST SEASON ROSTER						
Year	Team	GA	FGM	FTM	FTA	PCT.	AST	PTS	AVG
1942-43	Long Island	4	12	0	2	.000		24	6.0
1942-43	Philadelphia	7	18	8				44	6.3
1943-44	Philadelphia	5	2	0				4	0.8
1945-46	Philadelphia	6	5	4				14	2.3
1946-47	Philadelphia	4	15	18				48	12.0
Major League Totals		22	37	12				86	3.9

OSSIE SCHECTMAN

Oscar Benny "Ossie" Schectman (May 30, 1919–July 30, 2013) was an American professional basketball player. He is credited with having scored the first basket in the Basketball Association of America (BAA), which would later become the National Basketball Association (NBA).

Schectman was born on May 30, 1919, in Brooklyn, New York City. His parents were Jewish immigrants from Russia. He had three siblings. He played basketball and baseball while attending Samuel J. Tilden High School in Brooklyn, New York, and played under coach Clair Bee at Long Island University. He was a member of the team in 1939, when they won the National Invitation Tournament and National Championship. He was named to the Converse All-American first team in 1941

After obtaining his degree from LIU, Schectman played for Eddie Gottlieb's Philadelphia SPHAs in the American Basketball League. The Sphas joined the ABL in 1933 and won the league championship in 1942–43. He was second in the league in scoring with 199 points (10.5 average) in 1943–44. He played with the SPHAs until 1946, when he joined the New York Knicks of the Basketball Association of America.

Source: Ossie Schectman—https://en.wikipedia.org

Regular season

Year	Team	GP	FG%	FT%	APG	PPG
1946–47	New York	54	.276	.620	2.0	8.1
Career		54	.276	.620	2.0	8.1

DAVID POLANSKY

David Polansky (November 16, 1919–June 16, 2003) was an American basketball coach. As an assistant, he replaced Nat Holman three times as head basketball coach at City College of New York (CCNY). Polansky first took over in 1952 when Holman was suspended after the 1951 betting scandals wrecked the Beavers program. After Holman won reinstatement, Polansky remained his assistant in 1954 and twice relieved his boss again (illness in 1956 and retirement in 1959). He then coached CCNY for 10 full seasons before his own resignation in February  1971, after an 82–80 loss to Pace. Although Polansky had only six losing seasons in 15 years, he finished with a 127–135 overall record. Following his coaching career, Polansky purchased Camp Kent, a summer camp located in Kent, CT, and owned and directed the camp until it closed in 1982. In the decades following its closing, the Camp Kent community remained particularly close-knit, holding frequent reunions and maintaining lifelong friendships. In the social media era, the Camp Kent alumni community is more closely connected than ever, holding even more frequent outings and reunions.

Source: David Polansky—https://en.wikipedia.org

Coaching Record—David Polansky

Coaching Record

Season	School	Conf	G	W	L	W-L%	SRS	SOS
1952-53	City College of NY	Metro NY	16	10	6	.625	-8.86	-0.14
1953-54	City College of NY	Metro NY	18	10	8	.556		
1956-57	City College of NY	Metro NY	19	11	8	.579		
1957-58	City College of NY	Metro NY	17	9	8	.529		
1959-60	City College of NY	Metro NY	14	4	10	.286		
1960-61	City College of NY	Metro NY	17	7	10	.412		
1961-62	City College of NY	Metro NY	18	9	9	.500		
1962-63	City College of NY	Metro NY	18	8	10	.444		
Career			137	68	69	.495	-8.86	-0.14

LOU ROSSINI

Lucio "Lou" Rossini (April 24, 1921– October 21, 2005) was an American college basketball coach. He compiled a 357–256 record in almost 20 years of coaching, most notably with New York University (NYU).

In Rossini's first year as head coach with Columbia University, he guided them to a 21–1 record and an appearance in the 1951 NCAA Basketball Tournament. After Columbia, Rossini coached at NYU, leading them to three NCAA Tournament appearances and four National Invitation Tournament (NIT) bids in 13 seasons. Rossini last coached in the NCAA for St. Francis College in Brooklyn, from 1975 to 1979, and had a 55–48 record. He also coached the Puerto Rican national team in the 1964 and 1968 Olympics and the Qatar national team in the 1980s.

Two of his best players at NYU were Happy Hairston and Barry Kramer, who starred on the 1963 and 1964 teams. Hairston and Kramer advanced to professional careers. He also coached Puerto Rico's national team at the 1964 and 1968 Olympics.

Rossini died at his home in the Sewell section of Mantua Township, New Jersey, aged 84. The cause of death was Alzheimer's disease.

Source: Lou Rossini—https://en.wikipedia.org

LOU ROSSINI (continued)

Head Coaching Record

		Statistics Overview			
Season	Team	Overall	Conference	Standing	Postseason
Columbia Lions (Eastern Intercollegiate Basketball League) (1950–1954)					
1950–51	Columbia	21–1	12–0	1st	NCAA First Round
1951–52	Columbia	12–10	7–5	4th	
1952–53	Columbia	17–10	8–4	2nd	
1953–54	Columbia	11–13	6–8	5th	
Columbia Lions (Ivy League) (1954–1958)					
1954–55	Columbia	17–8	10–4	T–2nd	
1955–56	Columbia	15–9	9–5	T–2nd	
1956–57	Columbia	18–6	9–5	T–3rd	
1957–58	Columbia	6–18	2–12	8th	
	Columbia: 117–71		63–43		
NYU Violets (Metropolitan New York Conference) (1958–1963)					
1958–59	NYU	15–8	2–2	T–4th	
1959–60	NYU	22–5	4–0	1st	NCAA University Division Final Four
1960–61	NYU	12–11	2–1	T–2nd	
1961–62	NYU	20–5	3–2	3rd	NCAA University Division Regional Third Place
1962–63	NYU	18–5	3–1	2nd	NCAA University Division Regional Fourth Place
NYU Violets (Independent) (1963–1965)					
1963–64	NYU	17–10			NIT Semifinal
1964–65	NYU	16–10			NIT Semifinal
NYU Violets (Metropolitan Collegiate Conference) (1965–1967)					
1965–66	NYU	18–10	7–2	T–2nd	NIT Runner-up
1966–67	NYU	10–6	6–3	4th	
NYU Violets (Independent) (1967–1971)					
1967–68	NYU	8–16			
1968–69	NYU	12–9			
1969–70	NYU	12–12			
1970–71	NYU	5–20			
	NYU:	185–127	27–11		
St. Francis Terriers (NCAA Division I independent) (1975–1979)					
1975–76	St. Francis	13–13			
1976–77	St. Francis	12–14			
1977–78	St. Francis	16–9			
1978–79	St. Francis	14–12			
	St. Francis: 55–48				
Total:		357–256			

PRESS MARAVICH

Petar "Press" Maravich (August 29, 1915–April 15, 1987) was an American college and professional basketball coach. He received the nickname "Press" as a boy, when one of his jobs was selling the *Pittsburgh Press* on the streets of his hometown of Aliquippa, Pennsylvania, an industrial city outside of Pittsburgh. Maravich Sr. also served in the United States Naval Air Corps during World War II. Despite a long career as a coach, Maravich may best be remembered as "Pistol" Pete Maravich's father. Maravich graduated from Davis & Elkins College in 1941 and was a member of the Alpha Sigma Phi fraternity.

Press Maravich's first head coaching job at the college level was West Virginia Wesleyan College, 1949–1950. From there he went on to become head coach of his alma mater, Davis & Elkins, from 1950 to 1952. He had previously served as an assistant under Red Brown from 1947 to 1949.

Maravich was head coach of the Tigers of Clemson University from 1956 to 1962. He then went to North Carolina State University to be an assistant coach under Everett Case. Maravich took over the head coaching duties when health problems, primarily cancer, forced Case to retire early in the 1964–1965 season. Maravich led the Wolfpack to the Atlantic Coast Conference title that season. Maravich left for Louisiana State University in April 1966 where he coached his son, Pete Maravich.[4] Upon offering the LSU scholarship to "Pistol," "Press" told his boy that "If you don't sign this ... don't ever come into my house again." (*Pistol: The Life of Pete Maravich*). Pete, originally wanted to go to the West Virginia University but finally agreed to go to LSU if his dad bought him a car. (Pistol: The Life of Pete Maravich.) In spite of coaching his prolific son for half of his coaching career at LSU, Maravich had an overall losing record at the school. Maravich was replaced at LSU by Dale Brown in 1972. He then went on to coach the Mountaineers of Appalachian State, shepherding them through their early years in Division I, before retiring from coaching in 1975. Maravich returned to coaching in the early 1980s as associate head coach at Campbell University.

Source: Press Maravich—https://en.wikipedia.org

Year	Team	GP	FG%	FT%	APG	PPG
				Regular Season		
1946–47	Pittsburgh	51	.272	.517	.1	4.6
	Career	51	.272	.517	.1	4.6

Head Coaching Record
College
Statistics Overview

Season	Team	Overall	Conf	Standing	Postseason
West Virginia Wesleyan Bobcats (West Virginia Intercollegiate Athletic Conference) (1949–1950)					
1949–50	West Virginia Wesleyan	14–10			
	West Virginia Wesleyan:	14–10			
Davis & Elkins Senators (West Virginia Intercollegiate Athletic Conference) (1950–1952)					
1950–51	Davis & Elkins	18–11			
1951–52	Davis & Elkins	19–10			
	Davis & Elkins:	37–21			
Clemson Tigers (Atlantic Coast Conference) (1956–1962)					
1956–57	Clemson	7–17	3–11	T–7th	
1957–58	Clemson	8–16	4–10	6th	
1958–59	Clemson	8–16	5–9	T–6th	
1959–60	Clemson	10–16	4–10	7th	
1960–61	Clemson	10–16	5–9	6th	
1961–62	Clemson	12–15	4–10	6th	
	Clemson:	55–96	25–59		
NC State Wolfpack (Atlantic Coast Conference) (1964–1966)					
1964–65	NC State	20–4	10–4	T–2nd	NCAA 3rd Place
1965–66	NC State	18–9	9–5	2nd	
	NC State:	38–13	19–9		
LSU Tigers (Southeastern Conference) (1966–1972)					
1966–67	LSU	3–23	1–17	10th	
1967–68	LSU	14–12	8–10	T–6th	
1968–69	LSU	13–13	7–11	T–7th	
1969–70	LSU	22–10	13–5	2nd	NIT 4rth Place
1970–71	LSU	14–12	10–8	3rd	
1971–72	LSU	10–16	6–12	T–7th	
	LSU:	76–86	45–63		
Appalachian State Mountaineers (Southern Conference) (1972–1975)					
1972–73	Appalachian State	6–20	3–8	7th	
1973–74	Appalachian State	5–20	1–11	8th	
1974–75	Appalachian State	1–11	0–5		
	Appalachian State:	12–51	4–24		
Total:		232–277			

FRANK BAUMHOLTZ

FRANK CONRAD BAUMHOLTZ (OCTOBER 7, 1918–December 14, 1997) was an American professional baseball and basketball player. He was an outfielder for Major League Baseball's Cincinnati Reds (1947–49), Chicago Cubs (1949 and 1951–55) and Philadelphia Phillies (1956–57). He played two seasons of professional basketball for the Youngstown Bears of the National Basketball League during the 1945–46 season, and the Cleveland Rebels of the Basketball Association of America during the 1946–47 season. He was born in Midvale, Ohio.

Baumholtz played college basketball at Ohio University, playing the guard position. Baumholtz was a first-team All-American in basketball in 1941, his senior year, leading the Bobcats to the finals of the 1941 National Invitation Tournament, the most prestigious tournament in the country at the time. He was named the tournament's most valuable player. His No. 54 jersey hangs from the rafters of the Convocation Center. It was retired on February 4, 1995, which was declared "Frank Baumholtz Day" in the city of Athens, Ohio, and on campus and was the only number so honored at the school until 2007 when Dave Jamerson and Walter Luckett had their jerseys retired as well.

Source: Frank Baumholtz—https://en.wikipedia.org

Regular season

Year	Team	GP	FG%	FT%	APG	PPG
1946–47	Cleveland	45	.298	.776	1.2	14.0
Career		45	.298	.776	1.2	14.0

RALPH KAPLOWITZ

Ralph Kaplowitz (May 18, 1919–February 2, 2009) was an American professional basketball player. Kaplowitz played in the first two seasons of the Basketball Association of America (BAA), now known as the National Basketball Association (NBA), and was, at the time of his death, the oldest living person to have played for the New York Knicks.

Kaplowitz attended DeWitt Clinton High School and led his team to a PSAL championship. After graduating from Clinton, he attended New York University. He joined NYU's varsity team as a sophomore in 1939–40, was the team's second-leading scorer with 183 points, and was named to the Collier's Magazine All-America first team. In his junior year, Kaplowitz did lead NYU in scoring, and to a winning record of 13–6. At the start of his senior year he was named team captain, but was drafted into the US Army as an aviation cadet. After his basketball career, Ralph went on to thrive in other athletics. He is noted as winning multiple club championships at Old Westbury Golf and Country Club.

Source: Ralph Kaplowitz—https://en.wikipedia.org

RALPH KAPLOWITZ (continued)

Regular season

Year	Team	GP	FG%	FT%	APG	PPG
1946–47	New York	27	.259	.732	.9	7.2
1946–47†	Philadelphia	30	.291	.738	.4	7.0
1947–48	Philadelphia	48	.243	.783	.4	3.9
Career		105	.263	.749	.5	5.6

Playoffs

Year	Team	GP	FG%	FT%	APG	PPG
1947†	Philadelphia	10	.224	.815	.6	6.6
1948	Philadelphia	13	.344	.759	.5	6.6
Career		23	.283	.786	.6	6.6

SY LOBELLO

SY Lobello played basketball for Long Island University from 1938 through 1941. Lobello led the team in scoring for two consecutive seasons and tallied a then school-record 282 points during the 1938–39 campaign. During Lobllo's years at LIU the Blackbirds won two consecutive National Invitational Tournament Championships, and posted an undefeated season (24–0) in 1939–40. Lobello briefly played professional basketball before entering military service in 1943. Lobello was killed in action during the Battle of the Bulge in March of 1945.

Source: SY Lobello—https://probasketballencyclopedia.com/

Year	Team	League		GA	FGM	FTM	FTA	PCT.	AST	PTS	AVG
1937-38		L.I.U.(Frosh)	College								
1938-39		L.I.U.	College								
1939-40		L.I.U.	College								
1940-41		L.I.U.	College								
1941-42		Long Island Gruman Flyers Indep									
1942-43		Long Island Gruman Wildcats Indep									
1943-44		Brooklyn–New York	ABL	5	13	8				34	6.8
1943-45		U.S. Army	Military Service								
		Major League Totals		5	13	8				34	6.8

POST SEASON RECORD

Year	Team	League	GA	FGM	FTM	FTA	PCT.	AST	PTS	AVG
1941-42		Long Island Grumans WBT	3	0	0	0	.000		0	0.0
		Major League Totals	3	0	0	0	.000		0	0.0

Simon Lobello

He was a World War II Era casualty on March 3, 1945. ★ He served with honor in the United States Army. ★ Remembered by the people of New York ★ May his example inspire us to be strong and responsible global citizens. We can do great things. Together.

Simon Lobello

UPLOAD IMAGE

▌SERVICE OVERVIEW

Name	Simon Lobello
From	Queens County, New York
Born	December 16, 1919
Death	March 3, 1945
War	World War II
Branch	US Army
Rank	Private First Class
Group	13th Infantry Regiment, 8th Infantry Division
Cause	Hostile, Killed in Action
Awarded	★ Bronze Star
	★ Purple Heart

ORIGINS

Simon Lobello was born on December 16, 1919. According to our records New York was his home or enlistment state and Queens County included within the archival record. We have Corona listed as the city.

SERVICE

He had enlisted in the Army. Served during World War II. He had the rank of Private First Class. Service number was 32967715. Served with 13th Infantry Regiment, 8th Infantry Division.

CASUALTY

Lobello experienced a traumatic event which resulted in loss of life on March 3, 1945. Recorded circumstances attributed to "Killed in action". Incident location: Germany.

DETAILS

Pfc Simon Lobello enlisted in New York City, New York on 10 June 1943 ... He was a former LIU basketball star.

REMEMBERED

Simon Lobello is buried or memorialized at American War Cemetery Henri-Chapelle. This is an American Battle Monuments Commission location.

COMMENDATIONS

★ Bronze Star
★ Purple Heart
★ Combat Infantryman Badge
★ Marksmanship Badge
★ World War II Victory Medal
★ American Campaign Medal
★ Army Presidential Unit Citation
★ Army Good Conduct Medal
★ European-African-Middle Eastern Campaign

PLEASE NOTE THIS MIGHT NOT BE A COMPLETE OR COMPLETELY ACCURATE ACCOUNTING. FOR SOME AWARDS WE USE PROBABILITIES BASED ON KNOWN SERVICE DETAILS.

SAUL COHEN

Born and raised in the Bronx, New York, he attended DeWitt Clinton High School, Long Island University, and NYU Law School. After graduating high school at the age of 16, he received a full scholarship to play basketball at Long Island University. At LIU, he was a member of the Blackbirds 1941 NIT Championship Team, when the NIT was considered the most prestigious college tournament. He ended his career at LIU in 1943, an All-Metropolitan Selection. In 1943 he served in the army in World War II, going into the army with his Hall of Fame Coach, Clair Bee, and fellow LIU basketballers: Butch Schwartz, Irv Torgoff, Ossie Schectman, Pop Gates, Irving Rothenberg, Julie Bender, Art Hillhouse, Howie Rader, Dolly King, Freddie Lewis, Len Rader, Leo Merson, Marius Russo, May Scharf, Phil Rabinowitz, and Lou Simon, along with Assistant Coach Pic Picarello.

SAUL COHEN (continued)

Year	Team	League	GA	FGM	FTM	FTA	PCT.	AST	PTS	AVG
1939-40	Long Island (Frosh) College									
1940-41	Long Island College									
1941-42	Long Island College									
1942-43	Long Island College									
1943-45	Military Service									
1945-46	New York	ABL	21	42	36				120	5.7
1946-47	Brooklyn	ABL	33	129	111				369	11.2
1947-48	Brooklyn-Jersey City/UnionCity/Scranton	ABL	19	73	63	76	.829		209	11.0
1948-49	Utica	NYSL	7						35	5.0
Major League Totals			23.22	44	38				126	5.4

PLAYOFF RECORD

Year	Team	League	GA	FGM	FTM	FTA	PCT.	AST	PTS	AVG
1945-46	New York	ABL	2	14	7				35	17.5
1946-47	Brooklyn	ABL	3	6	3				15	5.0
1947-48	Scranton	ABL	2	1	2				4	2.0
Major League Totals			2	14	7				35	17.5

DICK HOLUB

Richard W. Holub (October 29, 1921–
July 27, 2009) was an American basketball player and coach.

A 6-foot-6 middle-born in Racine,
Wisconsin, Holub played college basketball at Long Island University, and
was a member of an NIT championship team in 1941. His college career
was interrupted by a stint with the Air
Force during World War II, but he
returned to school in 1946, and led
his team in scoring during the 1946–47 season. After being drafted by
the New York Knicks in the 1947 BAA draft, Holub spent the 1947–
48 season with the team, and then embarked upon a seventeen-year
coaching career at Farleigh Dickinson University. During his tenure as
coach, he achieved a 233–167 record. He also taught English at Farleigh
Dickinson. In 1981, he became an academic adviser for the University of
Connecticut's athletic department.

Source: Dick Holub—https://en.wikipedia.org

Regular season

Year	Team	GP	FG%	FT%	APG	PPG
1947–48	New York	48	.295	.633	0.8	10.5
Career		48	.295	.633	0.8	10.5

HANK BEENDERS

Henry G. "Hank" Beenders (June 2, 1916–October 27, 2003) was a Dutch American professional basketball player.

Beenders was born on June 2, 1916, in Haarlem, Netherlands, and migrated to the United States at age eight. He lived in Brooklyn, New York, and Scotch Plains, New Jersey, moving to Bridgewater Township, New Jersey, in the late 1960s. He attended North Plainfield High School in North Plainfield, New Jersey. He played the center position on the 1941 NIT champion Long Island University team, and was team captain during the 1941–42 season under Hall of Fame coach Clair Bee. He became one of the first international basketball players in the Basketball Association of America, which would later become the National Basketball Association, and was the first to reach the BAA Finals. Beenders averaged 12.3 points in his rookie season with Providence, which was 13th best in the league that season.

Source: Hank Beenders—https://en.wikipedia.org

Regular season

Year	Team	GP	FG%	FT%	APG	PPG
1946–47	Providence	58	.262	.704	.6	12.3
1947–48	Providence	21	.265	.638	.3	6.8
1947–48	Philadelphia	24	.333	.583	.3	2.5
1948–49	Boston	8	.214	.778	.4	2.4
Career		111	.265	.687	.5	8.4

Playoffs

Year	Team	GP	FG%	FT%	APG	PPG
1948	Philadelphia	12	.229	.538	.3	1.9
Career		12	.229	.538	.3	1.9

DOLLY KING

William "Dolly" King (November 15, 1916–January 29, 1969) was an American professional basketball player. He was one of a handful of African Americans to play in the National Basketball League (NBL), the predecessor of the NBA.

King was a multi-sport star at Long Island University during the late 1930s, playing basketball, baseball, and football. According to Clair Bee, King's coach in football and basketball, King once played an entire college football

game and an entire college basketball game on the same day. After college, King played several seasons of professional basketball with the all-black New York Renaissance before Lester Harrison signed him to the NBL's Rochester Royals in 1946. King averaged 4.0 points per game in 41 games with Rochester and participated in the league playoffs. King died of a heart attack in 1969, aged 52.

Source: Dolly King—https://en.wikipedia.org

DOLLY KING (continued)

Year	Team	League		GA	FGM	FTM	FTA	PCT.	AST	PTS	AVG
1936-37	Long Island (Frosh)	College									
1937-38	Long Island	College									
1938-39	Long Island	College									
1939-40	Long Island	College									
1939-40	New York Rens	Indep									
1940-41	New York Rens	Indep									
1940-41	Dolly King Five	Indep									
1940-41	Long Island Blcakbirds	Indep									
1940-41	New York Harlem Yankees	Indep									
1940-41	Dolly King Five	Indep									
1941-42	Long Island Grumman Flyers	Indep	23	96	19					211	9.2
1941-42	Washington Bears	Indep	14	57	34					148	10.6
1942-43	Washington Bears	Indep	19	54	47					155	8.2
1942-43	Long Island Gruman Wildcats	Indep									
1943-44	Washington Bears	Indep	29	80	41					201	6.9
1943-44	New York Rens	Indep									
1944-45	Washington Bears	Indep	10	35	21					91	9.1
1944-45	Long Island Gruman Hellcats	Indep									
1944-45	Rochester	Indep	3	12	8					32	10.7
1945-46	Washington Bears	Indep	10	43	26					112	11.2
1945-46	New York Rens	Indep									
1945-46	Wilkes Barre	PSL	7	34	34					102	14.6
1946-47	Rochester	NBL	41	52	60	97	.619		164	4.0
1946-47	New York Rens	Indep									
1947-48	New York Rens	Indep								0	
1948-49	Dayton	NBL	1	3	5	7	.714		11	11.0
1948-49	New Haven	ECL	1						26	26.0
1948-49	Mohawk	NYSL	24						368	15.3
1948-49	Scranton	ABL	14	64	48	68	.706		176	12.6
1948-49	New York Rens	Indep								
1949-50	Scranton	ABL	34	118	85	148	.574	33	321	9.4
1949-50	New York Rens	Indep								
1950-51	Scranton	ABL	35	83	81	127	.638	33	247	7.1
1951-52	Saratoga-Glens Falls	ABL	21	32	38				102	4.9
Major League Totals			42	55	65				175	4.2

338

DOLLY KING (continued)

PLAYOFF RECORD

Year	Team	League		GA	FGM	FTM	FTA	PCT.	AST	PTS	AVG
1940-41	New York Rens		WBT	4	20	9	13	.692		49	12.3
1941-42	Long Island Flyers		WBT	4	17	9	17	.529		43	10.8
1942-43	Washington Bears		WBT	3	9	6	10	.600		24	8.0
1943-44	New York Rens		WBT	4	13	6	11	.545		32	8.0
1944-45	Long Island Hellcats		WBT	1	1	1	3	.333		3	3.0
1945-46	Wilkes- Barre	PSL		4	12	4				28	7.0
1945-46	New York Rens		WBT	2	4	2	3	.667		10	5.0
1946-47	Rochester	NBL		11	30	31	43	.721		91	8.3
1947-48	New York Rens		WBT	3	1	3	3	1.000		5	1.7
1948-49	Mohawk	NYSL		3						29	9.7
1948-49	Scranton	ABL		6	31	27				89	14.8
1949-50	Scranton	ABL		8	7	7				21	2.6
1951-52	Saratoga	ABL		4	4	5				13	3.3
Major League Totals				29	94	64				252	8.7

CLAIR BEE

Clair Francis Bee (March 2, 1896–May 20, 1983) was an American basketball coach, who led the team at Long Island University in Brooklyn, New York, to undefeated seasons in 1936 and 1939, as well as two National Invitation Tournament titles in 1939 and 1941.

Source: Clair Bee—https://en.wikipedia.org

Basketball
Statistics overview

Season	Team	Overall	Postseason
Rider Roughriders (Independent) (1928–1931)			
1928–29	Rider	19–3	
1929–30	Rider	17–3	
1930–31	Rider	17–2	
Rider:	53–8 (.869)		
Long Island Blackbirds (Independent) (1931–1943)			
1931–32	Long Island	16–4	
1932–33	Long Island	6–11	
1933–34	Long Island	26–1	
1934–35	Long Island	24–2	
1935–36	Long Island	25–0	Premo-Porretta National Champions[5]
1936–37	Long Island	28–3	
1937–38	Long Island	23–5	NIT Quarterfinals
1938–39	Long Island	23–0	Helms Foundation National Champions
NIT Champions			
1939–40	Long Island	19–4	NIT Quarterfinals
1940–41	Long Island	25–2	NIT Champions
1941–42	Long Island	25–3	NIT Quarterfinals
1942–43	Long Island	13–6	
1945–46	Long Island	14–9	
1946–47	Long Island	17–5	NIT Quarterfinals
1947–48	Long Island	17–4	
1948–49	Long Island	18–12	
1949–50	Long Island	20–5	NIT Quarterfinals
1950–51	Long Island	20–4	
	Long Island:	360–80 (.818)	
	Total:	413–88 (.824)	

JACKIE GOLDSMITH

Jackie Goldsmith starred at Jefferson High School in Brooklyn and the Union Temple in the late 1930s before entering the US Army during World War II. Following the war, he joined Long Island University's basketball team in the fall of 1945. LIU finished 14–9, and Goldsmith was named Helms second team All-America and first team All-Metropolitan, leading LIU and the New York metropolitan area, scoring with 395 points (17.2 average). During the year, he set LIU game and season scoring records. Famed LIU coach, Clair Bee, called Goldsmith the best set-shooter in all of college basketball. Goldsmith played professional basketball during the 1947–48

season appearing with Toledo in the National Basketball League and with Portland of the Pacific Coast Basketball League. Goldsmith retired at the end of the season to concentrate on his other sports' interest— illegal gambling and point-shaving of college basketball games. Over the next six years, Goldsmith was heavily involved in the point-shaving scandals that rocked college basketball in the late 40s and early 50s. Goldsmith was arrested in April 1951 and pleaded guilty in May 1952 to bribery charges. Goldsmith was eventually sentenced to 2 1/2 to 4 years in prison for his participation in the scandal.

JACKIE GOLDSMITH (continued)

Year	Team	League	GA	FGM	FTM	FTA	PCT.	AST	PTS	AVG
1940-41	Brooklyn Union Temple	AAU								
1941-42	Long Island University	College								
1941-42	New London	CBL	4	12	5				29	7.3
1942-43	New London Bears	Indep								
1942-45	U.S. Coast Guard	Military Service								
1945-46	Long Island University	College	25	175	54				404	16.2
1946-47	Long Island University	College	21	84	32				200	9.5
1947-48	Toledo NBL		12	20	6	9	.667		46	3.8
1947-48	Portland	PCL	16						204	12.8
1948-49	Brooklyn	ABL	1	1	1	3	.333		3	3.0
Major League Totals			12	20	6	9	.667		46	3.8

POST SEASON RECORD

Year	Team	League	GA	FGM	FTM	FTA	PCT.	AST	PTS	AVG
1941-42	New London	CBL	1	0	1				1	1.0

JACK MOLINAS

Molinas grew up in Brooklyn and attended Stuyvesant High School. His parents owned a bar on Coney Island.

He attended Columbia University from 1950 to 1953 where he played basketball. In the 1952–1953 season he was the captain of Columbia's team and led the team in scoring. In 1953, he set a team record for most points scored in a game—a mark that was eclipsed a few years later by Chet Forte. The Fort Wayne Pistons drafted him third in the 1953 NBA Draft, and he played in 32 games before the league banned him for wagering on Pistons games. Molinas was selected for the 1954 NBA All-Star Game but was suspended at the time of the game and was replaced by teammate Andy Phillip. He later sued the NBA for $3 million, claiming the league's ban was an unreasonable restraint of trade. Judge Irving Kaufman ruled against him in the case. After playing in the minor leagues, he entered the Brooklyn Law School from where he graduated with a law degree. Before his admission to law school, the Bronx County District Attorney investigated his case and concluded that he had not committed a crime. The bar association also reviewed his case and admitted him to the New York Bar.

Molinas became the central figure in the 1961 point-shaving scandal. The gambling ring went on from 1957 to 1960 and involved 50 players from 27 colleges. Two of the most notable players ensnared in the scandal were future Hall of Famers Connie Hawkins and Roger Brown.

Molinas gave Hawkins $250 during his freshman year at Iowa, but never encouraged him to throw games. Although Molinas never implicated Hawkins in any way, both Hawkins and Brown were effectively black-balled from both collegiate and professional basketball, until signing with the upstart American Basketball Association in 1967. Hawkins also played in the ABL for its entire existence, 1961–63, and afterward appealed toward the NBA in allowing him to play again, starting in 1969 with the Phoenix Suns. Meanwhile, Brown spent his entire professional career in the rival ABA, leading the Indianapolis Pacers to three ABA titles before retiring from basketball in 1975; the Indiana Pacers retired his number (#35) on November 2, 1985.

In 1963, Molinas was convicted for his role in the scheme and was sentenced to 10 to 15 years in prison. He was paroled in 1968 after serving five years. Molinas was said to have contacts with New York City mobster Thomas Eboli. In 1973, authorities arrested and charged him with interstate shipment of pornography. He was due to stand trial on those charges at the time of his death.

At 2:00 AM on August 3, 1975 at age 43, Molinas was killed while standing in the backyard of his home in Los Angeles. Eugene Connor fired five shots while standing in the yard of Molinas' neighbor using a long-barreled .22 caliber pistol steadied on the fence. Molinas was hit in the neck, and his girlfriend and dog were both wounded as well. Police did not rule out a mob-related murder. His business partner Bernard Gusoff had been beaten to death in November 1974.

Source: Jack Molinas—https://en.wikipedia.org

Regular season

Year	Team	GP	MPG	FG%	FT%	RPG	APG	PPG
1953–54	Fort Wayne	32	29.9	.390	.759	7.1	1.6	11.6
Career		32	29.9	.390	.759	7.1	1.6	11.6

ACKNOWLEDGMENTS

I would like to acknowledge the following people who have helped me in the process. My wife Nancy and my sons Sam and Alex were an inspiration to me and invaluable in helping me through it all. Additional thanks to my friends Keith Kenner, Jorge Gomez, Marty Groveman, and Dane Matthews, who were supportive as well in their friendship and encouragement.

—Barry Cohen

Made in the USA
Columbia, SC
16 May 2021